WORK IN THE CHANGING CANADIAN SOCIETY

Mervin Y. T. Chen
Thomas G. Regan

BUTTERWORTHS
TORONTO

Work in the Changing Canadian Society
© 1985 Butterworth & Co. (Canada) Ltd.

Printed and bound in Canada

The Butterworth Group of Companies

Canada
Butterworth & Co. (Canada) Ltd., Toronto and Vancouver
United Kingdom
Butterworth & Co. (Publishers) Ltd., London
Australia
Butterworths Pty Ltd., Sydney, Melbourne, Brisbane, Adelaide and Perth
New Zealand
Butterworths (New Zealand) Ltd., Wellington and Auckland
Singapore
Butterworth & Co. (Asia) Pte. Ltd., Singapore
South Africa
Butterworth Publishers (SA) (Pty) Ltd., Durban and Pretoria
United States
Butterworth Legal Publishers, Boston, Seattle, Austin and St. Paul
D & S Publishers, Clearwater

Canadian Cataloguing in Publication Data

Chen, Mervin Yaotsu.
    Work in the changing Canadian Society

Bibliography: p.
Includes index.
ISBN 0-409-82335-X

1. Labor and laboring classes - Canada.   2. Canada -
Occupations.   3. Canada - Social conditions - 1971 -
4. Work I. Regan, Thomas G. II. Title.

HN103.5.C48 1984   306'.36'0971   C84-099562-8

Sponsoring Editor—Janet Turner
Editor—Priscilla Darrell
Cover Artwork—Doreen Huyghue
Cover Design—Gordon Sadlier
Production—Jim Shepherd

Preface

The aim of this book is to produce an account of the research done by sociologists in the fields of work and occupations. In writing the book, we have deliberately focused on the Canadian scene. Sociology students and other individuals interested in the topic of work will discover a text which takes Canadian content seriously, not an American text with Canadian addenda.

Our approach to work is both structural and social psychological. The subject matter of sociology is the web of social relations created by social interactions among groups and individuals. By the logic of the discipline sociologists tend to direct their attention predominantly to the social structure. However, social structures do not come into existence without people. Nor do individuals under the same structural conditions behave in the same manner. By taking both perspectives, we maintain a balanced view of the world of work.

As with most work groups the authors created a division of labour. Chen designed, developed, and wrote most of the text. Regan contributed Chapters 4, 5 and 8. Both shared the task of general editing and frequently used each other as sounding boards. The process was a growth experience.

We are indebted to many people. The book is an outgrowth of a suggestion by Bill White, Co-ordinator of Continuing Education at Acadia, that we develop a text for use in a program which he was developing in conjunction with the Canadian Employment and Immigration Commission and the Department of Education of Nova Scotia. An initial grant from the Commission and a sabbatical leave granted by Acadia University to Chen are gratefully acknowledged.

The book would not have been completed without the assistance, support, encouragement and constructive criticism of Drs. Oswald Hall, Merrijoy Kelner, and Anthony Thomson. Michael Corbett, Susan Robertson, Doreen Huyghue, and Kim Meade did preliminary research and proof-reading. The thoughtful suggestions of several other students also improved the quality of the book.

Elaine Schofield, Wendy Tupper and Yvette Cogswell typed the manuscript. Virginia Smith transformed it into a polished final draft. We owe her a special thanks for her diligence, consideration and skills in word processing. We are grateful to Paul Steele and the staff of the

Acadia Computer Centre and to Janet Turner and her colleagues at Butterworths for their enthusiasm and assistance. Priscilla Darrell's skillful editing and thoroughness helped to enhance greatly the quality of this work.

We wish to extend special acknowledgement to Drs. Frank E. Jones and Oswald Hall. They introduced us to topics about which we have written. They have remained sources of inspiration to us. Last but not least, our warmest thanks go to our wives, Ling and Jeanette, and to our children, Howard, Matthew and Jonathan. Our families have endured our absences from home and have been constant sources of moral and emotional support.

Wolfville, N.S   Mervin Y.T. Chen
June, 1984   Thomas G. Regan

Acknowledgements

The authors and publishers of these articles and textbooks have been most generous in giving permission for the reproduction in this text of work already in print. References, of course, appear where necessary and possible in the text. It is convenient for us to list below, for the assistance of the reader, the publishers and, in several instances, the authors for whose courtesy we are most grateful.

Every effort has been made to contact authors and publishers to obtain permissions. If the publisher is made aware of any errors which may have been made in obtaining permissions, the publisher will take steps to ensure that proper credit be given at that time.

Between the Lines	Shapiro, Martin. *Getting Doctored: Critical Reflections on Becoming a Physician*, 1978:14.
Canadian Sociology & Anthropology Association	Guppy, L.N. and J. L. Siltanen. "A Comparison of the Allocation of Male and Female Occupational Prestige." Reprinted from the *Canadian Review of Sociology and Anthropology*, Vol. 14:3 (1977) by permission of the authors and the publisher.
Carleton University Press Inc.	Kelner, M.J. "The Transition From Student to Practitioner: The Making of a Chiropractor," 1980: 6, 15, 16, 22. Presented at the Fifteenth Annual Meeting of the Canadian Sociology and Anthropology Association, Montreal.
Gage Publishing	Vincent, Claude L. *Policeman*, 1979: 36, 42, 44, 45, 46, 78, 99. Copyright © 1979 Gage Publishing Limited. Reprinted by permission of the publisher.
Fitzhenry & Whiteside	Haas, Jack and William Shaffir. "The Professionalization of Medical Stu-

dents: Developing Competence and a Cloak of Competence," in David Coburn, Carl D'Arcy, Peter New and George Torrance (eds.): *Health and Canadian Society: Sociological Perspectives*, 1981: 211, 215.

Kelner, M., Oswald Hall and Ian Coulter. *Chiropractors: Do They Help? A Study of Their Education and Practice*, 1980: 15.

Haas, Jack and
William Shaffir.

"Professionalizing Adaptations to Ritual Ordeals of Uncertainty," 1980: 5, 14. Presented to the Fifteenth Annual Meeting of The Canadian Sociology & Anthopology Association, Montreal.

Harper and Row

Hughes, Everett C. "Work and Self," in J. H. Rohrer and Muzafer Shiriff (eds.): *Social Psychology at the Crossroads*, 1951.

Meissner, Martin. *Technology and the Worker: Technical Demands and Social Processes in Industry*, 1969: 10.

The Institute for Research
on Public Policy

Menzies, Heather. *Women and the Chip: Case Studies of the Effects of Informatics on Employment in Canada*, 1981. Reprinted by permission of the Institute for Research on Public Policy, Montreal, Canada.

Prentice Hall Canada

Elliott, J. L. "Canadian Immigration: A Historical Assessment," in Jean L. Elliott (ed.): *Two Nations, Many Cultures: Ethnic Groups in Canada*, 2nd ed., 1983, Table 1, pp. 292-93. Table reproduced from McGraw Hill: W. E. Kalback & W. W. McVey. *The Demographic Bases of Canadian Society*, 1971: Tables 1.4 & 2.2.

Haas, Jack. "Learning Real Feelings: A Study of High Steel Ironworkers' Reactions to Fear and Danger," in

Jack Haas and William Shaffir (eds.): *Shaping Identity in Canadian Society*, 1978: 237.

Princeton University Press   Form, William H. *Blue-Collar Stratification: Autoworkers in Four Countries*, 1976: 136-37. Copyright © 1976 by Princeton University Press. Excerpt, pp. 136-7.

The University of Chicago Press   Lipset, Seymour Martin and Reinhard Bendix. "Social Mobility and Occupational Career Patterns," *American Journal of Sociology*, 57 (March), 1952: 180.

University of Minnesota Press   Caplow, Theodore. *The Sociology of Work*, 1954: 218.

Table of Contents

List of Tables

Chapter 1

Introduction

This book deals with work from a sociological perspective. It is an inescapable fact that humans are born into a society, are socialized by it, and live out their lives in it. They are the creators, and at the same time products of society. The web of social relations created by society and its members is the subject matter of sociology. To know something about the work people do and the way they do it, and to know something about work groupings are ways to further understand our society. Indeed, work exerts a profound influence. Most people spend some forty years as workers. Work, therefore, looms large in our lives. Not only are our own self concepts, life styles, social statuses, and children's life chances for the future greatly influenced by the work we do, even our life expectancy is to a large extent affected by our occupation. The sociology of work teaches us about society and about workers, including ourselves.

I. THE CHANGING MEANING OF WORK

Why do people work? Historically, and for many people in underdeveloped areas today, work is simply a requirement for sustaining life. However, people have come to depend on work for more than survival. Through the ages the meaning of work has changed and is still changing. In this section, we attempt to outline these changes.

Work is carried out in a social context. Its meaning is, therefore, embedded in the social order. In tracing the historical changes in the meanings of work in the Western world, Tilgher (1958), demonstrated this point clearly. To ancient Greeks and Romans, work, especially work with one's hands, was drudgery and degrading. It was the task of slaves. The honourable and ethical undertaking for citizens was to live in leisure with plenty of time to think truth and to acquire and practice virtue. For most Greek thinkers, agriculture was the only worthy type of labour for a citizen because it brought a livelihood and independence which they cherished.

Similarly, work is disdained in the Hebrew tradition. For the Hebrews, work was both a painful drudgery and a hard necessity. It was necessary not only because of physical survival, but more importantly for the expiration of the original sin committed by their ancestors. When work was accepted as a penalty, as an expiatory deed, it took on a religious meaning.

In early Christian times work gained respect, if not dignity. Still, it was not to be performed for economic gain. It was carried out only for the maintenance of the individual and the group in which the person was a member. It was not until the Reformation with the emergence of Calvin's doctrine that work was transformed into a "calling"—a sign of being among the elect; a sign of salvation. In this doctrine, work was perceived as the will of God. Profit was praiseworthy. However, it was not to be used for the earthly pleasure of the body. It was to be used to glorify God, to help establish the Kingdom of God on earth. How? To reinvest the profit for fresh adventures, which in turn bred new profits for further reinvestment, and on it went. To work hard, to live a frugal and disciplined life, to select a calling and to follow it through were crucial elements of the religious duty of the Calvinists. This is the Protestant ethic described by Weber (1930). Although unintended, the Protestant ethic had the effect of facilitating the development of the Industrial Revolution. In the process of industrialization, the Protestant ethic not only became the dominating ideology of work in modern times, it emerged as a "work ethic" in general in Western societies.

The "work ethic" is not, however, unique to Western civilizations. Work attitudes esteemed by Western societies are also found elsewhere. For example, industriousness, frugality, self help along with piety and loyalty are very much central to the ancient Confucian teachings. The path of evolution has undoubtedly been different. Excepting the religious origin, these beliefs are not at all dissimilar to those of the Calvinists. Furthermore, they are not just exalted ideals. They have been transmitted to the populace through proverbs, folkways and education.[1]

Under the strong influence of Confucianism, Japan naturally incorporated some of these ethics into its culture. Diligence, thrift, and achievement are certainly valued by the Japanese. These ideals are expressed in popular teachings. For example, Ninomiya Sonutuba, the Peasant Saint, exhorted his people to "work much, earn much, (and) spend little." Almost identical work attitudes exist among preliterate groups. For example, Firth (1926:17) has pointed out that "work for its own sake is a constant characteristic of Maori industry." Radcliff-Brown (1964:108) observed that "The Andaman Islanders regard laziness as anti-social behaviour."[2]

In Canada, as in other Western industrial societies, the sacred Protestant work ethic appears to be replaced by a secular version. Its moral connotations are nevertheless still abundantly clear. Only the persons who work are believed to be morally fit and deserving of respect and an adequate living. The derogatory label "welfare bum" manifests this morality. If a person cannot hold down a steady job, the character of that person is often subject to suspicion and negatively evaluated (Rinehart, 1975:8).

Recently, the changing attitudes towards work, or for some, the loss of the work ethic among Canadians, have attracted a great deal of research attention and that of the mass media. A research report based on a national survey (Burstein *et al.*; 1975) provides some empirical data about this.

The major conclusion of the survey is that Canadians have a "work ethic." The evidence of this conclusion is that 70 percent of those who were in the labour force reported that they work not only because they have to but also because they like to. The researchers also cited further indications that point to "the good health of the work ethic and the strong attachment of Canadians to work motives": (a) Canadians are, in principle, committed to work, (b) Canadians choose work over most leisure activities when a trade-off is necessary, (c) Canadians choose to work even during their leisure time, and (d) Canadians prefer working to being on unemployment insurance.[3]

Another point revealed by the survey is that the work ethic of Canadians is to a great extent coloured by an instrumental orientation. Among those who were in the labour force, 57 percent of men and 40 percent of women reported work as being the primary means of achieving the most important goals in their lives (the corresponding figures for those who were not in the labour force were 47 percent and 25 percent). These goals include both economic ones, such as money, accommodation, and property, and non-economic ones, such as family and friends.

The instrumental orientation is also manifested by the participants' responses to other questions in the survey. While the desire of achieving material goals through work was consistent in their responses to a number of questions, the motive for achieving non-material goals in work was not. For example, over 80 percent of the respondents disagreed with the statement: "To me, work is a way to make money and I don't expect to get any special satisfaction or enjoyment from it." But, when asked on what did they depend for personal rewards, altogether only 23 percent of those surveyed stated that they depend on work for personal satisfaction, 36 percent for self fulfillment. In both cases, family was a more important source of rewards.

Furthermore, Burstein and his associates probed what Canadians want from work by requiring the participants to rate a number of job features. They found that the single most important consideration in the minds of Canadians proved to be interesting work. The researchers also found that interesting work is most clearly related to: (a) being given an opportunity to develop special abilities; (b) being given a chance to do the things one does best, and (c) being given a lot of freedom in deciding how to do the work. From these findings emerges a somewhat ambivalent perception of work by Canadians. On the one hand, we do not depend too much on work for satisfaction and self fulfillment. On the other hand, we want to have interesting jobs.

How does one explain these seemingly contradictory attitudes? Peter Berger's analysis of "the problem of work" in industrial society furnishes us with a pertinent frame of reference. One of the inevitable consequences of the ongoing industrialization is that the nature of work is changing. As a result of rationalization of work, bureaucratization of the administrative machinery, mass organization for mass production and mass consumption, fewer and fewer jobs involve the totality of the person. "More commonly, the entrepreneur is replaced by the bureaucrat, the individualistic professional by a team, and the craftsman by a machine" (Berger, 1964:219). Under these structural conditions, the possibility of achieving self fulfillment in work is rather limited. At the same time there is an ideology of work which persistently presents the individual with the expectation that work is "meaningful" and "satisfying." Given the structural development in the occupational world, this expectation obviously has little chance of being met. On a priori sociological ground, Berger argues that the ideology of work will gradually adapt itself to its structural reality. He further argues that "privatism" partly constitutes such an ideological adaptation. By privatism Berger means the tendency in which individuals seek self realization and self identity ("who one really is") in the private sphere of life, especially the family.

In applying Berger's "theory" to the Canadian data, one may argue that the fact that most Canadians want "interesting work" is possibly a reflection of the prevailing ideology of work, and that only a small proportion of Canadian workers expect to achieve self fulfillment in work is possibly an indication of the ideological adaptation to the structural reality. While it is disputable that our society is a post-industrial society, industrialization is nevertheless an ongoing process. The latest technology (*e.g.,* microelectronics, informatics) brings rationalization of work and bureaucratization of organizations to an even higher level. It has been predicted by many researchers and specialists that an increasing number of workers will be displaced by sophisticated machines.

In response to real and potential structural changes, some changes in the concept of work also have been emerging. On the one hand, there is the development of the Quality of Working Life Movement which is based on humanistic values with the aim to humanize work. Many programs including job redesign, employee participation in decision making, decentralization of organizations and so on have been initiated. On the other hand, many writers argue that a fundamental change of the old notions underlying the work ethic is needed. Exactly what will evolve is uncertain. The most frequently suggested idea appears to be in the direction of the separation of work and employment (Cherns, 1980, Jenkins and Sherman, 1979, Watson, 1973, as cited in Anthony, 1977). While work is a personally oriented, lifelong pursuit, employment is a publically oriented, intermittent undertaking. If there is truth in these suggestions, the source of self identity and self worth would have to be found from somewhere else. This somewhere else is likely to be found from the new mechanisms developed to replace employment as a major device for the distribution of social and moral resources in our society.

II. A DEFINITION OF WORK

Exactly what do we mean by work? Its definitions perhaps are not often of much concern to most people. As Anderson puts it, definitions of work tell us little about it anyway. For some people, work is simply there, to be enjoyed or to be endured. For others, it may not be there, but they must strive to get it. However, for the purpose of studying and understanding work, at least a working definition is required. Dubin (1958:4) puts it this way: "By work we mean continuous employment, in the production of goods and services, for remuneration." Or, to put it simply: work refers to paid employment (Jenkins and Sherman, 1979).[4] Although this definition may seem narrow[5], it is adopted for a number of reasons: it characterizes the nature of work in an industrial society; it is probably the closest reflection of most people's perception of work; and, last but not least, paid employment is the most important mechanism for the distribution of social resources in Canadian society.

III. WORK AND SOCIETY

Work and society are inseparable. We shall analyze this close relationship in broad strokes in this section. To begin, we shall discuss

the division of labour in society in general. Sociologists and anthropologists often classify societies in terms of their basic modes of
subsistance (*e.g.*, Lenski & Lenski, 1978). Thus, there are hunting,
gathering, horticultural, fishing, agrarian, industrial, and post-industrial societies. To characterize societies in these terms is, in the main,
to state how their work is done.

As human life is predominately group life, work is carried out in
a social context. Since no individual is self sufficient, it would be
beneficial for individual members, and groups as a whole if necessary, if tasks are divided among the population. Thus, there is always
a division of labour in every group, small or large. This is the basic
thesis of Durkheim's *The Division of Labor in Society* (1947). From
this perspective, "The work that any individual performs is articulated with that of others who work, and with the containing social
structure by its location within the division of labour" (Braude,
1975:13).

Age, gender, strength, mental and physical skills are the common bases for the division of labour. However, the relative weight of
these factors change with the development of human societies. While
early societies are held together by customs, similarity, and the
authority of the elderly, the division of labour in more complex
societies finds its most explicit expressions in highly differentiated
but mutually dependent occupations. The more complex a society is,
the more complicated its division of labour will be. There are three
approaches to analyze the division of labour: functional division of
labour, social division of labour, and moral division of labour. Let us
discuss each of these approaches briefly.[6]

(a) Functional Division of Labour

This division of labour refers to the distribution of skills. That is,
the division is organized in terms of the level of skills of various
occupations. Some occupations, brain surgery for instance, require
highly specialized skills. Others, such as garbage collectors or
dishwashers, require few, if any. Obviously, the highly skilled specialists require more resources to train and are more difficult to replace
because they are scarce, whereas those who are unskilled or less
skilled require little training and are easily replaceable.

Although functional division of labour is the most general
approach, it is by no means the simplest. At the purely descriptive
level, no one disputes that all occupations do not have the same level,
or the same kind of skills. But when it comes to measuring the

functional contribution of a given occupation to the survival of the total system, it is not a straightforward matter. Garbage collectors may be easy to replace. But, are they less functionally important to the society than surgeons?

(b) Social Division of Labour

While the functional division of labour draws attention to the distribution of skills, the social division of labour refers to the distribution of prestige. The scarcest skills and the tasks which are considered as most essential to the functioning of a social system are accorded the most prestige. Thus, these different divisions of labour are two sides of the same coin: closely related ways of analyzing occupational differentiations. It should be added, however, that while occupational differentiation is universal, the degree and the form of differentiation vary from one society to another. They also vary from one time to another within the same society. They are greatly influenced by the level of technology and the prevailing value system of a particular society. For example, physicians enjoy much higher material rewards and prestige in Western societies than they do in socialist countries such as the U.S.S.R.

(c) Moral Division of Labour:

This division of labour refers to:

> ...the distribution of differing moral power attached to work tasks characteristic of a particular population. The question posed by the moral division of labour is: Who can do what to whom, and how severely? (Braude, 1975: 15)

How is the moral power distributed? Its distribution is manifested in the licenses and mandates accorded to various occupations (Hughes, 1959; Braude, 1975). A license may be explicit (*e.g.*, one issued by a government agency) or tacit (*e.g.*, academic degrees of college professors and the ordination of priests). It acknowledges the bearer's capability of performing the tasks that are appropriate and relevant to his/her occupation. It also legitimizes the bearer to work in a certain manner which others may not. For example, a man may know all there is to know about the structure and functioning of an automobile, but to set himself up as a grade A mechanic without a license would not only be illegal but also ethically indefensible.

Furthermore, a license is also a permit for the bearer to deviate.

The work of a surgeon is most illustrative. Both the law and social norms forbid us to cut other people with a knife. However, a licensed surgeon does just that. The physician:

> ...may deviate from societal expectations of moral behavior because of the rights accorded him by licensing as a doctor to behave morally in this fashion, in terms of the normative constraints implicit in the role (Braude: 1975:94).

Even the language which describes the action changes. The surgeon no longer cuts people with a knife. Rather, he/she makes incisions on a patient with a scalpel. What was illegal and improper before licensing is legal and proper now. A new set of norms for the particular occupational role is in place.

While a license defines what the licensee can and cannot do, a mandate implies that the person may tell others how to perform or behave. Hughes, who originally developed the concept, states that "a mandate defines, for both the practitioner and the client, conduct with respect to the matters concerned in their work" (1959: 447). For example, not only may a doctor treat the illness of patients, he/she is also in a position to instruct them on how to behave to remain healthy in the future. The fact that people voluntarily follow "doctor's orders" is a clear manifestation of the mandate of the physician. Thus, if an occupation is successful in defining values and conduct in a particular area of life, it has a license and a mandate from society, explicitly or implicitly.

The moral nature of an occupation's mandate is also manifested by the fact that to carry out their tasks the practitioners must have some "guilt or dangerous information" about their clients. In order to treat mental illness, the psychiatrist must have the access to the innermost thoughts of the patient. In order to advise and to absolve, the priest gets to know his parishioner's behaviour which may be legally punishable or socially damaging or both. The relationship between the two parties is based on a bargain and a trust. By the action of visiting a practitioner of an occupation, the client recognizes both the needed skills the specialist has and the propriety of the possession of private information about himself by the specialist. On the part of the practitioner, one accepts this information with mostly tacit agreement that one will not misuse it. The violation of this agreement on the part of the practitioner may be sanctioned by law, by peers, or by the client.[7]

Having dealt with the relationship between work and the division of labour in general, we shall now examine the relationship between work and some specific aspects of society. Work is essential to individuals who are the components of society. It is not only the source of survival for the greatest majority of people, it is also a source of self identity, and a link between the individual and the wider social structure. Social roles are allocated through many mechanisms, of which the occupational structure is one of the most important. Before an individual enters the world of work, time is typically spent on acquiring the knowledge and skills that can be used during the adult years of work. During retirement, one's former occupation becomes a major reference point in this stage of life.

Work and the Family

The relationship between work and the family is one of mutual influence. At the macro level, changes in the occupational system inevitably bring about changes in the family structure. The family, in turn, affects societal development. While there is no total or natural harmony, the agricultural mode of production and the extended family seem compatible. As a society becomes more industrialized, the nuclear family unit becomes the normatively dominant and numerically prevalent type.

On the other hand, "the family system may have an independent, facilitating effect on the modern shift toward industrialization" (Goode, 1982:190-91). Goode suggests that the family systems of the West have been different from those of other major civilizations for over a thousand years. Generally, those factors which may facilitate industrialization existed before its inception. Early adolescent marriage was not typical or the ideal. Ancestor worship did not exist. For crimes, individuals, not their families, were responsible. There was no clan system, and young people were expected to live independently upon marriage.

At the micro level, work affects the life of a family materially and socially. The occupation of the principal breadwinner often sets the tone, so to speak, of the life of the whole family unit (*e.g.*, shift work). Children's values, beliefs and career orientations are, to various degrees, affected by their parents' occupations (Kohn, 1969; Pineo & Looker, 1983).

While the occupational system in an industrial society and the nuclear family are compatible in some aspects, they are on the course of conflict in others. "Industrial enterprises, focused on profits (whether in the Soviet Union or in the United States) have little interest in the idiosyncracies and needs of aged parents, the emotional problems of adults, or the insecurities of children" (Goode, 1982:181). They tend to treat their workers as if they do not have responsibilities other than those of an employee. If adjustments have to be made, the employees are expected to adjust their familial roles to their occupational ones. Indeed, this single-minded expectation of the world of work is one of the major reasons that modern families, particularly dual-career families, experience so much stress (Skinner, 1980).

The family prepares future workers for the occupational world. In agricultural societies, the extended family is also a work unit. Work roles are hardly distinguishable from general familial roles. Working along with their parents and other adults, the children grow up with the family occupation. In industrial societies, where the educational system is more elaborate, this aspect of family socialization becomes limited. However, the work habits, motivation for work and sex roles learned in the family setting will still affect a person's orientation toward work and behaviour at work.

Marriage patterns and fertility rates also affect the world of work in a variety of ways. For some time now, Canadian women have tended to marry later and have fewer children. Consequently, the patterns of women's participation in the labour force have changed. Since more women are employed outside of the home, the consumption patterns of certain domestic commodities have changed, too. For example, there is a higher demand for prepared foods. These changes, in turn, bring about further changes in the world of work.

Work and Education

While the family is an important socializer, the educational system is even more so. Regardless of the dispute over the issue of whether the role of the educational system is to produce well-informed citizens or to train employable personnel, occupational competence is defined in terms of formal schooling. In fact, the educational system has not only been used as a sorting mechanism for the occupational world, it also has become the basis for the distribution of individuals within the total social system in both industrialized and developing societies (Moore, 1973).

The relationship between the occupational world and the educational system can be analogous to that between the consumer and the supplier. However, their relationship of mutual dependence is neither guided by a grand plan, nor is it in natural harmony. While the occupational world relies on education for scientific and technological developments and sophisticated skills, the adoption of these is rather uneven across the occupational spectrum. There is evidence of a considerable degree of deskilling of some occupations, as the educational requirements of those occupations remain higher than what is necessary.

Another strain, though not a direct one, in the relationship between work and education involves the question of whether those who attained a higher education are all best suited. It has been well established that a person's socio-economic background is a strong intervening factor between intellectual potential and academic attendance (Porter, *et al.*, 1973).

In brief, the role of education as preparation and the distribution into occupations is an indisputable fact. To be sure, there are strains in the relationship between work and education. Both the occupational world and the institution of education are systems of forces, each with its own needs, and those needs are not free of conflicts. What adds some more confusion to the relationship, as Hall indicates, "is that it is not clear what is exactly the optimum form the education should take for occupational education" (1975:312). Indeed, some governmental funding policies affecting schools and universities have rekindled the longstanding debate over liberal arts versus vocational emphases in education.

Work and the Government

Analytically the relationship between work and the government is twofold. The government can be perceived as an environment for work on the one hand; it can be perceived as work on the other. As an environment for work, government policies and regulations may facilitate or limit the development of certain types of work; or may stimulate or discourage certain occupational activities. The national energy policy of the federal government in the late 1970s which led to the contraction of oil exploration activities in Canada and the wage restraint policies exercised by both the federal and provincial governments in the early 1980s are good examples.

Government as a type of work is rather obvious. As the function of governments expand, their sizes increase. They have become some of the largest employers in recent years. As of 1983, the federal government had some 580,000 employees. The provincial governments had a total of about 285,000. Employees in all local governments in Canada totalled another 290,000. During the period from 1961 to 1983, the increases of employment in the three levels of governments were 165 percent, 185 percent, and 205 percent respectively (Foot, 1979; Statistics Canada, 1983).

The work of modern government is carried out by a great variety of occupations. Among those who seek public office, two occupational groups are prominent in Canada: lawyers are preponderant; business comes in a distant second. According to Porter (1965:391-93), 60 percent of federal cabinet ministers and 42 percent of provincial ministers were lawyers. Why should this be so? In his celebrated paper "Politics as a Vocation," Weber points out that the modern democracy as a rational state and the legal profession belong together. A lawyer's training in presenting arguments effectively is important in the management of politics (Weber, 1946). Cohn suggests three additional explanations. First, law and politics share a common subculture. A lawyer can learn the political system rather easily and quickly. Secondly, law is a profession in which the individual can control his own work arrangements more easily than in many other occupations. Finally, there are many role models of successful lawyer politicians (Cohen, 1969:563-74, cited by Hall, 1975:375-58).

Civil servants and other government employees belong to a wide range of occupations. While a considerable proportion of these jobs are clerical, there has been an increasing reliance upon experts and specialists at all levels of governments, a clear sign of the impact of technological change on the work of government.

Work and the Economy

The relationship between work and the economy is too obvious to necessitate an elaborate analysis. The fact that sociologists use a person's occupation as one of the major indicators of socio-economic status reflects the close relationship between work and the economy. Throughout the life span, occupations serve as a major link between individuals and the economy. They are significantly affected by their parents' occupations before entering the world of work themselves and by their own previous occupations when they are disengaged from it. Since over 80 percent of Canadians become employees to make a living, their economic status changes drastically, in case they are unemployed. As Hall (1975:238) puts it: "Economic factors alone do not determine an individual's position in the stratification system. They do, however, play an important role".

To sum up, we have discussed in this section the close relationship between work and society. In many ways this section has touched upon the major themes of the entire book. Work is systematically related to all aspects of society. Indeed, the study of work is one of the most fruitful avenues to acquire knowledge of society.

IV. THE PLAN OF THE BOOK

As it has been stated earlier, the subject matter of sociology is the web of social relations created by the social interactions among groups and among individuals. Thus, by the logic of the discipline sociologists tend to direct their attention predominately to the social structure. In general sociology, theorists examine the groups into which humans are born and different groups in which people play various roles throughout their lives. Group conflict, competition, coordination, and succession are the focal points of sociological research. In the field of sociology of work, researchers are preoccupied by groups into which people have organized themselves (such as work enterprises, unions, occupational associations, informal groups, etc.) or groups which are organized by bureaucracies and technology.

However, social structures do not come into existence without people. Nor do individuals under the same structural conditions behave in the same manner. It is true that society consists of and socializes individuals. But it is also true that society manifests its existence through individuals. To emphasize structural analysis to the extent of losing sight of the individual engenders structural determinism. Taking this view of sociology, our approach to work is therefore both structural and social psychological.

In Chapter 2 we describe and analyze the Canadian labour force. Following our definition of work, this chapter sets the boundaries of our treatment of work in this text. Chapter 2 is followed by five chapters dealing with various aspects of the social structure relevant to work. Chapter 3 attempts to answer questions such as: "Why does a person choose one occupation over others?" "How does a society allocate its human resources?" and "Is it choice or allocation?" Three theoretical approaches to occupational choice are discussed: fortuitous, rational decision making, and sociocultural influence approaches. Chapter 4 deals with the ways of learning to work. Chapter 5 discusses career channels and patterns in the occupational world. In each of these chapters we look into both the structural and social psychological aspects of these topics.

Chapters 6 and 7 are predominately structural analyses. Chapter 6 focuses on the structural inequality in intergenerational occupational mobility. Chapter 7 deals with structural inequality for women and the Native groups in the world of work in Canada.

The next three chapters concentrate on the organizational and technological aspects of work. Chapter 8 is an analysis of work organizations. We look into the types and functioning of formal organizations in which the greatest majority of Canadian workers find themselves. In Chapter 9 we discuss the counterpart of employing organizations—the labour union. Two major themes are explored in this chapter: the labour union as a limited countervailing power to management in a capitalist society and the changes in work and their impact on the development of unions. The nature of technology and its impact on the structure of the labour force, the work organizations, the characteristics of work and the worker are the foci of Chapter 10. We also make some speculations in this chapter, on the future of work: its relation to technology, the centralization or decentralization of authority in work organizations, and particularly what work might mean in the future.

The last chapter summarizes the major themes and conclusions of our analysis.

Notes

1. Confucius himself was a practitioner of his own teachings. When one of his disciples (by the name of Tsai Yu) was found spending the daytime in sleep, the Master said, "Rotten wood is unfit for carving, a wall of dirt unfit for plastering. As to Yu, what is the use of reproving him!" *The Analects of Confucius*, Book V, Section IX, translated by William E. Soothill, 1968:259.
2. These references were quoted in Burstein *et al.*, 1975:11.
3. It should be pointed out that all these findings are based on attitudinal responses. Although the researchers seem to be confident about the conclusion, there is always the gnawing question of validity in survey research: whether what people say they do *is* what they actually do.
4. Although we do not deal with it in this book, illegitimate, paid employment, such as professional theft and prostitution, may be regarded as work by this definition. We recognize the contributions of homemakers in producing goods and services and are quite aware that some writers consider housewifing an occupation (*e.g.*, Lopata, 1971). However, homemakers are not employees and are not paid a remuneration. Various suggestions have been made that they should be paid. But none have been adopted (see Wilson, 1982, Ch. 4).
5. For example, Braude provides a very broad definition: "work may be viewed as that which a person does in order to survive—physically or socially" (1975:12-13).
6. This discussion is largely based on Hughes' concepts (1959) and Braude's elaboration of these ideas (1975: 14-16).
7. From a sociological point of view, the Supreme Court of Canada's ruling (October 20, 1981; see the *Halifax Chronicle-Herald*, October 22, 1981, p. 48) that doctors and hospital workers are "privileged police informers" undermines the mandate of the medical profession because

it negatively affects the trust between the doctor and the patient. For a detailed discussion of the social control aspect of the moral division of labour, see Braude (1975: 95-101).

Suggested Readings

Berger, Peter
  1964. "Some General Observations of the Problems of Work," in Peter Berger (ed.): *The Human Shape of Work*. Chicago: Henry Regnery, 211-41.
Braude, Lee
  1975. *Work and Workers*. New York: Praeger, 3-30
Weber, Max
  1930. *The Protestant Ethic and the Spirit of Capitalism*. London: Allen and Unwin
Salamon, Graeme
  1980. "The Sociology of Work: Some Themes and Issues," in Eslan and Salamon (eds.): 1980. *The Politics of Work and Occupations*, pp. 1-42. Toronto: University of Toronto Press.

Chapter 2

The Canadian Labour Force

I. INTRODUCTION

However it may be defined, work is carried out by people. Since no individual is entirely self sufficient, the labour for survival has to be divided. In a minimally differentiated society, the division of labour may be very simple. As the society is more developed, the division of labour becomes more diversified and specialized. In order to understand the work world in contemporary Canada, a knowledge of its occupational composition is, therefore, essential. This chapter begins with a discussion of the definitions of the labour force. Section II presents a descriptive picture of the current Canadian labour in terms of age and sex and some other general categories. Section III examines the Canadian occupational structure. Factors which contribute to shaping the occupational structure of a society are discussed. Finally, in Section IV, some general trends and prospects in the occupational structure of Canada are described.

The distribution of skills and specialities in a society is defined in terms of a normative and evaluative framework (Braude, 1975:31). The best way of illustrating this is to note the changing responses of the Canadian government toward work, as represented in a variety of ways in which Statistics Canada has quantified information about Canada's workers through the years.

The original legal reason for conducting a decennial census was to determine representation-by-population in the federal House of Commons, as mandated by the *British North America Act*. However, many other important needs are also satisfied by a census. Governments, industry and private organizations wish to know the major characteristics of social and economic life in Canada at a specific point in time as an aid in their planning and decision-making processes.

The first census was conducted in 1851. It consisted of two parts: (1) a personal census, including items on trade and occupations; (2) an agricultural census, indicating the major characteristics of Canadian society in the mid-nineteenth century. The number of occupations recorded was small and there was no classification. In the 1871 census, the first under the *Census Act*, five broad industrial groups were recorded:

1. Agricultural
2. Commercial
3. Domestic
4. Industrial
5. Professional

and a residual group labelled as

6. Not Classified.

While the last group was labelled as "not classified," it included a number of occupational groups in the modern sense. Occupationally related work such as toolmaking for or by farmers and fishermen was not recognized as an industry of "any importance." Those who engaged in such occupations were denoted as "not classified."

The same occupational classification was used in 1881 census. Up to this point the occupations of females were not recorded in the census unless they were family heads who were farmers, servants, teachers, and so on. The reason for not recording the occupations of women is rather interesting. It was stated in the introduction that "females are engaged in many of the occupations in the tables but to give them separately would occupy too much space" (Vol. II:VI). It was not until ten years later that the occupations of females were documented for the first time (1891 census, Vol. I:VIII).

In the 1891 census, occupations were divided into six classifications, "according to their natural order of precedence" (Vol. II:VI).

1. Primary production.
2. Distributors.
3. Modifiers.
4. Personal service.
5. Professional service.
6. Engaged in non-productive occupations (Indian Chiefs, members of religious Orders, Paupers and Inmates of Asylums, Retired and Students).

Canadian society of the 1880s was still basically rural, but there were clear signs of industrialization. The census reported that there was an "upswing of numerous small industries" and the degree of specialization was evident. Many industries which had formerly been lumped together were now being recorded separately.

While work was being treated in more detailed fashion in the latter decades of the nineteenth Century, the enumeration was by industry or occupation but not by actual employment. Whether or not a person was actually working at a particular job at the time of enumeration made no difference. What was enumerated was whether the person had ever worked at the occupation at which he "appeared to attach the most importance" (1881 census, Vol. II, p. VI).

In the 1901 census, the concept of "gainful worker" was introduced and defined as:

> ...all workers except women doing housework in their own homes, without salary or wages and having no other employment, and children of 10 years of age and over who worked for their parents at home, or on the farm, or any other who worked for their parents at home, or on the farm, or any other work or chores while attending school.

A gainful occupation is that "...by which the person who pursues it earns money or in which he assists in the production of marketable goods...." In the subsequent four censuses, the definition of a gainful occupation remained very similar to this one.

For sound policy-decision making, the concept of "gainful worker" had its shortcomings, however. Since it implied what a person customarily did, regardless of whether he was working or not at the time of enumeration, it was not sufficiently precise enough to ensure that certain "marginal groups" (such as persons seeking work for the first time, part-time, intermittent workers) would necessarily be consistently enumerated:

> Because customary activity is based on an unspecified and open-ended reference period, the boundary separating the gainfully occupied and the remainder of the adult population cannot be clearly drawn (Denton & Ostry, 1967:4).

The concept of gainful employment tends to be associated with a particular view of labour supply, which Denton and Ostry call a "fixed stock" notion. In this view the total labour supply of the economy is more a stable pool of individuals grouping *pari passu* with the adult population rather than expanding or contracting in response to changes in the economic and social environment. However, the fixed stock notion is not adequate in a period of rapid social and economic transformation, such as during the war or economic crisis. The need for manpower statistics to produce economic intelligence for government policy purposes stimulated the adoption of the concept of the labour force in the 1951 census (Denton & Ostry, 1967:4-5).

Officially, the labour force refers to the population 15 years of age and over, excluding inmates, who were either employed or unemployed during the week prior to enumeration. It should be noted that the labour force in the census includes personnel in the armed forces, while the monthly Labour Force Survey does not. Unless it is specified otherwise, the term of labour force in this chapter refers to the census definition.

The definitions of "employed" and "unemployed" vary slightly from time to time. The version used in 1981 census is as follows:

1. The employed includes those persons who, during the week prior to enumeration: (a) did any work at all; or (b) were absent from their jobs or business because of own temporary illness or disability, vacation, labour dispute at their place of work, or were absent for other reasons.
2. The unemployed includes those persons who, during the week prior to enumeration: (a) were without work, had actively looked for work in the past four weeks and were available for work; or (b) had been on layoff for 26 weeks or less and expected to return to their job; or (c) had definite arrangements to start a new job in four weeks or less.

These official definitions, in the main, set the boundaries of the normative framework of the division of labour in Canada. Those who are not classified as employed or unemployed are by definition not in the labour force. Specifically, they are persons, who:

> ...in the week prior to enumeration, were unwilling or unable to offer or supply their labour services under conditions existing in their labour markets. It includes persons who looked for work during the last four weeks but who were not available to start work in the reference week as well as persons who did not work, have a job, or look for work in the four weeks prior to enumeration.

Since paid employment is a major, if not the only, mechanism for the distribution of social wealth in our society, this framework has considerable implications. First of all, these official definitions contribute significantly to the social definition of paid employment as work. For example, those who "were without work, had actively looked for work...and were available for work" are unemployed. Clearly, the word "work" in this sentence means "paid employment."

Secondly, those who are without work and are not actively looking for work are automatically relegated to a category of people who are officially perceived as "unwilling or unable to offer or supply their labour services. . ." As a matter of fact, most of them are willing and able to work; but there is no work available. Many of them are too frustrated to continue to search for work actively. Therefore, the unemployment rate calculated on the basis of "the unemployed" is often misleading. There are many more unemployed workers than the official rate indicates (Stirling & Kouri, 1979).

Thirdly, since housework is not an occupation under the definition of the labour force, it is, therefore, not defined as work. Consequently, much of women's contribution to the economy and the society in general by doing housework is not recognized.[2]

II. WHO WORKS

To get some idea of work in Canada, let us look at the bare labour force statistics. From the turn of the century to 1984, the Canadian population climbed from 5.3 million to more than 24 million. In the same period, the size of the labour force climbed from 1.8 million to approximately 12.2 million. Statistics for January, 1984 are presented in Table 2-1. Of the 12.2 million in the labour force, 10.4 million were employed in non-agricultural pursuits; about 479,000 were involved in farm related activities. The data also indicate that 1.3 million workers or 11.2 percent of the labour force were unemployed. Among them, proportionally, more younger than older Canadian workers were unemployed. The unemployment rates of the under 24 age group are particularly high, while those for men and women above 25 years of age are about the same.

Participation rate refers to the percentage the total labour force forms of the total population 15 years of age and over (excluding inmates) in an area, group or category. Up to 1961, changes in the labour force participation have had little effect on the historical growth of labour supply in Canada. As Table 2-2 indicates, the overall rate exhibited little long-run trend. Over the period between 1901 and 1961 the data show that the rate was remarkably stable in view of the profound economic and social changes that have occurred during these years. Apart from the sharp rise between 1901 and 1911, a consequence of the massive immigration of those years, the rate varied by less than a percentage point from the highest to the lowest level (Ostry 1971:17). However, since 1961 we observed another period of sharp increase of participation rates. Between 1961 and 1981, there was almost a ten percentage point increase in the overall rate (55.1% - 64.8%).

If we examine the participation rates of men and women separately, we can see that this trend is mainly because of the sharp

Work in the Changing Canadian Society

Table 2-1
The Labour Force by Age and Sex
Seasonally-Adjusted*—January 1984

Thousands

Total Labour Force	12,229
Employed	10,855
Agricultural	479
Non-agricultural	10,376
Unemployed	1,379

Employed by Age and Sex

AGE	TOTAL	MEN	WOMEN
15-24	2,339	1,209	1,130
25 & over	8,516	5,089	3,427
25-54	7,239	4,244	2,995

Unemployed by Age and Sex and Rates

AGE	TOTAL	RATES	MEN	RATES	WOMEN	RATES
15-24	537	(18.7)	314	(20.6)	223	(12.6)
25 & over	837	(8.9)	485	(8.7)	352	(9.3)
Total	1,374	(11.2)	799	(11.3)	575	(11.2)
25-54	744	(9.3)	423	(9.1)	321	(9.7)

*Fluctuations in economic time series are caused by seasonal, cyclical and irregular movements. A seasonally-adjusted series is one from which seasonal movements have been eliminated. Seasonal movements are defined as those which are caused by regular annual events such as climate, crop cycles, holidays and vacation periods. Source: Adapted from Table 1 of Labour Force Survey, January, 1984. Cat. 71-001 monthly.

increase of women in the labour force in the last decade. While there has been a relatively mild decrease in men's participation rate from 1961 to 1980, there has been more than 20 percent increase in women's during the same period. Women not only participate in the labour force more, they also stay in it longer. Looking across the age groups of women, we can see that prior to 1961 the highest proportion of women in the labour force was the 20-24 age group. After that, there was invariably a sharp decline in participation rates, as the age group goes up. However, this is not the case any more. There is still a decrease, but considerably smaller. As of the census time in 1981, more than three-quarters of the childbearing, childrearing group, two-thirds of the 25-34 age group, and well over half (53.2%) of the women in the 35-64 age group were still in the labour force.

Table 2-2
Labour Force Participation
Rates by Age and Sex (1901-1981)

	Both Sexes	Male						Female					
		14 yrs. & over	14-19	20-24	25-34	35-64	65 +	14 yrs. & over	14-19	20-24	25-34	35-64	65 +
1901	53.0	87.8	–	–	–	–	–	16.1	–	–	–	–	–
1911	57.4	90.6	–	–	–	–	–	18.6	–	–	–	–	–
1921	56.2	89.8	68.4	94.3	98.0	96.9	59.6	19.9	29.6	39.8	19.5	12.0	6.6
1931	55.9	87.2	67.4	93.9	98.6	96.7	56.5	21.8	26.5	47.4	24.4	13.2	6.2
1941	55.2	85.6	54.6	92.6	98.7	96.1	47.9	22.9	26.8	46.9	27.9	15.2	5.8
1951[a]	54.5	84.4	53.7	94.2	98.2	95.0	39.5	24.4	33.7	48.8	25.4	19.8	4.5
1951[b]	54.3	84.1	53.5	94.0	98.1	94.8	39.1	24.2	33.4	48.5	25.1	19.6	4.4
1961[c]	55.1	80.8	40.5	94.2	98.0	95.0	30.4	29.1	31.7	50.4	28.9	29.5	6.0
1971[c]	58.0	75.4	46.6	86.5	92.6	88.6	23.6	39.9	37.0	62.8	44.5	41.5	8.3
1976[c]	60.0	75.5	50.4	85.8	91.4	86.4	19.2	45.0	42.6	67.6	53.9	46.5	6.9
1981[c]	64.8	78.3	48.6	90.9	95.3	89.1	17.3	51.8	44.5	77.2	65.8	53.2	6.0

[a]excludes Newfoundland
[b]includes Newfoundland
[c]includes persons of 15 years of age & over.

Source: For 1901-1961 see Ostry, 1971: 18. For 1971, 1976, and 1981 data see the respective censuses of Canada. Reproduced by permission of the Minister of Supply and Services Canada.

III. OCCUPATIONAL STRUCTURE

The concept of occupational structure is used by sociologists to refer to the social pattern which is suggested by the distribution of the labour force across the range of existing types of work (Watson, 1980:149-50). Just as types of work in a society change over time, so does the occupational structure. What factors contribute to shape the occupational structure? What differentiating factors do we use to analyze the occupational structure? We shall discuss these factors and then proceed to describe the Canadian occupational structure.

(a) Industrial Development and Occupational Structure

The most powerful factors affecting the occupational structure of a society are the ones associated with industrialization. In the process where a society evolves from a rural-agricultural to an urban-industrial dominance, a wide complex of forces shape the demand for goods and services and hence, the derived demand for labour. Within industries, occupational requirements respond to a great variety of pressures, the most pervasive and compelling of which is undoubtedly technology. Technological advances often lead to the creation of new occupations or the extinction or modification of existing ones. When the combustion engine was developed, stage coachworkers were soon replaced by autoworkers. Computer programmer and system analyst are occupational titles unheard of before the invention of computer technology. The underlying logic of changes such as these is that "the new industrial system requires a wide range of highlevel skills and professional competency broadly distributed throughout the working population. Thus the old occupational structure is transformed by the emergence of more differentiated and specialized work force..." (Weeks, 1980:75).

As technological change is a constant feature of the industrial system, the transformation of the occupational structure is a continuing process. Industrialization begins, of course, in the industrial sector. Analogous to a piece of rock thrown into a lake, the effect of industrial growth ripples, sometimes waves, through other aspects of the society. The supply of necessary raw materials, components, and services to the industrial sector brings about the proliferation of a wide range of other occupations. These, in turn, have their own spin-offs. Thus, this dynamic process results not only in greater diversity and numbers of occupations but also a chain of the emergence of new and the disappearance of old occupations. As mentioned earlier, only five broad industrial groupings were recorded in the 1871 census. Today, *The Canadian Classification and Dictionary of Occupations*

(CCDO) identifies some 7,000 individual occupations which are classified into 500 Unit Groups, 81 Minor Groups, and 23 Major Groups (Statistics Canada, 1971). In the United States, the first edition of *The Dictionary of Occupational Titles* in 1939 had 17,452 entries. This number had risen to 21,741 in the third edition in 1965 (U.S. Department of Labor, 1965). These phenomenal increases exemplify the rapid growth and change of the occupational structures of the two societies.

(b) Societal Characteristics and Occupational Structure[2]

In addition to industrialization, the characteristics of a society also affect its occupational structure. "One such characteristic is a society's commitment to military prowess, both in numbers and in expertise" (Harvey, 1975:99). Nations such as the United States, the Soviet Union, the People's Republic of China and Israel maintain proportionally large military forces. This results in a substantially higher percentage of persons in military occupations than is found among less military-oriented nations, Canada being one good example. Furthermore, not only is the quantitative aspect of the occupational structure affected, but also its complexity and diversity as reflected in the numerous types of occupations in highly sophisticated military powers such as the U.S. and the U.S.S.R.

Other societal characteristics that might influence the occupational structure of a society include the form of government. Totalitarian regimes may have many policing and security related occupations with a sizable work force. In societies where religion has prominent status, religious occupations may be more differentiated and have a larger percentage in overall occupational composition. The religious hierarchies in Islamic countries and the Vatican offer good examples. The scale and complexity of a society's governmental bureaucratic structure may at least be partially affected by the sheer size of its population. Other factors such as climate and other geographical features of a society may, at various degrees, help to shape its occupational structure. In brief, what we are suggesting here is that, although industrial development is powerful, it is not the sole determinant of occupational structure. Many other factors may have their effects as well.

(c) The Occupational Structure of Canada

In this section we shall describe the occupational structure of Canada in terms of both industrial divisions and occupational groups to identify patterns and historical trends. In their attempt to explain the process of industrialization, Kerr *et al.* (1962) point out that a typical pattern is a continuing reduction in the proportion of the labour force employed in the primary sector (including agriculture, fishing, mining, logging) and a shift toward the industrial sector (including manufacturing and construction). At a later stage of industrial development, a further occupational shift occurs with an increasing proportion of the work force moving into the tertiary sector (including all work activities which produce services other than goods).

In terms of the proportions of the labour force employed in each sector of industry, the changes in Canada have followed the patterns observed above. The general trend of development from 1901-1981 is presented in Table 2-3.

It is apparent that the major changes in the industrial divisions of the Canadian labour force over the last 80 years have been the steady (drastic in the last 40 years) decline in primary industries, particularly agricultural, and the impressive rise in service producing industries (trade, finance, government, schools, hospitals and so on) in the last 40 years. The changes in the proportion of the secondary sector have been more moderate.

In 1901, 45 percent of the Canadian labour force engaged in agriculture. In 1941, there was still more than a quarter. Four decades later, there was only four percent. Together with fishing, logging and mining, less than seven percent of the labour force was involved with primary industries in 1981. It was in the 1951 census that the proportion of workers employed in the manufacturing and construction finally exceeded that in the primary industries. On the other hand, tertiary industries grew from 28 percent in 1901 to over 66 percent in 1981. As for the proportion of workers in the secondary sector, the fluctuations have been relatively small throughout this century. It should be pointed out that the industries in the secondary sector have never claimed more than a third of the labour force in Canada, one of lowest proportions among most industrial countries. In addition, the primary sector has played a dominant role in Canada somewhat longer than has been the case in other industrialized countries. (Smucker, 1980:77). Canada is not unique, however, in the experience of industrial shifts and those developments are common in broad outline, though not in precise details and timing.

The long run occupational trends depicted in Table 2-4 clearly indicate that the growth of the Canadian labour force in this century is characterized by two major occupational shifts related to the industrial shifts described above. First, there has been a marked shift away from agricultural pursuits: about 44 percent of the labour force were

Table 2-3
Percentage Distribution of
the Total Canadian Labour Force by Industry, 1901-1981

	1901	1911	1921	1931	1941*	1951	1961	1971	1981
Total (1,000x)	1752	2722	3173	3917	4447	5286	6471	8627	1204
Primary	45.0	39.5	36.6	32.6	30.9	21.1	14.2	8.4	7.0
Secondary	26.8	27.1	26.5	17.3	28.3	32.3	28.4	26.0	25.3
Tertiary	28.1	33.4	36.9	39.0	39.0	45.3	55.0	57.7	66.2
Other	–	–	–	11.1	1.8	1.3	2.4	7.9	1.5
Total	100.0	100.0	100.0	100.0	100.0	100.0	100.0	100.0	100.0

*The census of 1941 reported a separate category of "labourers" who were not included in the primary sector. These are included in the total of the secondary sector—manufacturing and construction.
Sources: calculated from censuses of Canada of the respective years.

Table 2-4
Percentage Distribution of the
Canadian Labour Force, by Occupation, 1901-1961

Occupation Division	1901	1911	1921	1931	1941	1951	1961
All Occupations (in thousands)	1899	2809	3312	4048	4652	5277	6458
Managerial	4.3	4.9	7.3	5.7	5.7	8.0	8.3
Professional & Technical	4.6	3.8	5.4	6.2	6.9	7.3	9.7
Clerical	3.2	3.8	6.9	7.0	7.5	11.0	12.9
Sales	3.1	4.7	5.7	5.3	4.9	5.4	6.4
Service & Recreation	8.2	7.6	7.0	9.2	10.4	9.7	12.3
Transport & Communication	4.4	5.6	5.5	5.2	5.1	6.3	6.1
Subtotal*	27.8	30.4	37.8	38.6	40.5	47.7	55.7
Farmers & Farm Workers	40.3	34.3	32.6	28.5	25.7	15.7	10.0
Loggers & Related Workers	0.9	1.5	1.2	1.1	1.9	1.9	1.2
Fishermen, Trappers & Hunters	1.5	1.3	0.9	1.2	1.2	1.0	0.5
Miners, Quarrymen & Related Workers	1.6	2.3	1.6	1.4	1.7	1.2	1.0
Subtotal*	44.3	39.4	36.2	32.2	30.5	19.8	12.7
Craftsmen, Production Process & Related Workers	20.6	18.4	16.1	17.8	22.4	24.7	23.6
Labourers	7.2	11.8	9.7	11.4	6.4	6.7	5.3
Subtotal*	27.8	30.2	25.8	29.2	28.8	31.4	28.9
Not stated	–	–	0.2	–	0.3	1.2	2.6
Total	99.9	100.0	100.0	100.0	100.0	100.0	99.9

*The broad groups are ours.
Sources: Totals of all occupations for 1901-1941 were taken from F.T. Denton and Sylvia Ostry, *Historical Estimates of the Canadian Labour Force* (Ottawa: DBS, 1967) Table 11, p. 29 (Adjusted data); for 1951 and 1961 were calculated from 1971 Census of Canada, Vol. III, Part 2 (Bulletin 3.2-2), Occupations: Historical for Canada and Provinces (cat. 94-716), Table 1. Reproduced by permission of the Minister of Supply and Services Canada.

farmers and other workers in primary occupations in 1901; about 30 percent were in those occupations by 1941; by 1981, only 5.8 percent were still engaged in these activities. Second, there is a decisive movement toward service type of occupations (including the first six groups in Table 2-4). About 28 percent of the labour force were in the occupations at the turn of the century. This proportion increased to 38.6 percent by 1931. In the subsequent decades, the changes were dramatic. By 1961, the proportion of these occupations increased to well over one-half, 55.7 percent, to be specific. This impressive change can perhaps be illustrated by way of an estimate. If the 1931 occupational distribution had not altered, there would, in 1961, be about 1.8 million farmers and farm workers; whereas, in fact, there were only about one-third of that number. Finally, while the movement toward service type of occupations has been dramatic, the effect of long run redistributional changes on the relative share of manufacturing and construction occupations (including draftsmen, production process and related workers, and labourers in Table 2-4) have been mild in comparison. The proportions of workers in these occupations were 27.8 percent, 29.2 percent and 28.9 percent in 1901, 1931, and 1961 respectively.

The occupational system in the census of Canada has changed since 1971. This change makes it difficult to compare with previous censuses. Table 2-5 presents percentage distribution of the 20 major occupational groups for 1971 and 1981. While these figures cannot be directly compared with those in Table 2-4, the general patterns are unmistakably similar. The largest increase is in the service type occupations. There is a noticeable decrease of primary industries. The change in the group of manufacturing and construction occupations is marginal. Clearly, these have been consistent patterns in the Canadian occupational structure.

Two other important patterns of the Canadian occupational structure are related to women's participation in the labour force. One is the dramatic increase of women in the labour force. The other is the unique distribution of women in various occupations. During the last 50 years, the number of women in the labour force has increased much more rapidly than that of men. Between 1931 and 1981, the female proportion of the labour force increased from 17 to 41 percent, while the participation rate increased from 21.8 to 51.8 percent. Why are more women working today? More women are working today in part because of the need for a dual income to support a family in an inflated economy (Connelly, 1978).

There are, however, other sociological factors encouraging the increase of working women. Current population trends are one such factor. The life span of Canadians has increased considerably during the twentieth century. In 1931, the average man lived 61 years, the

Table 2-5
Percentage Distribution of the Canadian Labour Force,
by Occupation, 1971 and 1981

Occupations	1971	1981
All Occupations (in thousands)	8,627	12,005
Manag., Admin., & Rel. Occup.	4.3	6.8
Nat. Sci., Engin. & Math.	2.7	3.4
Soc. Sci. & Rel. Fields	0.9	1.6
Occup. in Religion	0.3	0.3
Tech. & Rel. Occup.	4.0	4.1
Medicine & Health	3.8	4.3
Art., Lit., Rec. & Rel. Occup.	0.9	1.4
Clerical & Rel. Occup.	15.9	18.2
Sales Occupations	9.5	9.5
Service Occupations	11.2	11.9
Trans. Equip. Operating	3.9	3.8
Sub-Total*	57.4	65.3
Farming, Horti. & Animal Husb.	5.9	4.2
Fishing, Hunt., Trap. & Rel. Occup.	0.3	0.3
Foresting & Logging	0.8	0.7
Mining & Quar., Oil & Gas Field	0.7	0.6
Sub-Total*	7.7	5.8
Processing Occup.	3.9	3.9
Machining & Rel. Occup.	2.8	2.6
Prod. Fab., Assem. Repair	7.4	7.7
Construction Trades	6.6	6.4
Material Hand. & Operat.	2.4	2.0
Other Crafts & Equip. Operating	1.3	1.2
Sub-total*	24.4	23.8
Not Classified & Not Stated	10.4	5.0
Total	99.9	99.9

*The broad groupings are ours.
Source: Calculated from 1981 Census of Canada, Vol. 1, Table 1 (cat. 92-920).

average woman 64 years. By 1971, life expectancy had increased to 69 years for men and 76 years for women. By 1980, these figures have become 72 and 79 respectively. Since the difference between the life expectancy of men and women has been increasing, there has been a change in the ratio of widows to widowers. According to the 1981 census, there was about five widows for every widower.

In addition, the fertility of Canadian women is declining. By 1981, married Canadian women were averaging less than two children (1.4 national average). Since Canadian women are having fewer children, they are able to enter and re-enter the labour force. Moreover, many women, for a variety of reasons, have become principal breadwinners. This, too, increases the participation rate of women. Another factor is urbanization. this process has freed many women from the farms who are now seeking, or forced to seek, paid jobs in the labour market (Himelfarb and Richardson, 1979:146).

Finally, perhaps more significantly, changing roles also encourage women to work. Women today—unlike their mothers and grandmothers—have considerable freedom to choose how they will fulfill their sex role. An increasing number of women are actively seeking a meaningful career of their own, instead of playing the supporting role for their husbands and the family.

While more women are working and are staying longer in the labour force, they have not entered the occupational groups evenly. Table 2-6 shows the sharp contrast of distribution patterns between male and female workers. Men tend to spread much wider on the occupational spectrum. In contrast, women have a greater concentration in only a few categories. A number of questions can be asked in regard to this phenomenon. Has the increasing participation of women in the labour force changed the attitudes toward women and their status? What impact does it have on family, education, and women themselves? What impact does this phenomenon have on work organizations? To mention just a few. All these points have been vehemently debated issues. We shall return to them later in Chapter 7.

IV. FUTURE TRENDS AND PROSPECTS

The prediction of the future in social life is a risky task at best. The unstable domestic and international environments, the issues of national unity and energy, and the fluctuations in the economic cycles make it even more problematic. However, some speculations can be made by using available data.

Denton and Spencer (1980) attempted to project changes in the Canadian population and in the resulting labour force through 2051. Assuming a total fertility of 2.1 births per woman, they observe that the total population can be expected to increase from 22,993,000 in 1976 to 30,966,000 in 2001, and 40,758,000 by the middle of the next century. The most striking feature in this picture is the effect of the

Table 2-6
**Percentage Distribution of the Canadian Labour Force
by Occupation and Sex, 1971 and 1981**

Occupations	1971		1981	
	Male	Female	Male	Female
Manag., Admin., & Rel. Occup.	84.3	15.7	75.1	24.9
Nat. Sci., Engin. & Math.	92.7	7.3	85.9	14.1
Soc. Sci. & Rel. Fields	62.6	37.4	47.5	52.5
Occup. in Religion	84.3	15.7	73.5	26.5
Tech. & Rel. Occup.	39.6	60.4	40.5	59.5
Medicine & Health	25.7	74.3	22.4	77.6
Art., Lit., Rec. & Rel. Occup.	72.8	27.2	60.2	39.8
Clerical & Rel. Occup.	31.6	68.4	22.3	77.7
Sales Occupations	69.6	30.4	59.2	40.8
Service Occupations	53.8	46.2	47.7	52.3
Trans. Equip. Operating	79.1	20.9	78.9	21.1
Farming, Horti. & Animal Husb.	98.1	1.9	94.4	5.6
Fishing, Hunt., Trap. & Rel. Occup.	97.9	2.1	93.7	6.3
Foresting & Logging	99.4	0.6	97.8	2.2
Mining & Quar., Oil & Gas Field	82.2	17.8	77.8	22.2
Processing Occup.	94.3	5.7	93.2	6.8
Machining & Rel. Occup.	76.3	23.7	75.6	24.4
Prod. Fab., Assem. Repair	99.1	0.9	98.0	2.0
Construction Trades	97.6	2.4	93.5	6.5
Material Hand. & Operat.	80.3	19.7	77.4	22.6
Other Crafts & Equip. Operating	87.6	12.4	78.9	21.1
Occupations Not Elsewhere Classified	87.0	13.0	82.6	17.4
Occupations Not Stated	56.7	43.3	57.4	42.6
All Occupations	65.7	34.3	59.6	40.4

Source: Calculated from 1981 Census, Vol. 1, Table 1 (cat. 92-920).

post-Second World War "baby boom" which resulted in expanded school enrollments and which increased the number of workers of 16 to 19 years of age in the late sixties. By 1991 this baby boom generation will be entering its forties.

Unless the birth rate goes up again, for the first time in history, population pyramids will no longer be literal pyramids: wide at the base and narrow at the top. Actually, the population pattern will resemble a truncated diamond. Thus, there will be a larger proportion of the population working in 2001 than in 1976, but it will be an older and more mature population. Denton and Spencer projected that the overall labour force is to grow by some 45 percent by 2001. The female labour force is projected to grow by about 37 percent. The labour force of the 65 and over age group is projected to decrease for some years, in spite of the projected increases in the number of older people, which is a consequence of the declining male participation rates in this age group. In the case of women, the writers assumed a continuation of the trend towards lower participation rates among the young (under 20) and the old (over 65). Women in the age groups between 20 and 65 have assumed a continuation for some years to come of the recent strong increases in participation rates. For all ages of both sexes, the participation rates cease to decline and the older component of the labour force starts to grow.

These projections have several implications. Since a major shift in the distribution of members in the labour force by age can be expected, employment concerns may consequently shift from promoting opportunities in entry-level jobs to ensuring more stable occupational opportunities for relatively older workers. It is also quite conceivable that among workers in the 20-34 age bracket competition will be keen, both because of the proportionate increase in that group, and because it must compete with workers 35 and over who are smaller in number and will have the required skills and maturity.

The second implication of the population and labour force changes is for the economic burden of dependency in future decades. In 1976 the dependency ratio of Canadians younger than 20 and older than 64 to the population aged 20-64 was 0.81 (Denton and Spencer, 1980). That is, there were 81 people under the age of 20 and over 65 for every 100 people aged 20-64. This was the lowest ratio since the turn of the century in Canada. Looking into the future, Denton and Spencer (1980) projected that the youth dependency ratio would decline further between 1976 and 2011 and then remain approximately constant thereafter. That of the elderly, on the other hand, would rise sharply from 0.16 in 1976 to 0.31 in 2051, with most of the increase taking place after the year 2011. Will these changes of dependency ratios amount to a crisis? The writers reached a negative conclusion because:

...the net result of the fall in the young ratio and the rise in the elderly ratio is a somewhat lower overall dependency ratio for the remainder of this century and through the first decade of the next, as compared with 1976....(Denton and Spencer:1980:25)

While there will be a pronounced increase in the following decades, the overall dependency ratio will probably be no higher than it was in 1976. Thus, it appears that future increases in the older population would not impose an "unmanageable burden" on the economy or on the population of working age.

While the dependency problem may not become a crisis as many fear, there is trouble within the labour force. As the baby boom cohort is absorbed into the labour force, what do we do with the relatively older workers when those who are younger clamor for employment? The proportion of the 25-44 age group is projected to increase from 44.9 percent in 1976 to 56.5 percent of the labour force by 1991 (calculated from Denton and Spencer, 1980:23, Table 4). There are two possible solutions. One is economic expansion; thus, more employment opportunities would be available. The other is early retirement of the older workers, so that more younger workers can enter the rank of the employed. As international economy is in an era of a high degree of uncertainty, and the Canadian economy seems to be in a slow recovery after a lengthy recession, few people would anticipate an economic expansion as witnessed in the 1960s.

As for early retirement, while some writers suggest a continuation of the tendency towards earlier retirement among men over 55 (Denton and Spencer, 1980:22), there is also a revolt against mandatory retirement among older workers. It appears that this will remain a significant issue for some time to come.

While there are many projections of the population and the labour force in general, there is very little detailed projection of industrial and occupational distribution for the next couple of decades. However, there is enough information available which enables us to make a reasonable guess. As we have pointed out earlier, one of the striking features of Canadian economy in the last few decades has been the rapid expansion of service industries. In 1976, some 65 percent of the labour force was involved in the service industries. Many researchers project a continuation of this trend in the future. McCready foresees somewhat over 70 percent of the total labour force being accounted for as service industry employed by 1985, and maybe even higher thereafter (1977:254). Drouin and Bruce-Briggs (1978:100) suggest that white-collar occupations will continue to increase their share of employment, and will account for 66 percent of the labour force in the late 1980s. Two-thirds to three-quarters of growth in employment in the next ten years would come from white-collar jobs. This would largely be a result of the growing demands by consumers for medical, social, and personal services for a continuing improvement in living standards. It is said that the latest wave of technological change could increase the productivity considerably. If this is true, it is reasonable to predict that the work week will be further shortened, the demands for leisure-related services mounted, and the proportion of tertiary industries increased.

No discussion on future trends of the labour force is complete without a word about the level of unemployment. Currently, the overall rate is over 11 percent. The prospect is not bright. Most researchers project that unemployment will continue to be a major economic, social and political issue in Canada. Some say it will continue over the next generation (Drouin and Bruce-Briggs, 1978). Historically, Canada exhibits a higher unemployment rate than most, if not all, Western nations (Sorrentino, 1970; Moy and Sorrentino, 1977). There is a host of causes: its climate, its geography, the rapid growth in the participation rates, shifts of demands and accelerated technological change (Ostry, 1971), the changing attitudes towards work, increased demand for leisure, significant improvement in unemployment benefits, and, last but not least, the branch plant economy (Britton and Gilmore, 1978; Glayson, 1983). In short, the chronic problem of unemployment in Canada can be attributed as much to structural as to cyclical phenomena, to economic, social, and political factors.

One obvious and immediate consequence of unemployment is, of course, economic hardship. However, the social and psychological effects can be equally devastating, if not more so. It has been well-documented that job loss can lead to loss of self-respect, anxiety, depression, insomnia, strained family relations, domestic violence, and even suicide (Wadel, 1973; Hayes and Nutman, 1981).

Furthermore, most of these consequences are not limited to those individuals and families involved. They tend to spill over to the community, because they could put a strain on community medical and welfare facilities, especially when unemployment is massive in an area (e.g., lay-offs or plant shutdown). For instance, when workers in INCO, Sudbury, Ontario were laid off in 1982, a community-activities consultant had to establish a local stress management centre to deal with the situation (Glayson, 1983). It can be seen that unemployment is not only economically costly, but the human sufferings it causes are no more bearable.

V. SUMMARY

In this chapter we have posited an analysis of the Canadian occupational structure to answer the question "who works?". The normative framework, as signified by the official definition of the labour force was used for the analysis because paid employment is the most important mechanism for the distribution of wealth in this society.

After a discussion of factors associated with industrialization and societal characteristics which are accountable for the development of the occupational structure of a society, major patterns in the Canadian occupational structure were identified: a drastic decrease of primary industries, a dramatic increase of tertiary industries and moderate fluctuations in the secondary sector of industries. It was pointed out that these trends are similar to those experienced by most industrialized societies.

Some future trends and prospects were discussed in the last section. We suggested that the dependency ratio between the producing (20-64 age range) and non-producing (0-19 and 65+ age groups) populations may not reach a crisis level by the end of this century; the growth of the tertiary sector of the occupational structure is likely to continue; and, finally, for a variety of reasons, the unemployment rate in Canada will likely remain at a relatively high level.

Notes

1. For a further understanding of domestic labour, see the following works: Fox (1980); Luxton (1980); Wilson (1982, ch. 21); Lopata (1974).
2. Discussion in this section follows E. Harvey's ideas. See Harvey (1975:99).

Suggested Readings

Armstrong, Pat and Hugh
  1978. *The Double Ghetto: Canadian Women and Their Segregated Work*: Chapter I, "Women's Work in the Labour Force." Toronto: McClelland & Stewart.
Denton, Frank T. and Bryon G. Spencer
  1980. "Canada's Population and Labour Force: Past, Present and Future," in Victor W. Marshall (ed.): *Aging in Canada: Social Perspectives*. Don Mills: Fitzhenry & Whiteside.

Gingrich, Paul
    1978. "Unemployment: A Radical Analysis of Myth and Fact," *Our Generation*, 12(3):16-31.
Smucker, Joseph
    1980. *Industrialization in Canada*. Chapter 4: "Patterns of Change in the Economic Development of Canada." Scarborough: Prentice-Hall.
Stirling, Robert and Denise Kouri
    1979. "Unemployment Indexes—The Canadian Context," in John Allan Fry (ed.): *Economy, Class and Social Reality: Issues in Contemporary Canadian Society*, 1979:205. Toronto: Butterworths.
Wilson, S. J.
    1982. *Women, the Family and the Economy*, Part III, "Women's Work." Toronto: McGraw-Hill Ryerson Ltd.
Weeks, David R.
    1980. "Industrial Developent and Occupational Structure," in Esland and Salaman, *The Politics of Work and Occupations*, 1980:74-106. Toronto: University of Toronto Press.

Chapter 3

Occupational Choice

One of the most striking features of an industrial society is its rapid pace of change. New technologies are constantly developed and adopted. Thus, many occupations are rendered obsolete and many new ones are created. While many characteristics of work may change from time to time, one aspect remains the same; that is, occupational roles need to be filled by workers and individuals need to enter into occupations. Why does a person enter into one occupation over the others? How does a society allocate its human resources? Is the occupational distribution of a population the result of millions of individual choices or of societal allocation? These are the major issues which concern us in this chapter.

Although "occupational choice" is a commonly used term for the particular field or research dealing with the entry of people into work, its meaning is not as clear as it appears. Some researchers use it very inclusively. For instance, Ginzberg (1951) and Burchinal (1962) define occupational choice as the total development process involved in occupational attainment. Others use it in a more specific sense. Kuvlesky and Bealer, for example, define it to mean "only the psychological preferences or desires that an individual has regarding work status" (1966:267). As a result of this diversity of usages of the term, it is often difficult to compare the findings of the numerous studies.

Furthermore, as Sofer pointed out, the use of the word "choice" in the concept "occupational choice" has certain disadvantages. It can be taken to imply (1) "that people enter the occupations they do after careful and systematic consideration of the alternatives open to them"; (2) "that the attempt to implement preference is a distinct and discrete act"; and (3) "that the overall distribution of persons between occupations in our society is what it is as the result of the cumulation of several million personal decisions made in this way"(Sofer, 1974:13).

We will show that personal preference is only one of many factors affecting the way a person makes a decision when faced with concrete alternatives. There is also evidence that such choices are not necessarily systematic and in most cases the final decision of occupational entry is often the compromise between one's preferences and expectations. In addition, social structures play a crucial role in channelling people into one occupational stream or another. As a consequence, the overall occupational distribution of people is affected by these social influences.

Why then does the term "occupational choice" recur in scholarly publications from time to time? Sofer pointed out that this is partly a result of the fact that, "as in many branches of social science, the individual is the most convenient unit of research... and most studies of entry into occupations consist of research on the individual entrants" (Sofer, 1974:13-14). However, while personal preferences undoubtedly are important, the social processes and institutional forces are equally, if not more, crucial in determining an individual's entry into an occupation. A balanced perspective should be maintained in our attempt to understand the processes of "occupational choice."

I. APPROACHES TO THE STUDY OF OCCUPATIONAL CHOICE

In order to understand and explain the process of occupational choice, many researchers have attempted to conceptualize and theorize the phenomenon. Their endeavors fall into three broad categories: fortuitous, rational decision making, and socio-cultural influence approaches (Pavalko, 1971:45). These approaches are reviewed in the following pages.

(a) The Fortuitous Approach

To put it simply, in this view, the reason a person is a member of a certain occupation is more by chance than by choice. This approach regards "occupational choice" as a less purposive and deliberate selection of one among many occupations. Rather, it is perceived as a process of elimination.

For example, Katz and Martin (1962) have propounded this view in a study of nurses. They maintain that occupational choice is highly spontaneous, nonrational and influenced by situational pressures. As they see it, "the decisions which underlie embarkation on a nursing career for at least some persons revolve around limited situational contingencies in which the matter of nursing-as-career enters only tangentially or not at all" (Katz and Martin, 1962:149-50).

Caplow also indicates the adventitious character of occupational choice. He reported that (Caplow, 1954:218):

> The bases for decision are often trivial. A student decides to study law because he has gotten his highest grades in history courses, dislikes the idea of teaching, and knows that courses in history are required for entrance to law school. A grade school pupil elects the vocational high school because someone has told him that automobile mechanics get high wages. A high school sophomore transfers from the academic sequence to the clerical course to be with her best friend. The crucial decision to leave school and to go to work may reflect the most casual dissatisfaction or the lure of a passing opportunity.

Similarly, some of the authors' students who do not have a real interest in teaching pursue a bachelor of education to obtain their teacher's license "just in case."

While several studies have indicated that some people enter college teaching as the end product of drift (Stecklein and Eckert, 1958:44; Gustad, 1960:4), this perspective may be more appropriate in viewing the entry of work at the lower echelon of the occupational spectrum such as machine operator, meter reader, clerk and so on. These occupations require only short periods of "on the job training," or no training or experience at all. For explaining the entry into the professions which require a long period of preparation, the rational decision-making approach, which will be discussed presently, may be more accurate. It should be pointed out, however, that while the label "fortuitous" indicates the entry of an occupation by chance, or because of situational pressures, it is not entirely a lack of rationality. For example, one person whose original career choice was to become a recreational director became a nurse because of financial reasons. She described herself as being very people oriented. When finances caused her to shift her plans, she saw nursing as "a logical people-oriented alternative." Clearly, there is rational thinking in this case. As Ginzberg and his associates (1951) have pointed out, the fortuitous approach is correct in stressing the contingent factors but it is wrong in neglecting the fact that the way in which the person takes account of the external factors depends on how these factors are perceived.

(b) The Rational Decision-Making Approach

It should be made clear at the outset that the label "rational decision-making approach" is not a unitary and coherent theory. Rather, it includes several theoretical attempts to analyze the processes of occupational choice, which all depict that the coming together of an individual and an occupation has a large measure of rationality about it.

Some researchers conceptualize the nature of occupational choice as it is related to the maturation of the individual. The best known examples of this perspective are the work of Ginzberg and his associates (1951) and Super (1957).

Ginzberg's approach is developed from the perspective of a developmental psychology of adolescence. The emergence of occupational interests and a concern with values are viewed in the context of the individual going through a process of emotional change and maturation. The process of occupational choice is a series of compromises between a person's interests, capacities, opportunities and values.

Ginzberg divided the developmental process into three periods: fantasy choice (from early childhood to puberty, approximately from 6 to 11 years of age); tentative choice (early adolescence, ages 12-17); and realistic choice (ages 18 and above).

(i) The Fantasy Period

This period has been described in terms of the child's desires and thought about adult life. The occupational roles, such as doctor, nurse, cowboy, fire fighter or truck driver seem to have visibility in the child's world. While it is possibly true that these fantasies are influenced largely by what is visible, it should be pointed out that they need not relate to reality in any way.

(ii) The Tentative Period

During this period the person becomes more realistic. However, this realism relates to the individual's desires and aspirations and not necessarily with the position of the labour market. What is significant about this period is the fact that the individual recognizes that there is a problem of deciding upon a future occupation.

To highlight the general themes which influence occupational aspiration at this stage, Ginzberg has subdivided this period of tentative choice into stages of (i) interest, (ii) capacity, (iii) value, and (iv) transition.

(iii) The Realistic Period

In this period a choice is made with the objective of implementing it. It is during this period that compromises are often made between the person's capabilities, interests and so on and the available opportunities.

As with the previous period, this one is also subdivided: (i) exploration, (ii) crystallization, and (iii) specification. These sub-stages represent the individual compromising with the real situation and a progressive narrowing of the range of occupational choices through time.

While this framework systematizes an almost common-sense understanding of occupational choice, it has its shortcomings. First, as Pavalko (1971:46) pointed out, Ginzberg's scheme is both culture-bound and time-bound. It is culture-bound because the stages and corresponding age spans are closely tied to the American educational system. The choice periods could be viewed as reflecting the times at which the educational system forces decisions on the student.

It is time-bound because the age periods of 18 plus as a period of realistic choice may no longer be true. In the 1940s and earlier, "realistic" choice may have been made by a sizable proportion of people in their late teens. However, a large and increasing proportion of high school graduates are postponing a realistic choice of an occupation until early 20s by going to college or university.

A second criticism of this conceptualization is that choice was defined in terms of preference rather than entry or some other implementation of choice. However, choice means different things at different age levels. To a 13-year-old who desires to be an astronaut, it means nothing more than a preference, because at that age the need for taking action to realize that preference is rather remote. To the 20-year-old student of nursing, "choice" means a preference which has already been acted upon in entering nursing school, although the final stage of implementation is yet to come.

Furthermore, as we shall see later in this chapter, for groups with certain social characteristics there are considerable distances between their preferences and expectations. The discrepancy is even wider between their preferences and the implementations of the same. A second major contribution to our understanding of occupational choice is D. E. Super's work. In the following series of ten propositions he summarized his "comprehensive theory" as follows (Super, 1953:189-190):

1. People differ in their abilities, interests and personalities.
2. They are qualified, by virtue of these characteristics, each for a number of occupations.
3. Each of these occupations require a characteristic pattern of abilities, interests and personality traits, with tolerance wide enough, however, to allow both some variety of occupations for each individual and some variety of individuals in each occupation.

4. Vocational preferences and competencies, the situations in which people live and work, and hence their self-concepts, change with time and experience (although self-concepts are fairly stable from late adolescence until late maturity), making choice and adjustment a continuous process.
5. This process may be summed up in a series of life stages characterized as those of growth, exploration, establishment, maintenance, and decline, and these stages may in turn be subdivided into (a) the fantasy, tentative and realistic phases of the exploratory stage, and (b) the trial and stable phases of the establishment stage.
6. The nature of the career pattern (that is, the occupational level attained and the sequence, frequency, and duration of trial and stable jobs) is determined by the individual's parental socio-economic level, mental ability, and personality characteristics, and by the opportunities to which he is exposed.
7. Development through the life stages can be guided, partly by facilitating the process of maturation of abilities and interests, and partly by aiding in reality testing and in the development of the self-concept.
8. The process of vocational development is essentially that of developing and implementing a self-concept: it is a compromise process in which the self-concept is a product of the interaction of inherited aptitudes, neural and endocrine make-up, opportunity to play various roles, and evaluations of the extent to which the results of role playing meet with the approval of superiors and fellows.
9. The process of compromise between individual and social factors, between self-concept and reality, is one of role playing, whether the role is played in fantasy, in the counselling interview, or in real life activities such as school classes, clubs, part-time work, and entry jobs.
10. Work satisfactions and life satisfactions depend upon his establishment in the type of work, work situation, and way of life in which he can play the kind of role which his growth and exploratory experiences have led him to consider congenial and appropriate.

Similarly, Super also divided occupational choice into stages in terms of life cycle. There are six stages in his scheme (1957: Part 2):

1. Adolescence as exploration: developing a self-concept (roughly comparable to Ginzberg's period of "Tentative Choice").
2. The transition from school to work: reality testing (partially comparable to Ginzberg's period of "Realistic Choice").

3. The floundering or trial process: attempting to implement a self-concept (partially comparable to Ginzberg's "Period of Realistic Choice").
4. The period of establishment: the self-concept modified or implemented.
5. The maintenance period: preserving or being nagged by self-concept.
6. The years of decline: adjustment to a new self-concept.

In brief, Super maintains that occupational choice is purposive and it consists of the processes of formation, translation and implementation of the self-concept. The difficulty of this theory is that it involves a "chicken-egg" dilemma. "While it is possible that individuals may attempt to find work that is compatible with their personalities, it is at least equally possible that the kind of work people do may shape the kind of personality and self-concept they exhibit" (Pavalko, 1971:47). Studies on socialization of student nurses (Simpson, 1967), medical students (Merton, *et al.*: 1957), and policemen (Vincent: 1979) provide ample evidence to support Pavalko's alternative interpretation.

A variation of the rational decision-making approach is the so-called "Minimax strategy" (Sherlock and Cohen, 1966). These researchers proposed that occupational choice is a compromise between reward preferences and expectancies of access to specific occupations. In the process of deciding on an occupation, the individual tries to minimize one reward preference to maximize another. For example, their study of pre-dental students indicated that their decision to enter dentistry is the result of calculation of rewards and ease of access. while medicine might offer greater rewards than dentistry, it is less accessible. On the other hand, law or university teaching may be as accessible as dentistry; but they perceived these occupations as offering lower rewards. Dentistry was chosen because, from their perception, it offers both high rewards and reasonable ease of access.

Much of the research utilizing the rational decision-making approach to the process of occupational choice is psychologically based. researchers in this field examine the way in which the individual passes through a series of stages during which the self-concept grows as abilities, aptitudes and interest develop; or as in Sherlock and Cohen's study (1966), they examine the process of calculation. However, socialization experiences, perceptions, attitudes, interests and early work experiences are subject to structural limitations such as one's social class position, educational background and even location of residence and so on. It is on these limitations that the next approach put its emphasis.

(c) The Socio-cultural Influence Approach

While the rational decision-making perspective focuses on the individual's processes of psychological development, this approach, mainly the work of sociologists, attempts to identify and examine the limitations imposed by the individual's structural content. In this sociological perspective, the social characteristics are viewed as "external influences over which the individual has little or no control. In this way they set limits upon and constrain the kinds of occupational choices and decisions that individuals make" (Pavalko, 1971:51). In other words, this perspective emphasizes the "opportunity structure" to which the individual is exposed in contrast to those theories which see the occupation a person enters as an outcome of the implementation of that person's choice. Much of this literature concentrates on the individual's occupational preferences and/or expectations rather than the total process of occupational choice.

Many social characteristics have been studied in relation to their effects on occupational aspirations and expectations. Only the major ones, such as socio-economic status, parental education, sex, and ethnicity, will be discussed here. The influence of education is of special importance. Its effect on occupational choice will be discussed in a separate section.

(i) Socio-economic Status

Socio-economic status (SES) background is perhaps the most powerful overall factor which influences a person's occupational aspirations and expectations.[1] Numerous studies in Canada and in the United States consistently found that the socio-economic status of the family is positively related to the level of occupational aspirations and expectations. The higher the SES of a young person's family, the more likely that he is to aspire to the occupations with high prestige and rewards and is to expect to achieve these goals.

As an illustration, let us look at Brinkerhoff and Corry's study first (1976). By using a questionnaire, they collected data for 949 Grade XI students in Calgary. The sample was derived by stratifying the schools into three "broad groups based on average family income for continuous census tracts" (p. 264). Schools were then randomly drawn from each income level. Rural high schools in the surrounding school districts within a radius of 50 miles of the city were also included in the sample.

Occupational levels were based on Blishen's SES scale of occupations (Blishen, 1967). Those with scores 39 and below were considered *low.* those between 40 and 59 were termed *medium*, and those 60 and above were classified as *high*. Socio-economic status of the family was operationally defined by the respondent's father's occupation which was characterized the same way as the occupational levels (Brinkerhoff and Corry, 1976:267).

Students were asked: "Suppose that you were allowed to choose any job or occupation you liked for your life's work. What would you choose if you could have any job in the world?"(to measure occupational aspirations). "Some young people are not able to have any job they want. Realistically, what job or occupation do you think you will actually take up as your life's work?" (to measure occupational expectations). They found that, indeed, the higher the SES, the higher are the occupational aspirations and expectations (Table 3-1). While 40 percent of the high school students of high socio-economic backgrounds in this study aspired to high level occupations, only 25 percent of low socio-economic status did so. The influence of SES on expectations is somewhat higher than on aspirations (*Gamma +.27 vs .17*). The students appeared very realistic by taking into account their families' socio-economic statuses. This finding is consistent with that of some other researchers.

Table 3-1
Occupational Aspirations and Expectations of
High School Students in Calgary
as Influenced by Familial Socio-Economic Status,
by Percentages and Gammas*

Occupational Aspiration Level	*Low*	*SES Med*	*High*	*Occupational Expectation Level*	*Low*	*SES Med*	*High*
Low	37%	28	25	Low	45%	32	28
Medium	35	38	35	Medium	35	33	27
High	28 ·	33	40	High	20	35	45
N	284	324	315	N	278	319	314
Gammas**		+.17		Gammas		+.27	

*Adopted from Brinkerhoff and Corry (1976) Table 1 (p. 266)
**Gamma is a measure of association which assumes ordered classes of data. It indicates "...how much more probable it is to get like than unlike orders in two classifications..." (Goodman and Kruskal, 1954:749). For example, a gamma of .30 is interpreted to indicate that knowledge of rank differences on the one variable improves prediction of rank differences on the second variable by 30 percent above chance (see Brinkerhoff and Corry, 1976:266).

In his Canada-wide study, Breton reported that "the higher the occupational status of the boy's father, the more apt he is to choose a high status occupation" (1972:233). Somewhat differently, in his study of occupational goals in a predominantly blue-collar area in Toronto, Crysdale found that class differences influence expectations but not aspirations (1975:32). This slight inconsistency probably can be explained by the fact that Crysdale's sample was rather homogeneous with respect to SES. Under the influence of the homogeneous SES status, the school context of these students might have reduced the level of their aspirations (Brinkerhoff and Corry, 1976:268).

Additional evidence is provided by studies on social origins of members in different occupations or professions. For example, Jones (1976) reported that the proportion of physicians and lawyers with high social origin (father's occupation) is significantly larger than that of secondary school teachers and social workers from the same social origin (see Table 3-2 below).

Martin Shapiro (1978:14) expressed the same point about the social origin of physicians by using official statistics and his personal account:

> In general, medical students in North America are recruited from the economically privileged sectors of society. Over a decade ago, Canada's Royal Commission of Health Services reported that 54.4 percent of general practitioners and 65.8 percent of specialists in Canada, at the time of their entry into university, had fathers with professional or managerial occupations. In addition, 73 percent of all physicians had fathers whose occupational class, according to one index, was among the top 17 percent in the country; 15 percent of Canadian physicians have doctors for parents. The pattern is similar in the United States, where 58 percent of physicians come from professional or managerial backgrounds and about 17 percent have physicians as parents.
>
> Of 135 students in my medical course at McGill University, Montreal, I knew ten (and there were probably more) whose fathers were physicians. There were at least three in the class who were children of the elite (one was the son of the President of a large trust company, another was the son of the president of a large pharmaceutical company and the third was the daughter of the President of Liberia). Only a handful of students were from working class families and just one from a family that was genuinely poor. The rest were from the various strata of the middle class and upwards. In this sense we were probably representative of most medical school rosters today. We had a "relatively homogeneous social background", and few of us would have been thought destined for "lesser" careers.

(ii) Parental Education

Theoretically, one would expect that parents with higher education should be in a position to provide the opportunities, motivation,

Table 3-2

**Selected Social Origins for Four Professions in
Canada, by Percentages and Access Ratios (male sample)***

Origin (Father's Occupation)	% of Male Labour Force 1961	Physicians		Lawyers		Secondary School Teachers (Acad.)		Social Workers	
		%	a.r.**	%	a.r.	%	a.r.	%	a.r.
Professional & Technical Occupations	7.8	39.0	5.0	29.2	3.7	12.5	1.6	16.2	2.1
White Collar***	30.3	72.3	2.4	75.3	2.5	40.8	1.3	49.2	1.6
N		(249)		(243)		(152)		(179)	

*Adopted from Frank E. Jones (1976:149, 3)

**a.r. represents Access Ratio which was defined, by Jones, as the ratio of the percent
of the sample from a given occupational origin to the percent of the male labour
force in the same occupation.

***White Collar occupations—Canadian census class: clerical, sales.

and values which lead to higher level occupations. Methodologically, education is almost invariably a major component index of socio-economic status. Thus, it is reasonable to expect that the higher the parent's education, the higher the level of occupational aspiration and expectation. To cite Brinkerhoff and Corry again, they found that both parents' education has influences on their children's occupational "choice", particularly on the expectation aspect where the reality is more likely to be seriously considered (1976:268).

However, the findings on the relationship between this factor and occupational aspirations and expectations vary considerably. Breton found that the father's educational level has a greater effect on boys' (no data on girls') occupational choice than the corresponding level of the mother's (1972:234-35). Contrary to findings of both studies cited above, Crysdale (1975) suggested that the education of neither parent made much difference, although the mother's is more highly correlated with occupational preference.

(iii) Sex

Gender has been receiving increasing attention as an important structural factor in occupational studies. Discussions seem to cluster around several aspects of this factor: (i) whether women have higher or lower occupational aspirations than men, (ii) the range of women's occupational preferences, and (iii) the change of sex role and females' occupational choice.

Although Pavalko concluded in 1971 that "In general, women tend to have lower occupational aspirations than men" (p. 58), a close examination of empirical findings reveal that they are not conclusive. Brinkerhoff and Corry's study (1976) supported Pavalko's general conclusion. They reported that 40 percent of the Calgary boys aspire to high level occupations as compared to only 30 percent of the girls; similarly, 45 percent of the boys expect high level occupations as compared to 26 percent of girls (Brinkerhoff and Corry, p. 265; see Table 3-3).

These findings are also consistent with the general consideration that females' opportunity structure is different from that of males' because of the different patterns of socialization they receive—a point to which we shall return presently.

However, Breton (1972:230;292) found that Canadian youths of both sexes aspire equally to high status occupations (professional and managerial). On the other hand, Crysdale suggested that girls have higher occupational aspirations than boys (1975). These contradictory findings are likely a result of different occupation classifications

Table 3-3
Occupational Aspirations and Expectations of High
School Students in Calgary as Influenced by Sex.*

Occupational Aspiration Level	Boys	Girls	Occupational Expectation Level	Boys	Girls
Low	35%	23	Low	37%	31
Medium	35	37	Medium	37	24
High	30	40	High	26	45
N	541	399		532	395
Gamma	+.23		Gamma	+.24	

*Adopted from Brinkerhoff and Corry (1976:267, Table 1)

used in the various studies. For example, Crysdale used very broad census categories such as white-collar, blue-collar skilled, blue-collar semi-skilled, and unskilled. The white-collar category includes professional, managerial, owner, sales and clerical occupations. There is wide variation of prestige among these occupational groups. It is a well known fact that most female jobs are classified as white-collar but they are concentrated in the "clerical-sales-service" category. Since white-collar occupations are defined as high status in Crysdale's study, naturally he found most females aspiring to high status occupations.

Another concern is the range of women's occupational preferences. In general, the range of females' occupational preference is narrower. Even as preschoolers, girls choose fewer occupations than boys do (Kirchner and Vondracek, 1973; O'Hara, 1962). There is strong stereotyping of occupations in our society. There are men's jobs and there are women's jobs. Children seem to learn these stereotypes early in their lives. Tyler (1964) shows that the activity likes and dislikes of 10-year-old girls and boys are based on whether the activities are "appropriate" or "inappropriate" for their sex, rather than the "goodness" or "badness" of the activity. This sex-type notion of activity seems to start to shape the females' occupational orientation very early. Earlier research found that, even in first grade, girls did not develop skills and aspirations to match their interests (Tyler, 1951). Instead, the feminine value of helping others seemed to be the dominant force in guiding their aspirations and skill development (Tyler, 1964; O'Hara, 1962). Thus, in middle childhood, girls' activities and skills are often limited by being feminine. The result, not surprisingly, is a narrow range of occupational preferences. Furthermore, this phenomenon continues throughout childhood and adolescence. For example, Astin (1968) reported that of the 7000 ninth grade girls he studied in 1960, 16 percent planned to have careers in natural sciences or the professions (excluding teaching); except for nursing, these are male dominated fields. Four years later, only five percent of these same girls planned to have natural science or professional careers.

Females' occupational aspirations often decline in early adolescence. Moreover, this pattern of decline also occurs during college as many women give up plans to become high level professionals and plan to become housewives or middle level professionals such as teachers (Homall *et al.*, 1975; Klemmack and Edwards, 1973). This pattern of change is largely because of the type of sex role socialization females are subject to. Those who make sex-atypical choices in childhood are forced or discouraged by social pressures from family, school, or peers or by self-awareness in adolescence to shift from "unfeminine" and "unrealistic" career aspirations and/or plans to more appropriate sex role patterns.

In brief, the socialization of females has a considerable influence on their occupational aspirations. These influences range from those of the games played in childhood to cultural models provided by the media and by actual contacts. As a result, the range of females' occupational preference tends to be narrower than that of males. However, it is commonly believed that women's roles are changing rapidly under the strong drive of the women's movement. Do occupational aspirations of young women reflect any of these changes? This question leads us to our next point. To discover changes, there have been several large-scale studies undertaken in the United States. In a national survey in 1970, junior high school students were asked about their career plans, and their responses were compared with those of juniors from some of the same high schools in 1960. The girls of 1970 expressed much stronger interest in male-dominated occupations such as economist, lawyer and scientist, and fewer planned to enter female-dominated work roles such as nurse, office worker, and housewife (Flanagan, 1973). This is of course encouraging. However, another study revealed conflicting findings. College seniors of 1972 were compared with those of 1961 in this study. It was found that there was little change in the career orientations of either sex. Those traditional female occupations such as teaching, social work and nursing were still preferred by most women. Limited research in this area has been carried out in Canada. It has been reported that enrollment of females in law schools and medical schools has been increasing in this country (Coburn et al., 1981:36). Similarly, of all physicians in Nova Scotia, the proportion of female physicians increased from 6.3 percent in 1967 to 11.4 percent in 1977 (Brown, 1977: 78; Regan, 1978). This pattern is indeed consistent with the national trend. It can be seen from Table 3-4 that the proportions of women in medicine, dentistry, and law have been steadily increasing in the last century, although the percentages are still rather small (Coburn, et al., 1981:Table 4).

(iv) Ethnicity

Canada is an ethnically heterogeneous society. Given the cultural and socio-economic differences that exist in the various ethnic groups in Canada, it is conceivable that they also differ in terms of occupational aspirations and expectations. However, there has been very little research directly addressing this issue. Breton provided partial evidence that French Canadians have lower occupational aspirations than English Canadians. He compared the level of occupations preferred by French- and English- speaking boys in Quebec and the Maritimes in his 1972 study and found that the differences were mainly in Quebec. In New Brunswick, of the occupations they

Table 3-4
Percentage Female in Medicine, Dentistry and Law

Year	Medicine		Dentistry		Law*	
	Total	%Female	Total	%Female	Total	%Female
1891	4,448	1.7	753	1.5	4,332	0.6
1901	5,475	1.0	1,332	1.8	4,713	–
1911	7,410	2.6	2,183	7.6	5,204	0.1
1921	8,706	1.7	3,126	–	7,145	–
1931	10,723	2.0	4,039	0.8	8,208	0.7
1941	10,723	3.4	3,740	1.2	7,920	1.6
1951	14,325	4.6	4,608	1.5	9,036	2.2
1961	21,266	6.8	5,463	4.3	12,068	2.6
1971	28,585	10.1	6,430	4.8	16,315	4.8

*Lawyers and Notaries
Source: Adapted from Coburn et al. 1981: Table 4—Canadian Censuses of respective years.

had chosen, there was little difference between the two groups of boys in each category (p. 236). In Quebec, however, English-speaking boys had chosen high status, white-collar occupations more frequently (81.8%) than did their French-speaking counterparts (67.9%) (p. 237). It should be pointed out, however, that the political and possibly the economic relations between the two groups have changed considerably in Quebec since the publication of Breton's study. It is not unlikely that these patterns of occupational aspirations and expectations have changed as well.

Studies in the U.K. indicate that opportunities open to people of the West Indies or Asians are less than those for whites with similar ability, which in turn affects occupational aspirations of these disadvantaged groups (Watson, 1980:128-29). Studies in the U.S. comparing black and white youths almost invariably found that blacks have lower occupational aspirations than do whites (Pavalko, 1971:55-58).

II. EDUCATION AND OCCUPATIONAL CHOICE

Education is both a goal and a means at the same time. For some people, education should be valued because it is a "good-in-itself," or because it helps one to understand and appreciate the intellectual heritage of human civilizations; for most, education is important because of its relationship to the occupational world.

As a goal, education itself is unequally available to people. For example, in their book *Does Money Matter?* Porter *et al.* (1973:90-93) has provided convincing evidence that the higher the students' socioeconomic statuses, the higher the likelihood that they expect to go to university.

When it is considered as a component of the opportunity structure, education is a means to high status and high paying jobs. The type of school program (vocational versus university preparation) and the academic standing (grades) a student achieved not only have strong influence on educational goals and subsequently occupational choice, but also are directly affected by the same structural factors such as socioeconomic status, sex, parental education, and so on (Brinkerhoff and Corry, 1976:269).

The idea that education is a means can be expressed in another way. To paraphrase Moore, the school is the principal sorting mechanism for the adult occupational world in contemporary modernized societies (1969:871). The educational system is "a kind of maze through which young people pass and in which choices are both explicitly and implicitly forced upon them .The kinds and frequency of decisions that must be made are not evenly distributed throughout the educational process. Rather, major decisions must be made at scheduled times regardless of whether the individual is 'ready' to make those decisions" (Pavalko, 1971:64). Diagram 3-1 has summarized the choice points in the educational system and their relationship with occupational alternatives.

The first choice point is at the threshold of the high school. The type of high school (vocational or general) and the choice of program (general or university preparation) will all have occupational implications eventually. Here both the region of residence and the size of

Diagram 3-1*

Educational Choice Point	Decision to be Made	Occupational Consequence
1. Entering high school	Type of high school	Acquisition of specific occupational skills
	Type of program	Acquisition of prerequisites for college entrance
2. Completion of high school	Go to college?	
	no ⟶	Blue-collar work or low level white-collar work**
	yes	
	where? ⟶	Acquisition of specific occupational skills
		Ease of entering graduate and professional schools
3. Second or third year of college	Major	Restriction of occupational alternatives
4. Completion of college	Go to graduate or professional school?	
	no ⟶	Occupational entry
	yes ⟶	Preparation for work in specific occupation

*Source: Pavalko (1971:65)
**"or low level white-collar work"—our addition

community have significance. In more industrialized regions and larger communities not only are there more schools but more importantly wider variety of courses. The student would have more opportunities and choices.

The completion of high school would be a crucial choice point. The graduates have to make a decision of whether to go to university or not. If a person decided not to go, the entry into the occupational world would be the immediate problem. If the decision is to go, then the immediate questions would be, "which one and what program?" In this case, not only the decision of job entry is postponed, but the range of occupations to be chosen a few years later would most likely be very different. For the university students, normally there are two more choice points. One is the declaration of a major, which most universities require; the other is the decision of whether or not to go to professional or graduate school upon college graduation. As these points are closer to the end of a person's educational career, they obviously carry even stronger occupational implications.

This description portrays simplified and perhaps the model paths in the educational system. While the range of alternatives change, and in many cases they even become narrower (*e.g.*, professional school) as one advances in the educational system, the decisions are not entirely irreversible. Pavalko pointed out the mechanisms, which serve a "second chance" function, that exists in American higher education (1971: 64-65). These mechanisms which allow a student to shift from one educational route to another, or to change a major, exist in Canada as well. As a matter of fact, in more recent years it is not uncommon that people change their occupational career by going back to school to pursue new knowledge in a different field. The existence of these mechanisms allowing for alterations of decisions made earlier is important. Indeed, they are not only important but also necessary. Despite the development of counselling programs in high schools, the educational and occupational decisions that young people are required to make are not always made rationally. Inadequate information, misinformation or emotional considerations (*e.g.*, to be with one's best friend) are some of the reasons which may lead to undesirable occupational consequences. Thus, mechanisms which allow flexibility are important and necessary.

III. CHOICE AND ALLOCATION

At the beginning of this chapter, we raised the issue of individual choice versus societal allocation. We asked, "Is the occupational distribution of a population the result of millions of individual choices or of societal allocation?" In this section, we will address ourselves to this important issue. Furthermore, a balanced perspective which incorporates both individual and structural factors for the understanding of occupational choice will be suggested.

The allocation argument goes something like this. For the fundamental problem of survival, all societies must develop ways to divide the work that has to be done and mechanisms by which work roles are filled. The demands of massive production of goods, their efficient distribution and a wide variety of services for a high standard of living are characteristic of industrial societies. One of the effective ways of meeting these demands appears to be specialization where tasks are allocated to individuals who are experts in them. As a result, the division of labour in industrial societies is highly complex and the arrangements for manning the tasks intricate.

Although placing square pegs into square holes is of apparent import, the matching is not an easy task. Traditionally, the major mechanism was, and to a certain extent still is, the ascriptive system. This system of bringing people and jobs together assumes that some categories of people have, by birth, qualities that automatically fit them into certain occupations better than others. For example, occupational inheritance between father and son was common in history. Women in most societies were expected to become wives and mothers only; in some societies, they still are.

In modern industrial societies, contrary to popular belief, formal education becomes a sorting device or a placement mechanism for the occupational world (Moore, 1969; Berger and Berger, 1972). "(The) levels of the occupational hierarchy at which school-leavers enter depend primarily upon their educational achievements. Individuals' aspirations are of secondary importance; no matter how ambitious he may be, a beginning worker is unable to enter the job hierarchy at a level for which he is unqualified" (Roberts, 1975: 140). Within the educational system, there are many selection devices. In addition to numerous quizzes, tests, and examinations in academic subjects in schools of all levels, there are batteries of selection tests designed to help to channel students into various occupational streams or directions.

However, education is not an equal system. In an unequal society people are bound to enter the educational system from different levels of the social hierarchy. Numerous studies have shown that the kind of school a person enters, the economic ability to stay at school longer than others, attitudes towards school, ability of learning, motivation of achievement, program taken, or to be assigned to are closely related to the social class position of the family. In Section I of this chapter, we have shown the effects of socioeconomic factors on occupational preferences and expectations. In addition, schooling itself has profound influence upon its recipients' aspirations. Through a "hidden curriculum" the pupils unconsciously but unmistakably acquire "conceptions of their places in the social-pecking order, and as a result of such processes school-leavers' levels of aspiration become related to the stream through which they have passed within their secondary schools" (Roberts, 1975: 141). From these observations, Roberts claims that individuals' aspirations are, at best, of secondary importance; no matter how ambitious the person may be, a beginning worker is unable to enter the job hierarchy at a level for which he is not qualified (Roberts, 1975: 140). Furthermore, he claims that most people do not choose their occupations, they are chosen for them (Roberts, 1977).

The other side of the argument is what the rational decision-making approach propounds. Implicitly and explicitly, these theorists maintain that while the course of a person's vocational development may be influenced by external factors such as family background, education and so on, basically, occupational choice is an individual decision. For example, Ginzberg, in a recent article, insists that the individual is the principal actor in occupational choice, while acknowledging that the actual processes of career development are often inconsistent with his theory. He says (1972:175):

> Our greater sensitivity to reality factor in our present formulation of a theory of occupational choice does not obscure our conviction that the individual remains the prime mover in the decision-making process. While young people who grow up in adverse circumstances have fewer effective options through which to shape their lives and careers, all people have some options and the majority has a great many.

We have already pointed out that, for most people, the opportunity structure is so restrictive that their personal preferences are of little consequence. "The notion of individuals' ambitions and actual careers gradually moving into harmony is far more an expression of hope than a statement of fact. It is more typical for employees to have to tolerate a lack of it between their self-concepts and the demands of their occupations" (Roberts, 1975: 139). If these criticisms are valid, why then do the "choice" theories seem well received by both professionals and laymen? It seems that individualism is highly valued in our society. Thus, it is desirable that we do have complete freedom of what occupation we enter. Theories based on individual choice are, therefore, in tune with what we believe and naturally have a sympathetic audience.

While the approach of individual decision making to occupational choice is not strongly substantiated by facts, to say that most people are chosen for an occupation is probably guilty of structural determinism. Factors in the opportunity structure are best seen as constraints rather than determinants. Choice and structural constraints are two sides of the same coin. Every choice is made within certain structural constraints (Watson, 1980: 126). The difference is that some individuals may find themselves in a structural context where the range of choices is greater than that which exists for others. A white English-speaking Canadian with a good education and living in a metropolitan area, for example, will have a much wider scope of choice than an unqualified Indian female living on a reserve.

The best available model which incorporates both individual and structural factors is provided by Tony Watson (1980: 126-32). He suggests that the individual's approach to work is influenced by both objective and subjective factors. Objective factors include certain resources such as cash, skills, knowledge or physique. Subjective factors include the individual's motives, interests and expectations, such as to make a living, to achieve power or to gain job satisfaction. All these individual factors are, in turn, strongly influenced by structural factors and work related factors. The individual's family, class, gender, ethnic and educational backgrounds formulate the nonwork structural setting. The work related factors include the occupational structure and the prevailing job market. The relationships of these variables are displayed in Diagram 3-2.

Diagram 3-2*

NON-WORK STRUCTURAL FACTORS	INDIVIDUAL APPROACHING WORK	WORK SPHERE STRUCTURAL FACTORS
Class Family Education Race & Ethnicity**	(a) Resources of cash, skills, knowledge, physique	Occupational structure and prevailing labour market (number and type of job vacancies)
Gender Media & Peer influences	(b) Motives, expectations, interests and aspirations	

*Source: Watson, (1980: 127 Fig. 4.3)
**"Ethnicity"—our addition

In this model, the individual's approach to work is influenced by his or her own subjective and objective factors. These factors, in turn, operate within the constraints of the two sets of structural factors. The life chances are to a substantial extent influenced by the class-family-education cluster of structural factors. It is not accidental that most researchers use parental occupation as one of the major variables in predicting an individual's occupational aspirations and expectations. To a lesser extent, the knowledge and experience of siblings and more distant relatives are also influential. The relationships between social class and education and their effect on a person's occupational orientation has already been discussed above. It need not be repeated here.

All the nonwork structural factors operate to a large extent, as a shaping force of the individual's personality, values and interest. It goes without saying that the mental abilities and physique of the individual play their own limiting roles within the structural context. For example, many work careers, such as in sports or modelling, require certain physical characteristics. As the individual comes nearer to the point of entering the world of work, the values, interests and expectations begin to crystalize. They are matched against the jobs which are available and for which he or she is qualified. For most people, the final results of occupational choice are compromises between individual preferences and the structural factors in their environment.

IV. SUMMARY

For many years problems of occupational choice have attracted the interests of sociologists, psychologists, labour economists and members of other disciplines. In this chapter, various theoretical approaches to occupational choice have been introduced. While developmental psychologists pay more attention to the individual's decisionmaking, sociologists put more emphasis on the influence of the structural factors. It is our contention that choice and structural constraint are the two sides of the same coin. Watson's balanced view, where the interplay between individual and structural factors is taken into account, was thus introduced and discussed. A closely related issue to occupational choice are the processes through which we learn to work. It is to this topic we shall now turn our attention.

Notes

1. Following Kuvlesky and Bealer's suggestion, aspiration refers to "wanting or having an orientation toward a social object or goals," whereas expectation is "the individual's estimation of his probable attainment in reference to a particular goal area"(1966:273).

Suggested Readings

Breton, Raymond
  1972. *Social and Academic Factors in the Career Decision of Canadian Youth: A Study of Secondary School Students*. Ottawa: Manpower and Immigration.
Brinkerhoff, Merlin B. and David J. Corry
  1976. "Structural Prisons: Barriers to Occupational and Educational Goals in a Society of 'Equal' Opportunity." *International Journal of Comparative Sociology, 17*:261-74.
Crysdale, Stewart
  1975. "Aspirations and Expectations of High School Youth." *International Journal of Comparative Sociology, 16 (1-2)*: 19-36.
Ginzberg, Eli
  1972. "Toward a Theory of Occupational Choice: A Restatement." *Vocational Guidance Quarterly, 20(3)*:169-76.
Kuvlesky, W.P. and Robert Bealer
  1966. "A Clarification of the Concept 'Occupational Choice'." *Rural Sociology, 31:* 265-76.
Roberts, Kenneth
  1968. "The Entry into Employment: An Approach Towards A General Theory." *Sociological Review, 16*: 165-84.
Roberts, Kenneth
  1975. "The Developmental Theory of Occupational Choice: A Critique and an Alternative." In *People and Work*, Esland, Salaman, and Speakman, (eds.), 134-46.
Roberts, Kenneth
  1977. "The Social Conditions, Consequences, and Limitations of Careers Guidance." *British Journal of Guidance and Counselling, 5 (January)*: 1-9.

Super, Donald E.
　1980. "A Life-Span, Life-Space Approach to Career Development." *Journal of Vocational Behavior*, *16(3):* 282-98.
Williams, W. M. (ed.)
　1974. *Occupational Choice: A Selection of Papers from the "Sociological Review."* London: George Allen Unwin Ltd.

Chapter 4

Socialization to Work

This chapter describes and analyzes an ubiquitous sociological process, socialization to work. Although for many people work is not a central life interest (Dubin, 1956; Schein, 1974), it is an activity that constitutes a major focus in one's life. Hughes (1958) believes that one's work is as good a clue as any to the course of one's life and one's social identity. It is certainly a social routine that largely explains where one will live, with whom one will associate and even what one's children will become. Since it is widely thought that work is a central aspect of one's being, it is essential to understand both how people become workers and how work affects them.

Work is performed in a social context that is characterized by general norms and particular rules of conduct applicable to distinctive types of work roles. Work socialization consists of three phases. Firstly, the novice must learn the knowledge and skills that are necessary to perform the activities of a given occupational role. Secondly, he or she learns the subculture of the workplace in that one must "learn the ropes" or codes of conduct that are shared among one's fellow workmates. Thirdly, the novice experiences a transformation of identity through the internalization of his or her occupational role.

In general, then, socialization to work consists of the social and psychological adjustments of people to their work and workplace. The nature and degree of these adjustments are variables dependent on the nature of the job, and features of the work setting. The position taken in this chapter is that the contingencies of the job and the workplace are far more crucial to an understanding of the socialization of recruits than are specific attributes that these individuals initially bring to the workplace.

Most of our knowledge of work stems from the research of American and British sociologists. Only recently have Canadian sociologists directed their attention towards work and the workplace. We shall begin with a review of some research by Canadian sociologists that bears on the question of socialization to work. In presenting this material we shall introduce and illustrate concepts that are elaborated further in subsequent sections of the chapter.

Haas and Shaffir (1980, 1981) have analyzed the socialization of medical students at an Ontario medical school. Their findings are consistent with other studies of professional socialization (Becker et al., 1961; Bloom, 1973; Bucher and Stelling, 1977; Davis, 1953; Fox, 1957; Merton *et al.*, 1957; Olesen and Whittaker, 1968; Ross, 1961; Simpson, 1979) by showing that these students gradually formed professional self-images by the successful negotiation of the *rites de passage* embedded in their socialization. Moreover, their analysis highlights the centrality of expressive concerns of an occupation that is noted for its instrumentality.

Haas and Shaffir (1980: 5) argue that medical socialization involves:

> The moral and symbolic transformation of a lay person into an individual who can take on the special role and status claimed by the professional—a process that Davis (1968:235-251) labels "doctrinal conversion." In order for individuals to make such significant status changes, they must undergo public initiations or *rites de passage* that prepare them for their new role. A would-be professional must undergo a process of mortification, of testing and ritual ordeal before he/she is elevated into the special status and role.

Haas and Shaffir found that the socialization of these medical students confronted them with two sets of problems. The long-term goal of the socialization was to develop a practical competence and acceptance of professional responsibility. The short-term goal was to do well in school by adjusting to the expectations of their socializers:

> The students we studied attempt to define what is relevant and important to meet both immediate and future competency expectations. When the school's distinctive approaches do not fit with their perceived expectations, the students shunt them aside as they strive to develop a suitable professional competence. In their search for competence, students become preoccupied with learning the "core" of what they anticipate will be important for them to know in the long run, to meet professional expectations, and in the short term, to meet the requirements of those who evaluate them (1980:14).

Much of the medical socialization consists of acquiring a basic competency in the knowledge and skills of the trade. Competence is usually regarded as a measureable entity. Physicians must be able to apply their textbook knowledge to the art of diagnosis and healing. Haas and Shaffir observed that because of the vast amounts of knowledge that must be mastered and because of the exaggerated expectations they experienced, these students found that their competence and learning are assessed in situations in which they are weak, vulnerable and easily reminded of their incompetence.

Uncertain of what they should know or how they should apply it, these students attempted to project an image of competence by deflecting others from probing their ignorance. They found that this "cloaking" behaviour was often accompanied by initiative taking intended to impress their evaluators. These students seized upon opportunities which allowed them to generate a convincing demonstration of competence.

In realizing their short-term goals of doing well in school, these students recognized that they could satisfy faculty expectations by either being competent or by appearing to be competent. While the evaluation of competence ought to consist of an objective assessment of the students' instrumental abilities, it is in fact shaped by their expressive capacities. To convince others of their developing competence, these students engaged in selective learning and impression management.

These students grew more confident about their competence as they succeeded in their expressive demonstrations of impression management and were allowed to apply their knowledge in practical situations involving responsibility. As they took on increasing responsibilities that were granted to them they came to be defined and to define themselves as capable.

The adoption of a cloak of competence requires the initiate to turn off his or her real feelings. Gradually, the cloak is shed as new feelings of competence emerge. Initial attitudes and self-images are altered. Just as anxiety must be conquered, emotional empathy with patients is also abandoned. In their striving for competence, psychosocial concerns become less important as most students turn off their real feelings for patients.

These researchers conclude that the significant aspect of medical socialization is the passing of ritual ordeals. The ability to express a careful presentation of self is as important as the selective learning of instrumental skills. The rites of passage which these students experience as ritual ordeals force them to acquire both instrumental and expressive abilities which satisfy faculty expectations. The wearing of cloaks of competence and of emotional detachment gradually separates them from a lay culture. As this separation grows, they identify more closely with the profession by using symbols of the profession to support their new self-images.

While sociologists have paid a good deal of attention to professional socialization, little analysis has directly focused on the actual transition of recruits from an educational mode of socialization into the occupational roles for which they are being prepared. Kelner (1980) explores this transition by examining the socialization of chiropractic students. As in medicine, the transition from lay person to practitioner begins in the initial weeks of the induction period.

Canadian chiropractic differs from medicine in some important ways. First, chiropractic still is on the margin of the Canadian health care system (Mills and Larsen, 1981; Kelner *et al.*, 1980). The official stance of organized medicine has been that chiropractic theory and therapy are false and based on unscientific premises. Secondly, although chiropractors have grown in numbers and public acceptance, there is still widespread public ignorance about chiropractic doctrine. Finally, in recent years a substantial number of the new recruits report that they have chosen chiropractic after refusals from medicine and dentistry. Perhaps, because of its less established position, chiropractic education puts considerable emphasis on expressive considerations of the value of the chiropractic and of establishing an effective rapport with patients. The first two years of instruction are directed at the acquisition of instrumental activities. The students study the basic sciences, are taught to examine and palpate the spinal column and are introduced to the basic elements of spinal manipulation. Sixty hours of curriculum in the first year and 90 in the second year are spent developing chiropractic techniques.

Students practice their skills by doing spinal adjustments on one another, under faculty supervision. By the time they are admitted to the clinic, they have already learned a good deal about chiropractic techniques and are familiar with the major aspects of clinical treatment. In the third year students gradually become familiar with the operations of the clinic; first as observers and later as assistants to the fourth-year student-interns. In the final year, student-interns assume responsibility for treating their own patients under the general supervision of the clinic staff.

In her study of the clinic, Kelner observed that these students are concurrently exposed to two orientations. One is directed at the value of their technical competence and the other stresses the acquisition of expressive skills that keep the patients satisfied. With respect to the question of competence Kelner argues that the clinic allows the students to finally test the validity of their technical skill:

> When students find that patients are indeed helped by chiropractic treatment, the doubts that may have been troubling them are allayed...With the realization that their training has equipped them to successfully treat these ailing patients, comes the solid reassurance that only positive empirical results can provide...It generates sufficient self-confidence to any sense of inferiority students may have had about their chosen vocation, and enables them to discount the stigma associated with it. Once they have had the experience of healing, or helping to reduce pain and discomfort through application of chiropractic techniques and knowledge, the role of chiropractor is legitimated for them and they are well on their way to becoming practitioners (1980:15).

The students' expressive skills are simultaneously exercised through their work at the clinic. In order to graduate, interns must treat a minimum of 30 patients in their final year of study. This requirement creates a very practical problem, *viz.*, how to generate and maintain a clientele. Through the clinical experience the students become involved in the development of the expressive skills that fosters interpersonal relationships between their patients and themselves. Patients who seek care in the clinic return to the student-interns who have been treating them only if they are convinced they are getting competent treatment:

> The ability to persuade patients to continue coming back depends not only on command of technical skills, but also on mastery of the human aspects of treatment (1980:16).

Kelner argues that the clinical milieu is the critical element in the socialization of chiropractors. It is a structured environment in which recruits are simultaneously tested on their instrumental and expressive competency by forcing them to act towards patients in a manner that assures their return. Successful completion of the internship enables the student to readily shift from the clinic to private practice:

> The message is transmitted that in order to become chiropractors, students must not only acquire a sound base of chiropractic knowledge and skills, but must also develop their entrepreneurial capacities. Acquiring a clientele is the bridge to making a living as a chiropractor, and the clinic procedures encourage students to develop the type of abilities necessary for their future success (Kelner, 1980:22).

Like Haas and Shaffir, Kelner shows that the socialization of chiropractors involves the acquisition of the technical and social skills of the occupation. In both socialization settings, the initiates' competence and self-confidence increase as they are allowed to practice their respective arts on patients. Because chiropractic is more limited in scope than medicine, these students are not faced with as many ritual ordeals. However, since their doctrine is not as accepted as the doctrine of medicine, they do have feelings of uncertainty about both the efficacy of their training and their ability to survive as solo practitioners. During the clinic of the final year, these students are forced to deal with these uncertainties. The successful candidates emerge as competent and self-confident practitioners.

Chiropractors and physicians, despite real differences, are high status occupations. Typical of the professions and semi-professions, these initiates experience a lengthy educational method of socialization process. Vincent (1979) provides us with an analysis of a socialization that follows the training method and continues for months, not years. He reports on the induction of recruits into the police department of a medium sized Canadian city.

In the police force that Vincent studied the recruits are drawn from a heavily unionized, blue-collar working-class background. All applicants must satisfy citizen, weight and height requirements and have at least a grade eleven education. Applicants are interviewed by a selection committee that tries to ascertain their goals, honesty, ambition, and ability to function under pressure. Senior members of the force sit on the committee and the form of screening is a question and answer method with no psychological testing employed.

When openings on the force occur, those who have received the highest ratings by the selection committee are hired on probation. Recruits attend an in-service training course and are sent to the provincial police college for an introduction to basic police work. The latter program consists of two six-week periods. When not at college, recruits engage in ordinary police work under close supervision. The total probationary period is 18 months.

The instrumental knowledge and skills of police work consist of understanding various aspects of the law and police regulations and procedures, knowing how to select and fill out forms and how to make reports. They are constantly evaluated on the quality of their paper work and this factor as well as their abilities to follow procedures both demonstrate their competence to their superiors. As one sergeant commented:

> Hell, all these rules and regulations are there for a purpose. It sort of creates uniformity, a sense of unity and teamwork. Those damn hot-shot urban cowboys who want to by-pass all the rules, and run their own show, create more problems than they are worth. The ones who keep the rules and do a good job resent these fellows who watch too may television shows (Vincent, 1979:36).

The recruits learn the importance of following rules when they are called to give evidence in court or when others recount the problems that they experienced. As one constable stated:

> It was a long trial, lasting four days. We were expected to remember dimensions of rooms and exact positions of people after eight months. The lawyer was successful, and all charges were dismissed. I learned several things from this experience. I must be more exact and complete in making my notes because many of the cases are delayed for a long time and I have to depend on good notes if I want to have any hope of making the arrest stick and obtain a conviction (1979:78).

The influence of the peer group is also pervasive:

> The aspiring policeman makes a point of looking and acting like the other rookies. He takes his cues from them because at this time, for the most part, they are the only police he associates with, aside from his superior officers. It is

in a sense like a try-out camp in football. Only the exceptional veteran bothers with the rookies, and this seldom goes beyond acknowledging their existence. It is a puzzling, lonely, insecure period for the probationers and they group together for mutual support (1979: 44).

When the recruit graduates to patrol duty his reference group widens to include his partner and other experienced men. This enlarged reference group is essential because he learns the art of police work from these men: which approaches are approved of and which are frowned upon. Because the recruit is insecure he quickly adapts to his partners and operates according to their way of doing things.

Like medical and chiropractic students they engage in impression management as a means of demonstrating their competence and trustworthiness. This cloaking behaviour is especially true of their relations with superiors; as one sergeant put it:

While they're on probation they're really on their toes. Yessir, nossir. They almost make double genuflection everytime they pass by a sergeant. As soon as they are made permanent, they change quite a bit. I suppose they really don't change that much. They hold it all in to create what they conceive to be a good impression...Once they are on permanent staff...they are not quite as insecure. Oh, they still have to toe [*sic*] the line, but they learn the ropes real fast from the other guys (1979:45).

Much of the work of the police is routine. There are often long periods of inactivity that make the job boring. Most of the problems which they encounter are relatively simple but they must always be prepared to handle serious accidents, domestic disputes, holdups, etc. It is this element of preparedness that makes the job stressful and isolated. The recruit has to become street wise to assure his own safety and that of his peers. Vincent dramatically demonstrates the importance of crisis situations in shaping the attitudes, values and behaviours of policemen. It is with one's partner that the recruit learns how to exercise good judgment, stay cool and handle people. Equally important, he learns the importance of his partnership.

Because of the potential danger in answering any call and because the recruit must learn on the job, he is subjected to rigorous hazing by the more experienced men:

On the job the rookie is teased, cajoled and generally given a going over by the men. He is very unsure of himself and tries desperately to find out what is expected of him. He takes orders from superiors; but he works day in and day out alongside those fellow officers (1979: 42).

These ritual ordeals are very informal as are the rites of passage into acceptance by the veterans. Yet they are just as meaningful to these recruits as the more formal ones experienced by medical and chiropractic students. Indeed, the mockery, harrassment and bickering identified by Vincent are far more personal and debasing than the formal rituals of the professional schools. For the policeman the stakes are higher. If the recruit can not take the hazing he is regarded as untrustworthy. The good recruit will endure any amount of aggravation if it establishes his reputation of being dependable. He will often go out of his way to avoid the label of "being yellow" or a coward. Vincent (1979: 99) recounts this comment:

> When I hear the radio and there is real trouble I try to be the first one there. I don't want them to think that I'm yellow. I couldn't live among those guys if I thought for a moment that, in their eyes, I was gutless. I'm not talking about being afraid. We just have to overcome that. I'll put up with anything in my partner; he can be a closet-queen, cheating on his wife, you name it—anything. But if I know he won't back me up I'll do anything to avoid going out with him.

Vincent concludes that police socialization fosters the development of an occupational identity. He does not hold the view that the occupation makes the man, regardless of what he is at the outset. Nor does he see the policeman as a particular type of personality who through a process of self-selection enters into police work. He does, however, argue that the socialization process affects the values, attitudes and behaviour of the recruit; he is:

> ...affected deeply in his thinking by the constant and close links he has with his fellow officers. The young policeman is not competely passive in this interaction; he can disagree or question or refuse to change his attitudes in any way. He may even try to change the thinking of his partners. But as he works along day-by-day there is a gradual transformation, very subtle, but real, nonetheless. Because he shares so much experience and so many situations with his partner or partners his views begin to coincide more and more with the others'. It would be difficult for a police officer to survive on the job and not share most of the views held by his peer group (1979: 46).

The socialization of police recruits clearly differs from that of the professions. The basic training can be completed in a few weeks but an intensive apprenticeship is necessary in order to develop competence and self-confidence. They also experience insecurity, ritual ordeals, and engage in cloaking behaviours. Like their professional counterparts, they ultimately are tested in the area of direct contact with the public. Unlike these counterparts, they are not sheltered by the educational milieu of their socialization. They experience an informal learning via the school of hard knocks. The outcome is nonetheless the same. By the time that they are admitted into full membership, they have developed a strong sense of identification with the occupation.

Haas (1978) has studied the socialization of high steel ironwork-ers. In order to fully appreciate the induction process, he became a recruit, participated in the formal training program for ironworker apprentices and conducted his research while working on the con-struction of a 21-story office building. This occupation shares one of the atributes of police work, namely, a potential of danger. Haas's analysis focuses on how these ironworkers developed a shared per-spective towards fear and danger.

The formal training period is brief; consisting of classes on welding. The mark of the journeyman is his aptitude for "running the iron." It consists of a thoroughness in laying planking, in check-ing on safety precautions and in displaying a control of fear. Thus, the two most important lessons that the apprentice learns on the job are to make it as safe as you can by taking every precaution possible and to know that your partner is trustworthy.

Since high steelworkers' safety depends on the reliability of fellow workers, apprentice socialization largely consists of hiding one's fear and managing one's impressions in order to express self-confidence. The apprentice must accept danger and fear without allowing them to adversely affect his behaviour. An ironworker demonstrates his trustworthiness by acting with disdain to the dangers surrounding him:

> As a way of proving themselves to their work fellows, many seemed deli-berately to flaunt the situation by taking risks—they showed off by volunteer-ing for the most dangerous work activity, as a way of demonstrating their trustworthiness and enhancing their reputations (Haas, 1978: 234).

Haas further notes that suffering ordeals of personal abuse (which he calls "binging") is an institutional part of the apprentices' socialization. They are given the most demeaning tasks, called "punks" and through the media of horseplay, joking and banter are subjected to the deliberate castigation of veteran workers. The jour-neyman's perception of "binging" is nicely summarized in the fol-lowing conversation:

> On the top of the building, I talked with a journeyman about his constant kidding of new apprentices. I say, "Looks like you were busting Jerry, the firewatch, the other day" Abe, the journeyman answers, "Thats all right. I used to take it even worse than that and everyone was on my ass, all the time. If I took it these guys can take it. You've got to take it and dish it right back" (Haas, 1978: 237).

Haas concludes that the process of becoming an ironworker consists of adopting the attitudes towards fear that are shared by the group. These attitudes are seemingly contradictory. One denies fear in front of others but lives it privately and takes every precaution to ensure the safety of self and others. Furthermore, he views "binging" as a crucial socialization technique in that it simultaneously relates to the apprentices' competence and trustworthiness. First, it allows journeymen to teach without openly questioning an apprentice's competence. Secondly, it tests the worker's self control and thus his dependability. If, when subjected to personal abuse, the recruit loses his poise, his co-workers become aware that he may lose control in other threatening situations, especially, high above the ground.

In comparing this study to police socialization we can see that when reliance on workmates is regarded as essential for personal safety, the recruits' reputation for dependability is of paramount concern. The novices engage in acts of self-presentation to demonstrate their trustworthiness and the veterans subject them to informal yet crucial ordeals, the satisfactory endurance of which marks their passage to full membership. Haas notes that these processes parallel in many ways those described for other dangerous occupations such as pipeline construction workers (Graves, 1958), lumberjacks (Hayner, 1945), miners (Gouldner, 1954; Lucas, 1969), and combat personnel (Weiss, 1967).

I. PRIMARY AND SECONDARY SOCIALIZATION

The studies that we have just reviewed represent socialization to work as a distinctive type of interaction. The concept of socialization is far more general. It refers to any interactional process through which individuals develop a sense of who they are and how they relate to others. This sense of self and others is shaped by the acquisition of the knowledge, skills and attitudes which give one the ability to participate effectively in social groups. Socialization is the link between the individual and society. From the point of view of the individual, socialization is a means by which one acquires social identities and the actualization of one's potential. From the societal point of view, socialization explains how commitment to a social order is nurtured and maintained.

Social scientists have placed an emphasis on childhood or primary socialization. Accordingly, we know a great deal about how children develop their self-concepts and relations with others, but comparatively little about the complexities of adult or secondary socialization. Mackie (1980) explains that the main reason for this uneven focus is that primary socialization lays the foundation for all later learning and thus channels and sets limits for secondary socialization.

There is no question of the critical importance of childhood socialization. Nevertheless, socialization is a lifelong phenomenon with secondary socialization continuing the process of learning to participate effectively in groups. Within industrial societies secondary groups are quite diverse and we are socialized anew each time we enter a new group or a situation involving those of a different group. The study of secondary socialization, of which socialization to work is a part, underscores the plasticity or adjustment capacity of men and women.

The purpose of any socialization, then, consists of providing a newcomer with the knowledge and skills to assume a particular role and the ability to role-take, regardless of whether the other is father, lover, employer or workmate. The basic difference between primary and secondary socialization is specificity. Most adult roles and especially occupational roles are fairly specific in their content. One major reason for variation in the form and content of work socialization is the degree to which the "breaking in" period focuses on the formation of new values and new self-images.

II. CONTEXTUAL FEATURES OF WORK SOCIALIZATION

Van Maanen (1975) argues that although all work socialization is directed at acquainting the novice with the specific role demands of his or her new job, the intensity of this effort can best be understood by viewing the socialization to work as lying on a continuum. Some inductions are primarily concerned with the overt behaviour of the initiates. In these situations, little attention is normally paid to the recruits' underlying motivations or general value structure. At the other pole, there is a concern with "all facets of the general socialization equation." In these cases it is generally assumed that the recruit has some *â priori* motivations for membership in occupation.

Van Maanen places a particular socialization on this continuum by the use of a classification scheme consisting of four contextual variables: pattern, composition, length and formality. His set of variables is not complete but it does help to conceptualize some salient features that can be expected to influence both the form and content of the socialization process. A given socialization may have either a serial or disjunctive pattern:

> If the new member has been preceded by others who have been through the same situation and can instruct him about the setting, the pattern is considered to be serial. However, if the new member is not following in the footsteps of predecessors, the pattern is disjunctive (Van Maanen, 1975: 89).

Disjunctive patterns are most common when one's work is based only upon the acquisition of certain knowledge and skills. When one's job requires the worker to apply his or her knowledge and skills in an interactional context, a serial pattern offers the opportunity of learning the ropes on how to function in the workplace. A serial pattern also fosters the development of new values and self-images, for certain workmates can become significant others assisting the recruit in the formation of an occupational identity.

The second contextual variable is the recruit composition and refers to whether the novices are processed individually or collectively. A collective process increases the likelihood that the newcomers will construct reference groups among themselves. A reference group is a sociological term signifying a group comprised of significant others whose perspective is used by an individual as a frame of reference for defining his or her experiences and expectations. Since collective socialization literally places the recruits "in the same boat," each member may measure and interpret his or her progress and frustrations by comparing experiences with these significant others. This sharing promotes the creation of collective perspectives that ease the acceptance of new values and self-images.

Many who can not reconcile individual and collective perspectives come to the realization that they are not cut out for the line of work for which they are being socialized. Evan (1963) observed that collective socialization eased a person's passage into the work setting by fostering recruit peer groups that reduced strain and alleviated tension. Brueckel (1955) reached a similar conclusion in his study of the differences between individual and collective socialization into army combat units.

Whether becoming a journeyman steelworker or a physician, one's socialization typically confronts the newcomer with a set of problems and ordeals. Moore (1973) contends that the frequency with which initiates are put through some form of hazing might be interpreted as tactics to test their competence and self-image. Lortie (1968) agrees that these trials form the recruits' self-images and provide evidence of their competence and trustworthiness. Moreover, he maintains that the ordeals experienced during a collective socialization have a more profound effect on attitudinal change. Since these tests are common to the group, they are experienced not as individual but as shared ordeals:

> Candidates who shared the trial with others changed more than those who went it alone; sharing added to the impact of the experience (Lortie, 1968:255).

By sharing a common set of problems, collectively socialized recruits are more likely to develop a fellowship subculture. This subculture enhances one's identification with the occupational role for which the process is preparing the initiate.

The length of the induction period is the third variable in Van Maanen's set. It may vary from days to years. The length is typically a function of the complexity of the work to be learned and the importance that is placed on the formation of occupational values and attitudes. The longer the period, the more likely that it will be marked by transitional events. These *rites de passage* demonstrate to the initiate that he or she is gradually advancing to full-fledged membership in the occupation and aid in the development of a sense of belonging (Blau, 1955). As Hughes (1958:36) remarked:

> In general, the longer and more rigorous the period of initiation, the more culture and techniques are associated with it.

The final contextual variable is formality. In an informal socialization the newcomer's role as learner is unspecific. The novice, taught not by trained teachers but by experienced workers, enters the occupational role immediately and "learns the ropes" while on the job. While the novice will be subjected to ritual ordeals and status passages, these occur after the work role has been assumed and are simply measures of his or her acceptance by the established workers.

A formal socialization typically demands a rigid adherence to an institutional way of life during the induction period. The novice's status as learner is very specific and he or she is often sequestered for most or all of this "breaking in" period. Formality also appears to emphasize preparation for a particular status in life rather than for some particular work tasks. Rites of passage are frequently symbolized by the awarding of title, extra rights and the sharing of information which previously had been withheld. These events celebrate a sort of personal metamorphosis by providing temporal reference points which allow the person to say, "I am not what I used to be." Formal socializations typically conclude with a symbolic transition to full membership that gives explicit recognition to the member's new status.

It is important to recognize the interdependency of these four variables. Generally, the greater the emphasis that is placed on the formation of new values and self-images, the more likely the process will be serial, collective, lengthy and formal. This mix of contextual features is found for example in the socialization of chiropractors, physicians and other professionals. Policemen and high steelworkers experience a slightly different combination of these features but like their counterparts in high status occupations they experience ritual ordeals and status passages. All socializations involve some change in self-image, with the successfully socialized person emerging as a competent and self-confident member of his or her respective occupation.

III. STRUCTURAL FEATURES OF THE WORK WORLD

The way in which a given work socialization is organized is, itself, a function of the structural features of the occupational world, the nature of the work and the method of socialization. Work is always associated with an occupational role. The status of that role within the wider social structure is the most important structural influence on the socialization process. Its primacy is best appreciated by an examination of the relationship of occupational status to two other structural factors, namely, occupational choice and anticipatory socialization.

In Chapter 3 we attempted to summarize some theories of occupational choice. Although within industrial societies there exists a wide range of occupations, entrance requirements increase in proportion to occupational status. Formal schooling has increasingly become the principal sorting mechanism for the world of work. As Moore (1973: 871) has observed,

> ...many career choices are essentially negative in that educational qualifications are not met; indeed, if we accept the primacy of (structural) influences, we are not dealing with genuine choice but with outcomes.

If we were to study only social and economic variables we would have to admit that for the vast majority of people, meaningful choice of work does not exist.

Depending on the social status of the occupation into which one is being inducted, socialization to work may be either a kind of a commitment to a calling or more like a form of conditioning, a reluctant preparation for harsh realities. Either way, occupational status establishes a frame of reference against which workers evaluate their jobs and their alternatives. When the benefits of membership are substantial, the socialization can draw upon these rewards to support efforts to change the novice's attitudes and self-image. Schein (1968) succinctly calls this aspect the "price of membership." It can result in a psychological contract between the recruit's aspirations and the constraints and purposes of the socialization. On the other hand, to the extent that one's entry is more by default than by choice, the ability to affect attitudinal change is limited. Often the advantages of not working are almost preferable to the kind of work that is available.

Closely linked to the question of occupational choice is the concept of anticipatory socialization. This type of socialization is an interplay of fact and fantasy that serves as a rehearsal for future roles. It consists of learning both the behaviours and attitudes of role requirements, and visualizing oneself in the role. A good deal of primary socialization is actually anticipatory training for future adult roles. The expectations for occupational roles are often conveyed to adolescents by parental tutelage and example. The schools and the media are also agents of anticipatory socialization. DeFleur and DeFleur (1967) have studied the impact of television on occupational learning among children. They conclude that the information that television provides about occupations tends to be superficial and misleading. The most effective source of accurate learning proved to be personal contact with an occupation.

As one might expect, a child's knowledge about occupations is related to age and class background. Baxter (1976) studied perceptions of occupational prestige among a sample of Canadian boys. Not only did older boys' perceptions resemble adult perceptions of occupational prestige but middle and upperclass children also knew more about work roles and their relative prestige than did lowerclass children. If participatory socialization is accurate, it provides a basis for the acceptance of the values of the occupation to which one aspires. Merton (1957) states that such a preparatory orientation serves the twin functions of aiding one's rise into an occupation and of easing his or her adjustment after becoming a part of it.

The effects of parental tutelage and example are well illustrated by studies of medical students. Over a decade ago, the Royal Commission on Health Services reported that 54 percent of general practitioners and 68 percent of specialists in Canada had parents in professional or managerial occupations. Moreover, 15 percent of Canadian physicians have parents who were physicians (Judek, 1964). The pattern is similar in the United States, where 58 percent of physicians come from professional or managerial backgrounds and about 17 percent had doctors for parents (Gough and Hall, 1977). Oswald Hall (1948) has offered a widely-accepted explanation for this pattern, namely, that family and friends awaken an interest in medicine and give social support to those who choose to aspire to become physicians.

All socializations are influenced by the power of the socializers. Power is one's ability to induce others to carry out directives. Etzioni (1975) maintains that all organizations employ three kinds of power: coercive, remunerative and normative. Coercive power rests on the application of threat or application of sanctions. In the world of work, it is unusually evidenced in the generation of frustration. Remunerative power is based on the control of material resources and rewards. In occupational settings this control is exercised through the allocation of wages and other fringe benefits. Normative power rests on the allocation of symbolic rewards.

Socialization to the higher status occupations is likely to be characterized by a strong normative orientation. This orientation is aimed at the attainment of a high level of compliance to the demands of the setting. Etzioni calls intense compliance moral involvement. The professions and semi-professions seek to obtain moral involvement by stressing an "expressive" form of socialization aimed at the importance of the mission of the work that is performed by the occupation. On the other hand, as one moves down the status hierarchy there is an increasing emphasis on a remunerative orientation. This orientation is aimed at the attainment of acceptable levels of compliance. Etzioni labels these levels as calculative involvement. Many occupations influence behaviour by emphasizing an utilitarian form of socialization aimed only at the overt behaviour of the worker.

Although every occupation contains a mixture of these orientations, attention to the weight that is given to one or the other allows for an understanding of the direction and intensity of the socialization process. When a strong normative focus is present, socialization is both intense and directed at attitudinal change. When remunerative concerns dominate, socialization is only as intense as the instrumental demands of the dictates of work and is directed at the communication of basic skills.

IV. INTRINSIC AND EXTRINSIC FEATURES OF WORK

Clearly, our conceptualization of work socialization is incomplete without a discussion of the subject of the learning process, the work itself. There are a number of work attributes that play a significant role in the socialization of recruits. They are commonly grouped into two categories, namely, the intrinsic and extrinsic characteristics of work. Individually and in combinations these attributes offer the potential for work to generate rewarding experiences. It appears to be the case that one's motivation to work is directly proportional to the rewarding experiences which work can provide.

Hackman and his associates have compiled evidence that occupations, which ranked high on what they call the five "core" intrinsic dimensions of work, offer strong internal motivations for anyone assuming such a job (Hackman, 1969; Hackman and Porter, 1968; Hackman and Lawler, 1971). These dimensions are:

1. Variety–the degree to which the job requires one to learn different skills or perform different activities.

2. Task identity—the degree to which the worker is able to complete an entire process.
3. Significance—the perceivable impact that one's work has on others.
4. Feedback—the amount of information that one receives from significant others about the quality of one's work.
5. Autonomy—the amount of control that one is able to exercise over one's work.

All of these dimensions are closely tied to the technology of the workplace. If one's work is regulated by a highly standardized technology, such as the machine-tending of the textile industry or the conveyor-belt of the automative industry, there is little potential for intrinsically meaningful work (Blauner, 1964). Roy (1953,1954) has dramatically shown that for those who continually encounter routine and boring work the "game of work" cannot be played.

Centers and Bugental (1966) have demonstrated that intrinsic features have greater salience for those who are located on the upper end of the occupational ladder. For the remainder, the work itself is not very rewarding. Meaningless work results in heightened time-consciousness. If it were possible to measure "clock-watching," we should have a reasonably good indicator of the intrinsic qualities of a given type of work. When the work is not an end in itself, it becomes a means to other ends. Consequently, extrinsic considerations are seen as the most important characteristics of many occupations.

Of extrinsic work features, pay and security are probably the most discussed. For example, Blauner (1964) found that the principal meanings of work for the factory worker and especially the assembly line automotive worker were the size of the pay cheque and the nonwork life styles that a fairly steady job with good wages provides. Nonetheless, there is at least one other feature that is worthy of mention, *viz.*, the friendships that develop at the workplace. One's work offers an opportunity for fellowship. In a study of unemployment in Newfoundland, Wadel (1973) discovered that one of the most serious psychological adjustments for the unemployed is the loss of social ties with former workmates. The social routine of work is often the only experientially rewarding aspect of the job.

V. METHODS OF WORK SOCIALIZATION

The common denominator of all forms of work socialization is an effort to assure that the new recruits fit in. The contextual, structural and work variables that we have been discussing largely determine which method of socialization best communicates, in a clear and concise manner, both what is required of the initiate and how his or her compliance with these expectations can be obtained.

The Canadian research that we have reviewed focused on three methods of socialization: education, training and apprenticeship. Each of these methods varies both in the amount of effort requested of the recruits and the ability of the socializers to reward or punish them. Obviously, this list of methods could be expanded. However, we feel that the differences among added strategies would be slight and offer little additional substance to the discussion.

The great tradition of occupational preparation is apprenticeship. It is a process of learning by doing with the minor receiving instruction in the art of a trade by example of an experienced worker. This mode of socialization is primarily skills related and takes place within the work setting, with the responsibility for induction delegated to an experienced member. Apprenticeship is frequently found in craft guilds and police departments. In Van Maanen's terms it is serial, individual and fairly informal.

In recent years apprenticeship has declined and has been replaced by or combined with the training method of socialization. Like apprenticeship, the training method is primarily skills related. Also, it usually occurs within the work setting in which the initiate is to participate. While training is primarily based on an instrumental orientation, it often contains an expressive content:

> Organizations that conduct training programs conceive of them as imparting skills, but analysis of any particular training program always shows it to be concerned with the communication of values, the development of an ambiance, the rejection of prior affiliations and the development of an appropriate self-image (Caplow, 1954: 173).

Even the most instrumentally oriented program contains some expressive content which allows the new member to demonstrate the "proper attitude." Such demonstrations range from "being on time" to more elaborate manifestations such as "speaking the occupational line." The training method is serial and collective. The longer and more formal the training period is, the more emphasis there is placed upon the development of "proper attitudes."

While there are several reasons for the shift from apprenticeship to training (see Taylor, 1968), there are three principal ones. First, modern technology has eliminated the need for craftsmen in the traditional sense. In high technology industries it is no longer necessary for the great majority of the workers to be involved in more than a few steps in the operation. Most of these workers need only partial learning and routine repetition. Secondly, in comparison, training is more efficient in that it is less time consuming and more predictable. Craftsmen are not instructed in the art of instruction. Even the best of these workers may be poor teachers. Finally, if the basic skills are learned in the vocational school system, they are gained at public expense.

The training approach to work socialization is sometimes difficult to distinguish from the educational method. The latter typically refers to the systematic teaching of values and skills required for participation in a particular occupation. However, it differs from training in two principal ways. Firstly, its expressive content is more explicit and less specific. Secondly, it uses professional educators as opposed to vocational instructors. Moreover, it differs from the other methods in that it always occurs outside of the work setting. In this respect it is the "first wave" of socialization. This first wave emphasizes general skills and attitudes. The "second wave" occurs in the workplace and stresses specific behaviours and idiosyncratic nuances of the work setting (Van Maanen, 1975). In medicine and law the second wave is the mandatory internship and clerkship, respectively. In chiropractic it is the exit requirement to attract and clinically treat a minimum of 30 patients.

The educational method of work socialization is becoming increasingly common. Many trade schools, community colleges, and undergraduate university programs have received accreditation from various occupations. Graduates of these programs enter directly into full occupational membership. Whether education can truly be regarded as a method of work socialization depends on the degree to which the occupation for which recruits are being prepared directly influences the program of studies. Professional schools like law and medicine must satisfy the standards of their respective occupations. For example, graduates of Canadian medical schools must receive a license from the Medical Council of Canada or its provincial equivalent. Final year students must sit for terminal examinations which are set jointly by their medical school and the licensing bodies.

Generally, the scope of the educational method is broader than the role of requirements of a particular occupation. It combines both instrumental and expressive goals of socialization. The educational method is typically, serial, collective, lengthy and formal. Length and formality reach their zenith in professional education. As should be anticipated from our earlier discussions, professional education creates strong identifications with the novice's sense of identity becoming intimately tied to his or her professional role.

One variant of the apprenticeship method has not declined. It is called sponsorship (Hughes, 1958) and is found in high status occupations such as graduate schools of arts and science and in professional and managerial occupations. In these instances of high affect, the one-to-one sponsorship is likely to lead to an intense induction. Caplow (1968) suggests that sponsorship is common whenever an incumbent is viewed as the only one capable of forming his or her successor.

VI. SUMMARY

Everett C. Hughes had a great impact on the sociological study of work. A central feature of his approach was the concern for the common themes that run through seemingly disparate occupations:

> I believe that much of our terminology and hence, of our problem setting, has limited our field of perception by a certain pretentiousness and a certain value-loading. Specifically we need to rid ourselves of any concepts which keep us from seeing that the essential problems of men at work are the same whether they do their work in the laboratories of some famous institution or in the messiest vat room of a pickle factory. Until we can find a point of view and concepts which will enable us to make comparisons between the junk peddler and the professor without the intent to debunk the one and patronize the other, we cannot do our best work in this field (Hughes, 1978: 197).

In this chapter we have attempted to use the concept, socialization to work, in this generic and comparative sense. We have examined an individual's entry into the world of work by characterizing one's socialization to work in terms of Van Maanen's contextual variables (pattern, composition, length and formality), and by suggesting how these variables are influenced by the structural and inherent features of work and occupations. In this way one's initial socialization experiences can be viewed as on a continuum; with high status and intrinsically meaningful work at one pole and low status, intrinsically meaningless work at the other. Similarly, a given work socialization could range from one that is serial, collective, lengthy and formal to one that is disjunctive, individual, brief and informal. Whether or not one's socialization is the realization to a calling or a reluctant preparation for harsh realities, we should expect to find some evidence of ritual ordeals (ranging from solemn to trivial). Finally, we should expect that induction to work promotes some sense of identification with workmates and some adoption of an occupational ideology.

However, it has been argued that the very concept of socialization to work loses meaning as one moves down the status hierarchy from professional to unskilled work (see Krause, 1971; Kronus, 1976). Indeed, in a reflection on Hughes's influence, one of his students suggests that sociologists must follow his example and pay careful attention to those occupations at the lower end of the status ladder. He fears that the concepts that we have applied to high prestige occupations and the classical professions are "not so useful when applied to occupations at the opposite end of the continuum [*sic*], which are unskilled, unprestigeful and so on" (Solomon, 1968: 11).

Unfortunately, we are not able to thoroughly document the socialization of the unskilled in Canada. An examination of the American scene reveals that only 30 percent of the respondents to a 1963 national survey indicated that they learned their current occupation through specific and formal training (U.S.A., 1964). Nearly half of the respondents reported that they had some casual learning. By this they meant that they learned how to do the job from a friend or "just picked it up." Although this study probably underrepresents the role of formal training (see Taylor, 1968: 220-43), it still suggests that a great many jobs require only the most elementary forms of socialization. For the most part, this work is dull, routine and poorly remunerated. We surmise that the current situation in Canada bears some resemblance to this picture of the American labour force of the 1960s.

If such a large proportion of the labour force receives barely a rudimentary induction to work, can we seriously believe that the concept of work socialization can be meaningfully applied to them? We feel that any form of social interaction that allows people to identify with their work represents a socialization to work. A recent survey of the work ethic and job satisfaction in Canada (Burnstein *et al.*, 1975) found that a large majority (70%) of the respondents indicated that they worked more because they like to than because they had to. An even larger proportion (84%) stated that their work was more than just a way to make money; it was an activity from which they received at least some satisfaction or enjoyment. In a study of building cleaners in Halifax, Clark (1981) found that 64 percent claimed that they were proud of their work. These responses ranged from statements like "cleaning is my whole life" to simple acknowledgements that they take some pride in their work.

There is little doubt that for most of the semi-skilled and unskilled occupations, financial gain is the main incentive to work. It is not surprising that such workers would hold a strong instrumental orientation towards their jobs, with job satisfaction directly related to satisfaction with earnings. Nonetheless, work is a social routine and as long as the "game of work" can be played, novices will undergo some form of socialization, for indifference to the opinions, attitudes and values of one's peers is exceptional.

Suggested Readings

Braude, Lee
1975. *Work and Workers*. New York: Praeger.
Burstein, M., N. Tiernhaara, P. Hewson and B. Warrander
1975. *Canadian Work Values: Findings of a Work Ethic Survey and a Job Satisfaction Survey*. Ottawa: Department of Manpower and Immigration Canada.
Haas, Jack and William Shaffir, eds.
1978. *Shaping Identity in Canadian Society*. Scarborough: Prentice-Hall.
Hall, Oswald and Richard Carlton
1977. *Basic Skills at School and Work: The Study of Alberton, an Ontario Community*. Toronto: Ontario Economic Council, Occasional Paper 1.
Van Maanen, John
1975. "Breaking in: Socialization to work." pp. 67 - 130, in Robert Dube (ed.). *Handbook of Work, Organization and Society*. Rand McNally.

Chapter 5

Occupational Careers

One of the ways that sociologists attempt to describe and analyze the relationship between people and their work is through the employment of the concept of career. Like many sociological terms, career is used in a specific sense that differs from the popular usages of the same term. The popular meanings of career are usually evaluative and often perjorative. For example, the notion of "career woman" may be either complimentary or derogatory. As a compliment it denotes an evaluation of a woman who is engaged in full-time employment with the implication of some sort of continuing commitment (Pavalko, 1971). As a derogation it implies that a woman who devotes herself to a job automatically denies commitments to her family and domestic situation (Dunkerley, 1975).

As a sociological concept, career depicts both a path of movement within some form of social organization comprising progression through a series of interconnected statuses (Braude, 1975) and a "patterned series of adjustments made by the individual to the network of institutions, formal organizations and informal relationships in which the work of an occupation is performed" (Becker, 1952:70; Hall, 1948:327).

In the previous chapter we argued that induction to work promotes a sense of identity with one's workmates and workplace. This process of identification continues on the job and affects future life chances and job mobility. Sociologists typically deal with mobility in intergenerational terms. "Social mobility" generally refers to movement up or down in the stratification system over one or more generations. This type of mobility, measured by comparing the occupational status (or prestige) of parents and their children, is the subject of Chapter 6.

Career refers to a different set of phenomena. It places the focus on the mobility (*i.e.*, the change and movement) that occurs over the course of an individual's working lifetime. Moreover, as noted above, there are two dimensions to the concept of career: objective and subjective. Career consists objectively of a series of statuses one occupies during one's working years. Subjectively, a career is the moving perspective in which the person sees his or her life as a whole and interprets the meanings of his or her various attributes and actions (Hughes, 1958).

I. OBJECTIVE DIMENSION OF CAREER

As a type of status passage a career is "worked out in some organized system without reference to which it cannot be described, much less understood..." (Hughes, 1958:8-9). The type of work and the division of labour required to perform the work are two important organizational influences on the direction and timing of an individual's career. Glaser and Strauss have effectively argued that all status passages develop a shape:

> The shape of a status passage is determined by combining its direction and temporality. The term shape refers to the line—course of the passage—that results from graphing a status passage when using directions and timing as the two axes (Glaser and Strauss, 1971:57).

The direction of a career refers to the movement among the statuses in an organizational or occupational hierarchy. It can include promotions, demotions and simotions (or changes that do not differ in status terms). The temporal aspect of a career consists of such matters as schedule, regularity, prescribed steps, speed and pace. As a combination of directional and temporal concerns, the shape of a career emerges as periods of rises, dips, and plateaus. A basic property of shape is the distance that the worker has travelled during the career.

The two basic career shapes are vertical and horizontal. A career that is vertically mobile consists of movement upward or downward in some organized system of status or prestige. Caplow (1954) has delineated several ways in which this type of mobility can occur. First, a person may move from one occupation to another of higher or lower status. In industrialized societies such as Canada, many workers experience periods of preliminary and tentative employment, described by Davidson and Anderson (1937) as the floundering stage and by Miller and Form (1949;1964) as the initial work stage.

Lipset and Bendix's (1952) classic "Oakland Mobility Study" reports on the work histories of 935 persons. They found that changes in jobs within the same occupation were far more common than the phenomenon of switching occupations. Nonetheless, for certain categories of workers, there was considerable switching:

Although many persons have experience in a wide variety of occupations, most of it will be homogenous to the extent that it will be either manual or non-manual. The departure from this conclusion are generally of two major types.
1. Individuals whose occupational career is predominantly manual may have brief experiences in nonmanual occupations, especially in small business, sales and lower white-collar positions.
2. Individuals whose career is predominantly non-manual quite often have spent some of the occupational career in manual positions, generally briefly and generally early in their career (Lipset and Bendix, 1952:180).

Blau and Duncan (1967) offer similar evidence concerning movement from one's first job to later jobs. Among self-employed or salaried professionals, 79 percent stated that their first job was that of a self-employed professional. However only five percent of persons in managerial positions reported that their first job was of this type. The majority of the craftsmen in the sample reported a wide variety of semiskilled or unskilled first jobs. The only groups of workers who reported the degree of occupational stability found among professionals were farmers and farmhands. Three quarters of the farmers reported their first job as either farmer or farm labourer. These findings suggest that switching occupations is uncommon at both the top and bottom of the occupational status hierarchy while relatively frequent at the intermediate levels.

A recent Canadian study indicates that the American pattern also is evidenced among a sample of approximately three thousand Ontario males (Ornstein, 1981). Unfortunately, this analysis uses occupational status scores as opposed to occupational categories. These scores provide a measure of occupational standing that it is known to be quite stable, but they make it impossible to deal with the important differences between occupational categories. Nonetheless, among men in the top occupations, 70 percent reported that their first job had the same occupational score as their current job, suggesting that there are very few "departures" from this occupational level. Among those in the lowest occupational standings, 24 percent began their careers at this level, suggesting that there is considerable switching in the lowly occupations.

If we concentrate on careers within a single occupation, vertical mobility occurs through promotion, demotion, and seniority. Promotions and demotions involve a change in one's position, as when a naval officer receives command of a ship or a locomotive fireman becomes an engineer. Such mobility typically involves a change in function or the acquisition of broader (or narrower) functions. Seniority is sometimes difficult to distinguish from promotion for seniority also involves changes in status and privileges. Technically at least, promotion is based on merit while seniority is based on longevity. However, in occupations that have limited opportunities for promotion, the seniority system often compensates for the absence of vertical channels. Finally, vertical mobility may occur when one's occupation, *per se*, experiences a change in status. The literature on "professionalization" (Vollmer and Mills, 1966) offers examples of individuals experiencing vertical mobility in the sense that they are carried along by the changes occurring in their occupation.

A worker experiences horizontal mobility when his or her change of occupations or functions within an occupation does not entail a change in status. For example, a manager may move from one plant to another or a junior partner in a law firm may switch his or her area of specialty. Martin and Strauss (1956) suggest that horizontal and vertical mobility often mesh and mutually support each other. They argue that horizontal movement affords the worker "breadth of experience" training and testing for potential vertical moves. Such horizontal movement becomes a necessary condition of further vertical mobility. However, "too much horizontal mobility may actually act as a demotion"(Martin and Strauss 1956:107). Unless horizontal moves terminate in vertical moves, the worker's career goes "out of shape" compared to those associates who continue to climb up the organizational hierarchy.

A typical career consists of a series of moves within an organization both horizontal and vertical. For some workers their career lines peak earlier than for others: few reach the top; some stop at lower echelons. These objective aspects of career allow the sociologist to "see" the social organization of the workplace. The interlocking of individual careers, each with vertical and horizontal movements, adds up to an organized system.

II. SUBJECTIVE DIMENSION OF CAREER

The subjective dimension of career highlights how one perceives, interprets and modifies the shape of one's career as a lived experience. While the structural features of career have a significant influence on the shape of an individual's movement within an organization or occupation, he or she is not a passive reactor to the social structure of the workplace (Stebbins, 1970). To appreciate the dynamic character of human agency, the student of occupational careers must grasp not only the change and stability of movement underlying the concept of career but also the subjective impact of temporal and directional sequences upon the person.

Participation in a career is a major basis of the formation of one's identity. Goffman (1961:25) regards the concept of career as a crucial link between the private world of the individual and the shared or social world of norms, expectations and statuses. However elusive an identity may be, Strauss (1959) points out that a central aspect of it is the individual's response to the appraisals that others make of one's conduct. Our response to the appraisals made of our work activity looms large in the development of an identity. Indeed, Strauss (1959) posits that the shaping of one's work identity is the prototype of identity formation in Canada and the United States.

By completing the "breaking in" period that was examined in Chapter 4, the recruit symbolically moves into a new status. Each subsequent change of status brings a corresponding change in one's personal identity. Moreover, the person takes on the attributes associated with his or her new position. With the passage of time one is fully aware of the investment of self that goes into one's career. This investment is most noticeable in terms of feelings of commitment, success and failure.

Varying degrees of commitment surely exist in all occupational careers (see Glaser, 1968). One's work, nonetheless, ties one's personal fate to socially sanctioned patterns of behaviour. A sense of career involves "expectations of and commitment to activities and outcomes at some future time, however ill defined it may be" (Braude, 1975:142). Most workers develop some sense of commitment to their jobs simply because of the amount of time and energy that they direct towards their working life. Even when the goals that they pursue as workers are not their "central life interests" they develop some commitment to the job; otherwise work loses all meaning.

The recognition by one's fellows of one's performance as in a promotion gives one a sense of purpose and self-esteem. It also bestows additional privileges that are socially desirable. The subjective impact of promotion is obvious. However, a much stronger evidence of the importance of the subjective dimension of career occurs in the analysis of failure. The most obvious manifestation of failure is dismissal. With dismissal the worker is socially deprived of his or her status. Such an action can have such profound effects on individuals that management is reluctant to employ this practice; moreover, unions find ways to prevent it.

Less severe acknowledgements of failure, as in demotion, are frequently deliberately obscured so that only a few people are aware that a demotion has occurred. More (1962) has outlined eleven forms of demotion:

1. lowered job status with same salary;
2. lowered job status with lower salary;
3. retained status with lower salary;
4. bypassed for promotion;
5. changed to job with less desirable function;
6. retained status but with decreased span of control;
7. exclusion from a general salary raise;
8. increasing the steps in the hierarchy above given position;
9. movement from line to staff authority;
10. transferred out of direct line of promotion;
11. elimination of position and reassignment.

To be sure, these eleven forms do not exhaust the possibilities. Martin and Strauss (1959) note that horizontal mobility and honorary promotions are often forms of demotion. Goldner (1965) found that individuals often experience "zig-zag" mobility which combines demotions and promotions to the point that the affected person is not sure that a demotion has occurred.

The subtlety of many of these forms of demotion allows the affected individual to salvage some self-esteem by obscuring the fact that a demotion has occurred. Obscured demotions may simply be denied, especially if one continues to receive fringe rewards such as trips, salary increases and so forth. When denial is not possible, many organizations attempt to minimize the humiliation as a result of socially recognized failure. When the stigma of lost status is strong, Goffman (1952) suggests that efforts are made to "cool-out" the unfortunate person to a level of self-appraisal and career expectations which allow the person to save face.

The "cooling out" of a demoted person occurs in the face of absolute failure, *i.e.*, when one must give up all aspirations linked with an occupation or position. When the stigma of failure is less severe, Glaser (1964) suggests that the adjustment to "comparative failure" involves a "cooling down" of one's expectations to a level that is commensurate to his or her new career shape. The key to both "cooling" processes is a redefinition of one's self-image so that he or she can accept the change in status.

A common method of cooling observed by Goldner is a shift of attention to another aspect of self:

A man engages in a number of activities of which his work may be only one. To compensate for a defeat in any one of these spheres of activity he may increase his investment in another sphere...This is one of the chief reasons why many managers consider the West Coast and other "desirable" geographical assignments as ideal places to go after being demoted. Such locations afford special opportunities to shift attention to family and leisure activities (1965:277).

Another form of cooling occurs when the demotion is redefined as a release from the tension of authority and responsibility associated with the position. More (1962) found that some men express a sense of comfort at being able to return to familiar and easier tasks.

Unless the demoted person can be effectively "cooled," demotion can have a negative effect on both the individual and the organization. The person may show negativism, bitterness, resistance to orders and a defeatist attitude. Such damage to self-esteem has organizational repercussions in decreased productivity, loss of loyalty to the organization and increased turnover and absenteeism (Martin and Strauss, 1959; More, 1962; Whyte, 1948).

By fastening attention on the subjective dimension of career one can shed light on the worker as an active participant in the workplace and clarify the important linkages between work statuses and personal identity. It also provides a fresh perspective on the complex policies that organizations employ for partial and complete failures. From the standpoint of organizational structure, the subjective dimension of career focuses on the sociopsychology of the structural relationships that constitute the social system of a workplace.

III. CAREER PATTERNS

While only individuals have careers, they pursue them within the context of particular occupations. Whether or not an occupation is pursued within a formal organization or outside of such an organization, its members experience a rather distinctive career pattern. An occupational career pattern is an ideal typical representation of the myriad of individual career shapes that occur within an occupation. Within a given occupational career pattern the actual shapes of individual careers display a considerable degree of variation. Ritzer (1972:46) illustrates the relationship of career shape to career pattern:

> Let us take the case of the college professor, who usually has four career steps open to him: instructor, assistant professor, associate professor and full professor. While many individuals proceed in an orderly manner through these steps, many others have more disorderly careers in academia. An individual may be an instructor, move to industry for a few years, return to academia as an assistant professor, work for the government, return to academia as an assistant professor, and so forth. Such individual variation and disorder does not negate the fact that an orderly pattern is associated with the occupation.

Career patterns differ in terms of the social and technical division of labour within an occupation *per se*, or within the division of labour of a formal organization. Occupations with a relatively simple

technology evolve a division of labour based on the interchangeabil-
ity of personnel. Such a division of labour results in a "flat" hierarchy
of statuses. Since there are few higher statuses, the occupational
career pattern is primarily horizontal. Conversely, in occupations
with a highly developed technical division of labour, the status
hierarchy is organized in terms of acquired skills. The greater the
technical division of labour, the "taller" the hierarchy. In occupations
with tall hierarchies, career patterns are primarily vertical (Martin
and Strauss, 1956).

An occupational career pattern may exist simply as a part of the
occupation's subculture or it may be modified by the subculture of
the formal organization in which members of the occupation work.
In the latter case, occupational career patterns are contingent upon
the social structure of the workplace. Since formal organizations
usually bring together a number of occupations, their complex
division of labour typically results in tall hierarchies which offer the
potential for frequent promotion through the many statuses that
constitute the hierarchy. Moreover, formal organizations frequently
exhibit a high ratio of managers to those who are managed and this
structural feature enhances vertical mobility because many careers
terminate in prestigious administrative positions—thus offering the
possibility of another avenue for career movement (Wilensky, 1960).

Occupational careers within formal organizations are also
affected by two other features of these organizations. While the
criteria for and timetables of advancement are fairly identifiable for
any occupation, the degree to which they are well articulated varies
and this articulation is most pronounced in formal organizations.
Because the technical and temporal criteria of promotion are fairly
clear and explicit, everyone in a formal organization has a stable set
of expectations, rules of conduct at various statuses and institutionalized channels through which to move. For management, this stabili-
zation provides a known method of moving persons through statuses.
For the worker it allows a basis for shaping his or her career. For both
mangement and the worker, institutionalized career patterns may
contribute to the efficiency of operations for the mobility hierarchy is
ordered and stable, hence predictable (Tepperman, 1975).

Some occupations exist solely within formal organizations. All
occupations exist within a larger social structure that affects their
own social organization and career patterns. For example, economic
factors focus or inhibit the expansion and contraction of occupations. In expansionist periods, mobility generally increases as additional positions are created. Similarly, the demographic characteristics of a society affect the number of recruits, the competition for
positions, and the amount of movement possible within a career. All

of these factors interact with one another. While it is difficult to establish the primacy of influences in the shaping of individual careers, it is possible to identify their relative influence, at given times, on occupational career patterns.

High prestige occupations are characterized by variable but stable career patterns (Ritzer, 1972). As we have observed in Chapter 4, initiates to these occupations undergo the most rigorous preparatory period of individuals in any occupation. The professions, however, have extremely diverse career patterns. Lawyers comprise an occupation that has a fairly tall hierarchy. The division of labour is stratified in terms of the types of work settings: solo practice, group practice, law firm, and government (Krause, 1971). This division of labour is also a social stratification in terms of prestige and reward. Solo lawyers draw their clientele from wage earners; group practices specialize in corporate affairs; law firms are most specialized and selective, while government lawyers are totally on salary. In addition to the diverse forms of practice, the law firm offers a series of well-defined steps leading to the top, *i.e.*, becoming a senior partner.

In contrast to lawyers, college professors form an occupation with a relatively flat hierarchy. Within the university setting it consists of four well-defined statuses. In some colleges and universities promotion is largely on the basis of seniority. In others, merit in terms of teaching and publications are the bases for advancement. Regardless of the type of institution, the final status, full professor, is the most difficult to achieve. In most universities one or more books and a number of articles are required in order to be considered for a full professorship. Although some advance to administrative posts and others leave to take positions in the business world, the career pattern of academics is rather constricted. Once one becomes a full professor, there are few channels for further mobility.

An examination of the mobility of Canadian university professors during the 1960s and 1970s illustrates the influence of demographic and economic factors on career patterns. Canadian universities experienced a period of rapid growth in the 1960s. This period was followed by one of nongrowth and potential decline. Additionally, there is a fairly fixed amount of resources (senior positions, tenure and money) in the university system. For these coldly impersonal reasons Holmes (1974:2) asserts that:

> ...the future for an ambitious 25 year-old is far less bright than it was in the heady 60s. Prospects for academic promotion will grow dimmer...

Other high prestige occupations offer virtually no mobility in career pattern terms. Physicians, for example have a very flat hierarchy. Although there are many transitional statuses in the socialization of medical students, once an individual has become a full-fledged physician, he or she has in most cases reached the pinnacle of his or her career (Ritzer, 1972). National data (Canada, 1980) indicate that 51 percent of Canada's 35,432 active civilian physicians are in general practice. To further one's mobility requires returning to a residency program in a medical or surgical specialty. On becoming a specialist, there is very little opportunity for further advancement. While the career patterns of these occupations offer only limited mobility, they provide a set of highly stable opportunities and expectations (Wilensky, 1960).

The career patterns of managers and senior executives are less stable than the professions but offer the greatest potential for career mobility (Krause, 1971; Ritzer, 1972). Generally, executives have had a less involved preparatory period. Most hold a bachelor's degree but it is becoming increasingly common for them to have a master's degree in business administration. In a study of 483 top executives drawn from a broad cross section of Canadian business, Dimick and Murray (1978) found that less than one executive in five (18 percent) had no postsecondary education. Seven percent had some university education but no degree. Another 11 percent had some professional designation other than a university degree (CA, RIA, etc.) and 64 percent had university degrees. Further analysis of their data suggested that:

> ...the extent of post-secondary education among executives is strongly associated with organization size and associated, but not as markedly, with position level within an organization. The technostructure of large organizations appears to make such education a necessary, if not a sufficient, condition for membership (1978: 376-377).

Dimick and Murray also reported that proportionally more executives in primary and secondary industries had university degrees than did executives in the service sector. Additionally, companies with few product lines or slow rates of technological change were managed by people with relatively low levels of formal education. Since these companies tended to be in the service sector, namely, retail, insurance, banks and transportation, Dimick and Murray (1978:380) concluded:

> Thus it appears that educational requirements of top management are in a sense a response to technological change and complexity. Where those factors were less important, university education was apparently somewhat less emphasized in a hiring or promotion decision.

Managerial career patterns often appear to simply consist of a series of well-defined steps through a set of statuses leading to the pinnacle of an organization. It is a popular myth that anyone with ambition and skill can rapidly climb to the top. However, there are a number of organizational features that affect these career patterns. Executives enter industry with varying occupational backgrounds. The most common are skills in production and operations, finance and accounting, marketing and sales, or highly-narrow or specialized skills that comprise what is called the staff. Staff positions consist primarily of personnel, planning, engineering and research, and development functions. The greatest opportunity for upward movement to top positions is through the traditional line functions of production and operations management. Dimick and Murray found this pattern existed in all but the very large companies. They argue that because of their complexity, these large companies appear to draw senior executives from all aspects of the organization, including staff, in order that they can develop breadth and thus be able to interface between functional areas.

Regardless of the mode of entry into an organization few make it to the top. The critical years of the executive career in terms of reaching the top appear to be the first decade and a half, or from about the age of twenty-five to forty. During this period, those who have realistic opportunities for senior positions are clearly separated from those who have already peaked at lower echelon positions (Krause, 1971). In the Dimick and Murray (1978) sample, the average age of top management was 49 years and they had been in their present position for an average of three and a half years.

Unlike the higher level occupations that we have been discussing, middle level occupations typically offer more constricted career patterns. In Chapter 4 we noted that the semiprofessions (*e.g.*, teaching, nursing, and social work) are characterized by a socialization process similar to the established professions of medicines, law and the sciences. While members of these occupations experience little upward mobility, their career patterns are marked by a good deal of horizontal mobility. The single major route for upward mobility for members of the semi professions is the assumption of administrative positions. Relative to the number of teachers, nurses and social workers, there are very few such positions. Further, administrative work is not regarded as a meaningful option for many semiprofessionals for, in effect, it is a movement out of the occupation for which they have trained. On the other hand, demotion, in any formal sense, is also a very remote possibility for semiprofessionals.

With respect to horizontal movement, two fairly distinct patterns appear to exist. One could be called the "desirable location" pattern. It consists of moving from one workplace to another in search of the "right" kind of environment. For school teachers this search consists of locating the right kind of principals, colleagues and students or classrooms with a good student-teacher ratio (Becker, 1952). For nurses, it often means selecting a hospital or clinic in which they can perform the type of nursing duties that they value. For social workers, horizontal mobility is frequently in search of particular types of clientele. The second pattern could be labelled the "in and out" syndrome. Because of the prevalence of young women in the semi professions, careers are often halted by marriage or childbirth and resumed again when the children are in school. Krause (1971) posits that these two career patterns bear no clear relation to the performance of the individual and in general appear to be reactive rather than planned.

The skilled trades offer another example of rigid and highly restricted career patterns. Once in his or her selected trade, the journeyman craftsman has virtually nowhere to go. While most are proud of their craft, the only form of mobility open to them is geographical. Seamen, carpenters, electricians, etc. can find similar work in many locations but all of these movements are horizontal. Most are high school graduates and the combination of highly-specialized training and lack of higher education makes it impossible to change occupations or assume administrative positions. The one option open to them is the possibility of going into business for themselves.

In terms of the career patterns of the skilled occupations and semiprofessions, the policeman is an exception. The new policeman begins at the lowest status on the force—foot patrolman. Promotion is typically based on assessment with respect to clearly defined criteria. In the Canadian police force studied by Vincent (1979) there are five factors, each contributing a possible twenty points to a total possible score of one hundred. Those who obtained the highest scores were listed as next in line for promotions when such positions became available. While passage through the ranks was generally slow because of seniority and the very low turnover rate in personnel, an upwardly mobile officer had the benefit of a formal promotional mechanism for ascending through a fairly tall hierarchy of statuses. Additionally, members of large police forces have an opportunity to "move out and up" by seeking a higher status position in a smaller department.

As one would suspect, the career patterns of the semiskilled and unskilled occupations are characterized by virtually no upward mobility. In a comprehensive study of the American occupational structure, Blau and Duncan (1967:424) concluded that those who start their working lives in the manual occupations experience little career mobility. Just as it has been argued that the concept of socialization to work loses meaning when applied to semi- and unskilled work, so too the "developmental" aspect of career seems missing, especially in contrast to the higher level occupations (Krause, 1971).

Increasing mechanization has both expanded the number of semiskilled occupations and reduced promotional opportunities for the blue-collar and clerical worker. At one time promotion to foreman or office supervisor was a possibility for these workers but now these positions are becoming the entry points for managerial recruits. Such positions offer these recruits some experience with production and supervisory problems as part of their training for middle and upper management jobs.

Since the career patterns of most middle and low level occupations are characterized more by seniority in one status than by a series of status passages, the subjective dimensions of these careers may not be measured in terms of their work history but in terms of their "purchasing career" (Krause, 1971). To compensate for the absence of occupational status mobility, these workers may embark on purchasing careers based on the accumulation of funds to be spent on objects that are prestige and status symbols. For example,. Langner (1970a; b) noted that the women of the New York Telephone Company were extremely "goods oriented." In occupations with blocked career mobility, one's time and effort spent on the job is not for advancement but for the pay cheque.

IV. CAREER CONTINGENCIES

Career patterns provide a frame of reference that allows an individual to assess his or her career shape and the potential for future advancement. Even among those occupations that have a developmental career pattern, people do not advance at the same pace. The success of an individual in regulating the pace and direction of his or her career (and hence control of its shape) is a function of personal attributes (such as ability, ambition and education), formal criteria for promotion and informal influences on the promotional network. The ultimate shaping of a career is the result of an interplay between the agency of the individual and the formal and informal features of the workplace.

The sociological study of careers has shown that certain non-work related statuses often operate as critical contingencies that serve to modify or redirect the shape of an individual's career. When individuals with similar formal criteria are competing for promotion, their social background and social assets may become deciding factors. Among the professions, the acquisition of a sponsor has been shown to be a crucial contingency on an individual's career. A sponsor is one who occupies a superior status within the occupation and is able to pull an aspirant along with him or her.

Hall (1946) presents an extreme example of a sponsorship system that dominated all promotion procedures among a group of physicians. Among the physicians studied was an "inner group" involved in the lucrative specialized fields of medicine and occupying the dominant posts in the area's hospitals. Its sponsorship process effectively controlled the local medical practice by sponsoring the entry of new members into the group. Unless a physician had a willing sponsor from this inner fraternity, he or she was not likely to achieve much career mobility.

Sponsorship, as Hall describes it, means that established members of an occupation actively intervene in shaping the careers of their juniors. It is a process in which seniors discover bright newcomers, show them the ropes and coach them through the status hierarchy (Strauss, 1959: 109-24). In a study of the careers of lawyers Smigel found that sponsorship was a factor in the attainment of partnership in a law firm:

> Associates often try to place themselves so that they can be in a position to work for the partner who they think can do them the most good (1964:107).

He concluded that in a situation involving two or more associates of equal ability, personality and social background, the strength of the sponsoring partner would tip the scale in favour of one candidate or the other.

A strict seniority system may limit the importance of sponsorship as length of service becomes the single most important criteria for advancement. However, even in firms where seniority is regarded as important, sponsorship occurs. In a study of management Dalton found that junior managers in their "search for mobility ladders sharpened their sensitivity to the attitudes and attributes of superiors and induced competition to please" (1951:414). Dalton also notes that the likelihood of sponsorship and promotion was related to ethnicity, religion, participation in certain clubs, political affiliation and membership in the Masons (Dalton, 1959). Similarly, Hughes reports that in his study of an English factory in Quebec, promotion was a vote of confidence:

> In general, there is probably a strong bias in favour of appointing for higher positions a man of the kind liked and trusted by the appointing group (1943:53).

More recently, Beattie (1975) concluded that informal discrimination against Francophones in the federal civil service slows their rate of upward career mobility in comparison to Anglophones. This discrimination is part of the sponsorship system that exists in the federal civil service:

> Sponsorship for promotion, and the compatibility between senior and junior employees which sponsorship entails, often become prime factors in the promotion process. Those who lack sponsors or are felt by senior employees to be incompatible may find their upward climb slowed down. The Francophone minority many of whom are conscious of personal difficulties in using the English language, are prone to feel that they are outsiders. Because of these difficulties with the English language and their interest in French Canadian culture, sociability with Anglophone superiors is hampered and the possibilities of sponsorship lessened (Beattie, 1975:170).

In most of the studies mentioned above, gender was also found to be a salient contingency. In a study that focused on female physicians Kosa and Coker (1965) hypothesized that gender status would be a crucial contingency to the extent that there is perceived incongruency between gender and work statuses. Nursing and teaching are occupations in which role obligations are congruent with a female status. On the other hand, in medicine and law there is a perceived incongruency between gender and these work statuses.

A female physician is confronted with a series of distinctive problems. First, the public is reluctant to accept a female doctor. Secondly, she is not fully accepted by her male colleagues. This lack of professional acceptance takes many forms. Medical schools have a stricter selection criteria for women than men (Shapiro, 1978). Hospital committees on privileges erroneously assume that many female physicians do not practice. This assumption is based on the fact that pregnancy and childrearing do limit their involvement in the crucial early years of their career (Ritzer, 1972).

Because of these conflicts, Kosa and Coker observed that female physicians prefer part-time positions which give some time to fulfill sex role expectations. For those who seek mobility via the specialities, pediatrics, psychiatry and public health are the major preferences. These specialities offer work tasks that are perceived as more congruent with gender status.

Businesswomen also find themselves placed in incongruent statuses. Based on a sample of businesswomen in India, Australia and Canada, Ross (1979) suggests that women find it difficult to make the necessary adjustments that would make them acceptable in their male colleagues' informal groups both in and outside the office. The price of acceptance into informal male cliques is their involvement in heavy drinking, off-coloured language and frequenting "low class" pubs. These activities are often foreign or distasteful to a woman's conception of her femininity. Additionally, the women studied reported an uneasiness in entertaining male clients and colleagues.

The main problem in entertaining was their embarrassment as well as that of their male guests when they paid the bill. Secondly, spending large portions of time with males was especially difficult for singles, widows and divorcees. In these cases there was always the possibility of the "suspicious wife" syndrome. Wives often have a hidden but great influence on businesswomen's careers:

> Once derogatory rumors begin to spread about a businesswoman's conduct they are difficult to squelch (Ross, 1979:433).

While the price of membership is high, acceptance in the informal cliques of male colleagues is as important to businesswomen as it is to businessmen. These groups are frequently the channel for subtle forms of information that are essential for one's work and promotion. Ross concludes:

> If women are not able to share fully in the networks of communication upon which business decisions depend, they are not of "equal" use to their firms, even though they appear to perform "equal work" (1979:434).

Vincent (1979) presents similar reasons for policemen's resistance to the hiring of females for police work. These men believed that the presence of women everywhere on the job would add to existing tension and create awkwardness. They acknowledged that a female presence on the force inhibits their language and the comradeship that exists among the males. They also worried about the reactions of their wives and were concerned about the potential for additional problems for their marriages. However, when women were finally admitted to the force these men conceded that some benefits had ensued. Female police officers were often a calming influence on domestic disputes and were able to deal more effectively with a woman who is involved in a crime. Nonetheless, these men were convinced that female officers were not able to manage violent situations or an emergency where the use of physical force was required to resolve a problem.

Governmental promotion of affirmative action and equal opportunity programs attest to the significance of gender and ethnicity as mobility barriers. A more detailed examination of this issue is the subject of Chapter 7. Other than these two ascribed statuses, age can also be a mobility barrier. Age is a career contingency in the sense that acceptable age ranges are identifiable for the various strata of an occupation. While these age ranges are not usually defined explicitly, they exist nonetheless in terms of some of the criteria used by superiors in determining who is promoted. For example, a person may be overlooked for promotion because he or she is "too old" or, less frequently, "too young."

One function that these timetables perform is to act as guidelines for the development of expectations concerning one's career shape. Age peers serve as a reference group to which one may make comparisons when forming judgements about one's own success and accomplishments. These timetables also reflect the more general cultural norm that authority should increase with age and that younger persons should show deference to their elders.

In occupations where breadth of experience is regarded as an important attribute of a worker, age related norms help to account for a number of regularities in the association between seniority and work activity. Apprentices, helpers and assistants are typically younger than journeymen, those who are helped or those who are assisted. These titles identify transitory statuses that represent early phases in one's career. In some occupations, formal rules exist concerning the length of time one must spend in a status before moving up to a higher status. When timetables are well defined, one who does not move out of a given status and into a higher position by a certain age will likely never move further up the hierarchy. Age, in a sense, begins to work against the probability of mobility.

Age norms are also related to the importance attached to seniority in occupations that offer little opportunity for upward mobility. Because of the severely-truncated career patterns found in these occupations, they are relatively heterogenous with respect to age. A seniority system uses the length of time in a job (which becomes a proxy for age) as the principle for differential distribution of privileges and responsibilities among people who otherwise occupy the same status.

Age is frequently associated with the psychology of the worker. Various models of career stages (Buhler, 1935; Miller and Form, 1964; Super, 1957) indicate that by one's late forties the average worker enters a maintenance stage in which he or she prefers to do those things that he or she can do well and does not attempt to break new ground. In a study of Montreal real estate agents, House (1974) quotes an agent who explains his reasoning for not risking a career move:

> Look. I'm sixty now, hey. I've got my own little corner here. I have made my contacts, the people that know about me here. It would mean starting all over again, if I were to move into industrial [sales].

By their mid career most workers have a fairly clear idea of how much further they are likely to advance. For many this is not a tranquil period but one that Jacques (1965) calls "mid-life crisis." Mid career signals middle age, *i.e.*, that one has as much or more time behind oneself as ahead of oneself. Hall (1976) argues that as people move into the maintenance state, they experience a variety of attitudinal changes including feelings that one is less mobile in the job market and a heightened concern with security. While many workers may not experience anxiety associated with awareness of the aging process, most cannot avoid the critical adjustment that occurs in the status passage from working person to retired person. Accordingly, we now turn to the sociological effects of retirement.

Attitudes towards retirement are changing. Many sociologists have argued that one is "pushed into retirement," *i.e.*, that retirement forces the worker from an occupation against his or her wishes. A large body of research suggests that this "push" phenomenon constitutes a severe crisis for the retired worker. In this literature, work is viewed as integrating workers into the social structure by determining identity patterns of participation and life style (Maddox, 1966, Simpson *et al.*, 1966a). Contrary to this negative view of retirement, Atchley has found that an increasing number of people are attracted or "pulled into retirement." His research suggests that more and more people see retirement as "active, involved, expanding, full and busy; as fair and good; as hopeful and meaningful" Atchley, 1976:28). Two recent Canadian studies (Canada, 1979; C.R.O.P., 1978) support Atchley's views.

Studies that give a negative view of retirement are based on the belief that attitudes towards work and retirement are closely related. Research conducted during the last decade indicates attitudes towards work are weak predictors of attitudes towards retirement (Fillenbaum, 1971; Goudy, *et al.*, 1974; Glasmer, 1976). While the wish to continue working does depend on attitudes towards one's work, especially to the extent to which work fulfills some needs, these work related attitudes have a stronger effect on decisions to retire than outlooks on retirement. But what about the retirement experience itself? Attitudes towards retirement are directed towards retirement as an abstract future possibility. In actuality, retirement is the final status passage in a worker's career. It moves the person out of the world of work and into a rather ill-defined world of leisure. It is this lack of definition of what it means to be retired that makes this status qualitatively different from the other statuses in a worker's career.

Retirement constitutes a severe identity crisis only for those who regard work as a central life interest. While most workers form bonds of attachment to some aspects of their work, the extent to which it is a central interest varies by occupation and organizational setting (Dubin, Hedley and Taveggia, 1976). Feelings of job deprivation are most likely to occur among those who had not achieved job related ambitions (Simpson *et al.*, 1966b). While initial adjustment might be easier for members of the middle and low level occupations, long-term adjustment is more likely for higher level workers who, in comparison with the lower level workers, typically develop broader social ties outside of their work statuses (Simpson *et al.*, 1966b; Rosenberg, 1970). The importance of these social ties lies in their relationship to the use of "the free time" that confronts the retired person. Most people have an ambiguous expectation that the pursuit of leisure activities will use up the large blocks of time that had previously been devoted to working. Yet most people do little definite planning for retirement. Riley and Foner (1968) and Simpson *et al.* (1966c) found that those who do some planning for retirement demonstrate higher morale and fewer feelings of job deprivation following retirement.

V. SUMMARY

Many approaches to occupational careers focus on either the psychology of the worker or the sociopsychology of the workplace (Osipow, 1979; Whiteley and Resnikoff, 1972). Sociologists add to and complement these approaches by drawing attention to the subjective and objective dimensions of career. By identifying the important linkages between work statuses and personal identities the sociology of careers show the worker to be an active participant in the shaping of his or her career. However, careers are also an objective phenomenon that exist within some organized system. They cannot be properly understood without reference to the type of work and the division of labour in which they are located.

Each occupation has a rather distinctive career pattern. Some occupations are characterized by a tall hierarchy of statuses based on a complex division of labour with movement following well-known timetables. Others have flat hierarchies with ill-defined criteria for and timetables of advancement. Generally, the high prestige occupations exhibit stable career patterns. Even among those which offer only limited upward mobility, they nonetheless provide a stable set of opportunities and expectations concerning the developmental aspects of career. In contrast to the higher level occupations, the middle and lower level ones are typically characterized by constricted career patterns offering few or no developmental features. In these occupations seniority replaces mobility as the central feature of one's career.

The study of career patterns illustrates that the ability of individuals to shape their own careers must be examined through a lens that focuses on the total picture. That bigger picture shows that the scope of individual career opportunities is closely associated with the organizational and structural features of given occupations. A careful examination of the whole picture also shows that personal attributes and interpersonal dynamics also serve as critical contingencies that may modify or redirect a person's career, other structural features notwithstanding. Sponsorship is an old and ubiquitous influence, even in occupations with clear and measurable criteria for advancement. Gender and ethnicity are other potential barriers that must be hurdled in the exercise of shaping a career.

Finally, an examination of age norms enlightens our understanding of the sociopsychology of careers and offers a vantage point from which to examine retirement. Retirement is the last passage in one's work career and, as such, draws attention to the relationship between work and the larger social order. One's attitudes towards and adjustment to retirement are associated with one's experiences as a worker. For some, retirement creates a severe identity crisis; for others, it is awaited with joyful anticipation.

Suggested Readings

Beattie, Christopher
  1975. *Minority Men in a Majority Setting*. Toronto: McClelland and Stewart.
Glaser, Barney G.
  1968. *Organizational Careers: A Sourcebook for Theory*. Chicago: Aldine.
Ross, Aileen D.
  1979. "Businesswomen and business cliques in three cities: Delhi, Sydney and Montreal." *Canadian Review of Sociology and Anthropology, 16 (4):*425-35.
Vincent, Claude L.
  1979. *Policeman*. Toronto: Gage.

Chapter 6

Occupational Mobility

"What chance does a garbageman's son have to become a doctor?" Questions like this one underline the issue of intergenerational occupational mobility. In a broader sense, it implies there is a close relationship between occupations and social stratification. The examination of this relationship is the burden of this chapter. It consists of three sections. First, by exploring the reasons why occupations have become one of the most important indicators of social status, we shall analyze the close relationship between occupational ranking and the overall social stratification system. Secondly, the various scales of occupational ranking are introduced. These scales serve as frameworks for the analysis of vertical mobility. Finally, patterns of occupational mobility between generations as they are manifested in Canadian society are discussed.

I. OCCUPATIONS AND THE STRATIFICATION SYSTEM

When two strangers meet, one of the first few questions asked would be, "What do you do for a living?" It seems that this piece of information helps people to define their relationships. By knowing the occupation of a person, people could make a fairly good guess at the education and the level of income of that person. Thus, the relative status of the participants in the situation is established. Answers to the question may reveal information other than just an occupational label. For a woman to say "I am just a housewife" or for a garbage collector to say "I do sanitation work for the Department of Health," it indicates the importance of occupational identification, the ascribed statuses of occupations, and their resultant placement in the social system.

To analyze the various relations between occupations and the stratification system, we shall raise and attempt to answer three important questions: Why do occupations occupy different positions within the stratification system? Why has occupation become a major indicator of a person's placement in the social structure? What are the determinants of the status of an occupation?

One of the basic theoretical issues in sociology is to explain social order and disorder. Why do occupations occupy different positions within the stratification system is one of the questions raised in addressing this issue. To answer this question, we shall briefly outline two well-known theories of social stratification: functionalism and conflict theory.[1]

Functional Theory of Stratification: This view of social stratification was developed by two American sociologists, Kingsley Davis and Wilbert Moore (1945). They argue that, for the fundamental problem of survival, all societies must develop a way of assigning people to various positions or occupations. Once the positions are filled, the incumbents have to be motivated to perform their roles adequately. If all positions are equally important, all tasks are equally pleasant, and all people are equally talented, then it does not make any difference who is allocated to what position. However, this is not the case in any society at any time. Some people are more talented than others. Some jobs are more pleasant than others. Moreover, some jobs are more important than others for the survival of the society. Some jobs require more skills and training. Since this is the case, the society must develop a system of rewards to induce its members to fill the positions which have varying amounts of appeal. Davis and Moore suggest that the rewards may take forms of material (or money), leisure and prestige. But all of them are differentially distributed according to positions. The system of differential rewards leads to a stratified society. From this functionalist point of view, social inequality is not only inevitable but also functional for the survival of the society.

If functionalism is the best known theory of social stratification, it is also the most criticized. This is no place to review the dialogue and debate between Davis and Moore and their critics.[2] However, the points which are most relevant to us here should be discussed.

One of the major criticisms of the functionalist perspective is that it is extremely difficult to determine which jobs are more important for the society. Tumin (1953:387-94) notes that, in a factory, unskilled workers are as important as the engineers, since the workers are the ones who produce. Davis admits that it is difficult to determine the exact functional importance of a position. But it is not so difficult to establish which category of workers is more difficult to replace (Davis, 1953:394).

Another criticism is that the functional explanation is valid only if there is equality of opportunity. But in a stratified society there is no equal access to opportunities to develop and use one's talent. For example, those who are from a high socioeconomic background would have greater access to education regardless of individual potential. Thus, inequality in one generation would limit the possibility of developing talent in the next. Furthermore, empirical studies (*e.g.*, Pike, 1970) have demonstrated repeatedly that inequality in one generation affects the motivational aspect of succeeding generations. Davis's response to these criticisms is that it does not really matter how the important positions are filled as long as they are filled (1953:395-96). He admits that the moral connotations of this argument may be undesirable, but it is analytically sound. However, it is undeniable that social stratification does have negative consequences, no matter how logically sound the analysis may be. Some of the negative consequences are the possibility of losing some potential talent which may otherwise contribute greatly to society and the differential effects on motivations of people.

Another point related to the lack of equality of opportunity is that high status families, with their wealth and power, are in a position to pass the advantages on to their children. Those who occupy important positions, therefore, may be there because of inheritance rather than because they are the most qualified people for those positions. This is clearly a dysfunction of social inequality which Davis and Moore ignore.

Regardless of these and other criticisms which have been levelled against the functional approach, the debate continues. The debate is partly kept alive by ideological differences. Many critics consider that the functional perspective is derived from a conservative ideology. It is thus a rationalization rather than an explanation of social inequality. However, despite the heated debate, no one has been able to disprove, empirically or logically, the basic idea in Davis and Moore's formulation; namely, if positions are to be filled competently there must be some minimal differentiation of rewards (Wrong, 1964).

The Conflict Approach: According to this approach, inequality is a matter of power and control. Those in the upper levels of a stratification structure hold a monopoly of the society's scarce resources and use their monopoly to dominate others. Conflict theories, then, argue that those with wealth, power and prestige are in control of the distribution of rewards. As a result, occupations are given certain statuses; the stratification system takes the form it does in capitalist societies such as Canada.

The conflict approach to social stratification is largely based on Karl Marx's ideas regarding class conflict. For Marx, human history has been a class struggle between the powerful and the powerless, the exploiters and the exploited. Capitalist society is no exception.

Although the capitalists are in the minority, they are able to control the workers by creating a belief system that legitimates the status quo in which they hold all the advantages.

In a less grand scale but the same vein of reasoning, theorists such as C. Wright Mills (1959), John Porter (1965), and W. Clement (1975), maintain that large organizations control both the private and public sectors. These large organizations in turn are controlled by a small elite of people with common background. With the overwhelming amount of power, the elite controls the rewards and thus the stratification system.

Theories are tools. Like any other tools, they have their limitations. For example, it is difficult for conflict theorists to explain why powerful leaders of organized crime find it almost impossible to gain widespread public prestige and those who are accorded extremely high prestige (*e.g.,* Nobel Prize Winners) are without power. It is equally hard for functionalists to explain the fact that women occupying positions identical to those held by men (in terms of both functional importance and occupational title) are not as highly rewarded. Exceptions such as these suggest that neither of these theories can by itself adequately account for the existence of stratification structures. Both appear to reflect different aspects of the development of social inequality.

While social stratification is a universal feature of human societies, occupation as a major indicator of a person's placement in the social structure is a relatively recent phenomenon in history. One of the early observers of the links between a person's occupation and status is Durkheim. In his *The Division of Labor in Society* (1947), he maintains that industrialization leads to specialized functions which, in turn necessitates a more specialized division of labour. It also separates people according to occupational groups. Since members of an occupation share similar skills and interests, a solidarity develops through their interaction. According to their importance to a particular society, a ranking of these solidarities develops through time.

More recent writers also note the increasing importance of occupation as an indicator of social status. For instance, Caplow points out that "There appears to be a consistent tendency for occupational identification to displace such other status-fixing attributes as ancestry, religious office, political affiliation, and personal character" (1954:30). Similarly, Blau and Duncan note: "In the absence of hereditary castes or feudal estates, class differences come to rest primarily on occupational positions and the economic advantages and powers associated with them" (1967:vii). Empirically, it has been found that occupation is of fundamental importance for general social ranking in industrial society. The most famous example is perhaps W. Lloyd Warner and his associates' exhaustive studies of social class in various American communities (1941;1942;1944; 1949). By using the reputational approach they found a high correlation between social class level and occupation. In fact, they have developed an occupational scale which may be used to reveal a person's general social class level (Warner, *et al.*, 1949:140-41). Other factors are also important in determining status. However, they too tend to be strongly affected by occupation. For instance, family background, upbringing, and social participation are highly related to occupation. The income, power, and style of life of the occupation have consequences for general social status in the broader community (Miller and Form, 1980: 591).

The discussion so far has made clear the point that in industrial societies occupation has become a major indicator of a person's placement in the social structure. The question that should be raised here is why. In explaining the reasons for the close relationship between occupation and social status, Caplow has discerned three major trends in modern industrial societies which are as follows:

   (i) aggregation;
  (ii) differentiation and
 (iii) rationalization (1954:19-25; 30-31).

Aggregation refers to increasing size of social groupings, particularly large-scale work organizations. The sheer size leads to "the substitution of formal groupings for informal groupings, and the substitution of regulatory mechanisms for voluntary coordination of human activities." Both the separation of home from the workplace and the bureaucratization of urban society in general, produce a high degree of anonymity and impersonality in human relations. Social interactions become fragmented. Only a part of the personality, rather than the total life history of the individual, is involved in most interpersonal relations. Thus people tend to define their relationships with others in functional terms. And, after sex, age and race, occupational designations or position titles become the most convenient shorthand method for recognizing others in casual interaction with many unrelated people in an urban environment.

Closely related to aggregation is differentiation which refers to the fragmentation of work processes brought about by the Industrial Revolution and the resultant occupational specialization on a large scale. With specialization, the attributes of each position become more abstract, particularly to the lay community. The requirements of each occupation, its importance and responsibilities, and the competence of its members are beyond the judgement of lay persons. They are, therefore, forced to respond primarily to an occupational title rather than to individual characteristics. This process of differentiation to which Caplow refers, also promotes strict authority systems within work organizations. While organizations consist of people, the hierarchical offices are also independent of specific individuals. Again, the response is to positional titles rather than personal characteristics or performance.

Rationalization refers to the substitution of the formal control of behaviour for informal, personal and spontaneous controls. This leads to the specification and standardization of work. The assignment of people to positions is, or is supposed to be, based on merits rather than on personal relationships or ascribed attributes. According to Caplow, this means that the assignment of occupational functions is "scientific," "appropriate," and "efficient." As this proceeds, it leads to the assumption that "the occupational label is a fair index of intelligence, ability, character, and personal acceptability. The modern reliance upon occupation as a measure of a man takes for granted the existence of high correlations between occupational position and all other attributes" (p. 31). Whether or not these correlations are exaggerated is beside the point, as Caplow rightly pointed out. What is important is the prevalence of the general belief that formal control is rational; that a person's occupational status is an effective indicator of personal attributes which are associated with corresponding social status.

Now that the reasons why occupation is a major determinant of social status in industrial societies have been discussed, the next question to be answered is: On what bases are occupations ranked? This is a reasonable question. To answer it, however, is no easy task. The evaluation of occupations appears to be closely related to the values of the culture in which it takes place. Since industrial societies are characterized as complex and heterogeneous, social values are also divergent. Thus, evaluations of an occupation are not always consistent among different groups. In addition, responsibility, rewards, functional status, and potential for upward mobility of an occupation may change through time; historical connotations often linger. These factors make the identification of characteristics which contribute to the ranking of various occupations a rather difficult task. Furthermore, we do not have sufficient knowledge about just how social evaluations of work role characteristics converge to assign a specific evaluation to each work role by people (Reiss, 1961:11).

These difficulties should not prevent us from exploring possible determinants though. Reiss suggests that the social evaluations attached to work in a society may be thought of as referring to (i) the kind of work a person does and (ii) the situation in which one works (Reiss, 1961:10-11). We shall follow his suggestion and Hall's elaboration (1975:242-44) to discuss the major characteristic related to these two factors.

One characteristic related to the kind of work a person does is the nature of the task. Whether one manipulates symbols, physical and/or social objects contributes to the differentiation of status. In general, more prestige is attached to the manipulation of symbols than to the manipulation of tools and materials. Caplow states that "all cultures emphasize certain central symbols, and the occupational functions attached to these always confer a degree of power and respect" (1954:44). However, there is some evidence to suggest that social manipulation also gives high status (Hall,1975:242). For example, the nature of the task of some executives is mainly involved with the manipulation of people. However, this does not mean that manual work invariably ranks lower than symbolic-social forms of work. Nor does it mean the differences between these forms of work are always clear-cut. While some craftsmen enjoy higher status than lower level white-collar workers, the work of a dentist involves the manipulation of tools and instruments to a large extent.

The second factor affecting the status of an occupation is the prerequisites for entry, as we have partially discussed in Chapter 3. These include, for example, the amount of education, training, and/or experience required, and the presence of certification or licence. With few exceptions, in general, the status of an occupation increases as the entrance requirements become more stringent. This explains the high status of the professions among white-collar workers and craftsmen among blue-collar workers.

Another determinant of the status of an occupation is the kind of social organization for the task. By this Reiss means whether the work is carried out individually or in groups. Although he does not specify which type of social organization gives higher status, it appears that work performed on an individual basis carries higher status, since individual work implies that the worker can accomplish the task without supervision. As some work is increasingly controlled by technology, the importance of this factor may decrease.

According to Reiss, the structure of interpersonal relations on the task and the type and amount of responsibility also affect the status of an occupation. Those occupations which are in a supervisory position enjoy higher statuses than those which are supervised.

"Responsibility for social or symbolic activities yields a higher status than responsibility for physical objects." In most cases, the more responsibilities, the higher the status (Hall,1975:243).

In addition to the kind of work a person does, the work situation also plays a role in determining the status of an occupation. The work situation, in turn, includes a variety of factors: (i) the institutional setting of work, (ii) the rewards of the job, (iii) the type of industry, and (iv) the nature of employment itself. These factors are discussed as follows:

(i)   the institutional setting of work: here the general trend is that a factory has a lower status than an office, and a research laboratory has a higher status than a machine shop (Hall, 1975:243).

(ii) The rewards of the job: these include income, recognition, tenure, retirement benefits, and so on. Although it is generally true that the higher the reward (income, for example) the higher the status of an occupation may be, it should be pointed out that the rewards that work situations offer vary tremendously. Individuals with the same title and responsibilities can receive highly varied rewards (Hall, 1975, 145-47).

(iii) The type of industry: it appears that depending on the level of technology and the state of economy of a society, various amounts of status are accorded to industries. For example, currently in Canada, the oil industry seems to yield more status than the fishery industry. As Hall points out, "within a community, various employing organizations occupy different statuses" (1975:243). Workers in automated factories usually enjoy a higher status than those who work in nonautomated factories.

(iv) Finally, the nature of employment itself; that is, whether it is public, private, or self-employment. Self-employment has traditionally been enjoying high status. Private employment usually has higher status than public, except in the case of elected public officials in high positions such as premiers and members of parliament (Hall, 1975:244).

According to Reiss, occupational status is evaluated in terms of the combination of the nature of the work and the situational aspects. Furthermore, while the work-related attributes tend to be more universal, the situational factors are more subject to local variations. Knowledge of the differences between work settings is most evident at the local level (Hall, 1975:244).

In conclusion, although there are considerable difficulties in determining occupational status in an accurate and objective manner, every occupation does have characteristics that can be evaluated according to the criteria discussed above.

II. THE SOCIAL GRADING OF OCCUPATIONS

Having introduced some theoretical explanations of status differences of occupations, having discussed the reasons why occupation has become a major indicator of social status and some of the factors which account for the differentiation of occupational status, it is time to introduce the various scales of occupations. The development of these scales reflects that the ranking of occupations is a social fact rather than purely a creation of the social scientist. What is more important, however, is the necessity of having some standard measurement of occupational status in order to analyze occupation mobility.

In general, sociologists use two kinds of scales of occupational ranking; namely, prestige scales and socioeconomic scales. Prestige scales are judgement scales. A sample of people are asked to place, according to their judgements, a group of occupations in relative social standings. The aggregated judgements of the people in the sample produce a scale of ratings of these occupations. A socio-economic scale, on the other hand, takes socio-economic characteristics such as income and level of education into consideration. Thus, it is a more "objective" type of measurement.

Although prestige scales are subjective in nature, it is an important dimension of any social stratification system. As Hall puts it, "Occupations do not have prestige, rather they are given it by the public. Since the public acts on the basis of its interpretation of an occupation,...prestige is an important component in the ranking of occupations" (1975:245). The best known and most widely used prestige scale in the United States is the one produced by the North-Hatt or National Opinion Research Center (NORC) survey, conducted in 1947 and since expanded and refined. With the objectives of securing a national rating of the relative prestige of a wide range of occupations and of determining the standard of judgement people use in evaluating occupational status, the original study asked a national sample of 2,920 persons to rank ninety occupations ranging from U.S. Supreme Court judge to shoeshiner (Reiss, 1961). Each of the ninety occupations was ranked by the respondent on a five point scale (excellent, good, average, somewhat below average, and poor). The final rankings were obtained by a scoring system that gave an

Table 6-1
Score and Rank of Selected Occupations*

Occupation	Score	Rank
U.S. Supreme Court Justice	96	1
Banker	88	10
Psychologist	85	22
Author of novels	80	31
Radio announcer	75	40
Bookkeeper	68	50
Garage mechanic	62	61
Truck driver	54	70
Night watchman	47	81
Shoeshiner	33	90

*Source: All the occupations ranked, the scores and the proportion of the respondents giving each response are shown in Reiss, 1961: 54-57.

occupation that received 100 percent *excellent* a score of 100 and those that were unamimously rated as *poor* a score of 20. There was not a total concensus on any of the occupations, of course. The above are examples of the scores and rankings of some of the ninety occupations in the NORC study.

The most well-known and the only national study to date of occupational status conducted in Canada is by Peter Pineo and John Porter (1967). They had a sample of 793 persons who rated the social standing of 204 occupations. This was a replication, with necessary adaptations, of the 1962 NORC study which, in turn, was a replication of the 1947 NORC survey. It was carried out both in English and French. Respondents were asked to sort cards with names of occupations on a ladder of "social standing." The final scores of the 204 occupations are "a transformation of the mean which makes it adopt a range from 0 to 100" (Pineo and Porter, 1967:29).

Provincial premier received the highest score (89.9 and 93.6 from the English and French respectively). Federal political occupations (*e.g.*, member of the Canadian Cabinet, member of the House of Commons) received high scores also. Professional occupations ranked highly, particularly physician, university professor, County Court judge, and lawyer. The lowest rank of occupations were newspaper peddler and garbage collector. To test if the ranking test was being taken seriously, the two researchers included two nonexistent occupations, "biologer" and "archaeopotrist." These two occupations ranked reasonably well, but the proportion of "don't know" responses was high: 44 percent for "archaeoportist" and 30 percent for "biologer." Several occupations with strong regional characteristics (*e.g.*, "whistle punk" and "troller") also received high "don't know" responses.

Table 6-2 shows the results of this study by major Census Classification (1961 Canadian Census Classification). Table 6-3 presents an alternative way of classifying the occupations into socio-economic categories. Table 6-4 lists prestige scores of some selected occupations.

The result of the Canadian study and those arrived at in the United States in 1949 and 1962 are highly correlated (.98). These very high correlations strongly suggest that over a period of time these prestige rankings between the two countries have been very stable. High correlations were also found when these rankings were compared with those arrived at in other Western industrial societies. The relatively high degree of stability may be taken as a strong indication that occupational prestige is a general and socially shared notion (Hodge *et al.*, 1966:318). This does not mean, however, that there are no shifts in the position of specific occupations within their general groupings (see Nosanchuk, 1972).

While the ranking of occupational prestige appears to be stable over time and between societies, studies of occupational prestige are

Table 6-2
Occupational Prestige Scores by Major Census Classifications

	Number of Titles	*Mean Score*	*Standard Deviation*
Owners and managers	27	60.38	15.71
Professional occupations	46	64.11	10.95
Clerical occupations	14	37.46	7.23
Sales occupations	11	36.99	12.91
Service and recreation occupations	23	37.17	15.92
Transport and Communications	13	41.72	12.83
Farmers and farm workers	6	34.98	10.01
Loggers and related workers	3	27.87	11.25
Fishermen, trappers, and hunters	2	23.50	0.32
Miners, quarrymen, and related workers	5	33.12	7.22
Craftsmen, production process workers	43	36.55	8.00
Laborers not elsewhere specified	3	21.47	6.02

Source: Pineo and Porter, 1967. Reprinted from the Canadian Review of Sociology and Anthropology, Vol. 4:1(67), pp. 34 & 35, by permission of the authors and the publisher.

Table 6-3
Occupational Prestige Scores by Socio-Economic Categories

	Number of Titles	*Mean Score*	*Standard Deviation*
Professional	21	72.04	8.16
Proprietors, managers, and officials, large	15	70.42	12.99
Semi-professional	29	57.73	8.29
Proprietors, managers, and officials, small	23	48.79	8.91
Clerical and sales	23	38.57	8.90
Skilled	27	38.76	6.98
Semi-skilled	34	32.91	7.71
Unskilled	18	23.46	6.23
Farmer	6	34.98	10.01

Source: Pineo and Porter, 1967. Reprinted from the Canadian Review of Sociology and Anthropology, Vol. 4:1(67), pp. 34 & 35, by permission of the authors and the publisher.

Table 6-4
Prestige Scores of Selected Occupations

Occupation	*Score*
Physician	87.2
University professor	84.6
Civil engineer	73.1
High school teacher	66.1
Registered nurse	64.7
Job counsellor	58.3
Insurance agent	47.3
Stenographer	46.0
Travelling Salesman	40.2
Airplane mechanic	50.3
Machinist	44.2
Plumber	42.6
Bus driver	35.9
Steel mill worker	34.3
Paper making machine tender	31.6
Quarry worker	26.7
Cod fisherman	23.4
Filling station attendant	23.3
Janitor	17.3
Garbage collector	14.8

Source: Pineo and Porter, 1967. Reprinted from the Canadian Review of Sociology and Anthropology, Vol. 4:1(67), pp. 34 & 35, by permission of the authors and the publisher.

not without methodological problems. A major problem encountered in the NORC studies was the different amounts of knowledge the respondents have about the occupations being rated. While almost all of the respondents could rank occupations such as physician, lawyer, school teacher, or carpenter, more than half of them were unable to rank nuclear physicists. It was also pointed out that their ability to rank varied with the respondent's education, socioeconomic status, and the type of community lived in (Reiss, 1961:10-18).

Another problem encountered was the ambiguity in the basic question when the respondent was asked to give his or her *personal opinion* or the *general standing* that an occupation had. The respondents were not instructed what to do when their personal judgement of the social standing was at variance with that of the community at large. There appeared to be some uncertainty about whether the respondent's own opinion of the job's standing or his opinion of the general community evaluation is required. The researchers assumed that the question was workable "because cases of this discontinuity between personal evaluation and perceived community evaluation are rare" (Pineo and Porter, 1967: 28-29).

In an attempt to provide a more objective method for describing and measuring occupational status, researchers in both the United States and Canada have developed scales using the combined measures of education and income. Occupation is "the intervening activity linking income to education" (Duncan, 1961: 117). In general, education prepares a person for an occupation from which the person derives an income. By characterizing an occupation according to the prevailing levels of education and income of its incumbents, both its "social status" and "economic status" can therefore be estimated (Duncan, 1961: 117). It has also been proven that socioeconomic measures are highly correlated to prestige ratings of occupations.

In the United States, the most well-known and widely used socioeconomic scale was developed by Duncan (1961: 107-38; 139-61). In Canada, it is the one constructed by B. R. Blishen. The original occupational class scale based on 1951 census information was published in 1958 (Blishen, 1958). It was subsequently revised and updated twice; once in 1967 and most recently in 1976 by using 1971 census data (Blishen, 1967; Blishen and McRoberts, 1976). The most commonly used by researchers to date is the 1967 scale which was based on 1961 census data. To construct this index, scores based on "the percentage of males in each occupation whose income was reported to be $5,000 or over during the preceeding 12 month period and the percentage who had attended at least the fourth year of high school were calculated" (Blishen, 1967: 43). Scores of 320 occupations were obtained. These occupations were ranked in terms of their socioeconomic scores. Based upon the use of the ten digits of the individual index values, the occupations are divided into six classes (Blishen, 1967: 51). Table 6-5 shows the six occupational classes, rank intervals, number of occupations in each class, and some examples of each class.

Table 6-5
Occupational Classes by Blishen's Socioeconomic
Index, 1961

Socioeconomic Index	Rank Interval	No. of Occupations (N=320)	Examples
70+	1-24	24	Chemical engineers (76.69)* School teachers (70.14)
60-69	25-50	26	Accountants and auditors (68.80); owners and managers, health & welfare services (60.07)
50-59	51-86	36	Security salesmen and brokers (59.91); musicians and music teachers (50.93)
40-49	87-138	52	Nurses-in-training (49.91); photographic processing occupations (40.05)
30-39	139-241	103	Engineering officers, ship (39.86); coremakers (30.0)
Below 30	242-320	79	Baby-sitters (29.99); Trappers & hunters (25.36)

*Numbers in brackets are socioeconomic scores of individual occupations.
Source: Blishen, 1967: 44-50.

The Blishen index and the Pineo-Porter prestige scale are in close agreement. A correlation test of the socioeconomic scores and the prestige scores for 88 matching occupations produced a high coefficient of .919. This verifies Duncan's speculation two decades ago that the three variables (*i.e.*, education, income and prestige) are socially tied together (Duncan, 1961: 116-17). We should not be too surprised by this general agreement though. Himelfarb and Richardson note that through socialization we learn to use the similar criteria to evaluate occupations (1979:185). The fact that people can even rank fictitious occupations (such as "biologer" and "archeopotrist" in Pineo and Porter, 1967) indicates strongly that they do not need to know much about an occupation in order to rank it.

However, contrary to Pineo and Porter's assumption mentioned earlier, there is some difference between personal opinion of an occupation and the perceived community evaluation of the same.

> Researchers find important differences when people are first asked to rank occupations the way they think most people would and then as they personally feel. Many manual workers feel lawyers and accountants are overrated and coal miners and farmers are not given their just due (Richardson, 1977: ch. 4; Coxon and Jones, 1978). In other words, while people know what they are supposed to think—what are the relevant criteria—lower-class people have not necessarily internalized the values of the upper class (Himelfarb and Richardson, 1979:185).

While the close agreement between the types of scales is well-established, there is one important issue which these scales do not address. That is the issue of gender in the social evaluation of occupations. In the case of the Pineo and Porter study, there is no differentiation between male and female occupations. In terms of their sample, it was reported that the sex distribution in the sample is not significantly different from that in the census (1967: 27). However, this does not necessarily mean that this prestige scale is free of sex biases. Guppy and Siltanen (1977:321) suggest that:

> An implicit sex bias is inherent in the construction of occupational prestige scales. One is more likely to think of a female worker when ranking a secretary and male worker when ranking a physician. Thus, the sex of the worker may enter into the construction of occupational prestige scales, but the degree to which this variable affects the ranking of occupations is unknown.

From their comparative study, Guppy and Siltanen found that men and women in similar occupations do not share the same allocation of prestige. The average score of the male prestige scale is 50 units higher than the average score of the female prestige scale (1977:327). They also found that the sex composition of occupations explains over 50 percent of the occupational prestige differences between males and females. Based on these findings, the researchers suggest that "the effects of the sex of the worker and sex composition of the occupation on the social evaluation of occupations are sufficient to warrant the use of separate scales for male and female occupational prestige" (1977: 329). However, the researches so far have not followed their own suggestion to develop such scales. Guppy and Siltanen further suggest that a female-based occupational status scale is essential if researchers are to continue the use of occupational socioeconomic scales in studying social stratification (1977: 329). We shall see presently that this last suggestion has received a response.

While there is no specific differentiation of gender in the Pineo-Porter prestige scale, the socioeconomic scales developed by Blishen (1967 and 1976) used data of the male labour force only. The reason for this was based on the assumption that "the family's social status is dependent upon the occupation of the husband rather than the wife when both are working" (Blishen, 1967: 42). However, this assumption is not supported by empirical findings. Marie R. Haug suggests that if the wife's status position is higher than that of her husband, it tends to raise the status of the family (1973:85-97). Furthermore, Acker finds that if the wife is unemployed in the labour force and is a housewife, the status of the family is lowered because housewifing is a low-status occupation (1973:936-45).[3] Similarly, Samson and Rosi (1975) suggest that the wife's race, occupation and education do have an effect on family social status, though it is not to the same extent as the effect of the same characteristics of the husband. Finally, Guppy and Siltanen's recent work (1977) outlined above indicated that the ranking of occupational prestige differs according to the sex of the incumbent.

In response to these suggestions, Blishen and Carroll developed a socioeconomic index for employed women (1978). This scale is based upon education and income levels in 465 occupations having female incumbents in 1970. They find that across the occupations studied, there is a close similarity between men and women in terms of occupational stratification by educational level, but there are considerable sex differences by income (p. 352). More specifically, "women tend to be concentrated in a small number of occupations requiring high levels of education and yielding relatively low income, while men are especially concentrated in occupations which require less education and provide higher income" (p. 356).

However, the sex differences in occupations are obscured by the socioeconomic index which is based on a combined calculation of education and income levels. The average socioeconomic score for women in the 1970s employed labour force is even slightly higher than that for men (42.26 and 40.95 respectively) (p. 356, Table II). Given this basic weakness, Blishen and Carroll caution researchers against "the exclusive use of occupationally based socio-economic indexes, such as the present ones, in the study of sexual stratification" (1978: 358). We suggest further that, for the very reason that these scales tend to mask the status differences between employed men and women the same caution should be extended to researchers in the entire field of social stratification, not just sexual stratification. While the construction of a socioeconomic scale for women is one step toward the right direction, Blishen and Carroll's end product does not seem to be that useful a research tool because of its weaknesses.

Despite the various problems of measurement of occupational status, some mobility studies have been conducted in Canada. The findings of some of these studies are introduced in the next section.

III. INTERGENERATIONAL MOBILITY IN CANADA

At the beginning of this chapter, we asked "What chance does a garbageman's son have to become a doctor?" To answer questions such as this one is to identify the mechanisms by which the life chances of parents influence those of their children, and to measure the extent to which social advantages or disadvantages are passed down from generation to generation. More specifically, one must identify to what extent socioeconomic background affects a person's educational and occupational attainment. The search for an answer or answers has been the motivation of many sociologists who conduct generational mobility studies.

To date, published mobility studies in Canada are relatively few in number and have small sizes (Pineo, 1976). One major study by a group of sociologists has completed its data collection stage. The results are yet to be published. Nevertheless, intergenerational mobility data about Canadian society have been accumulating recently. Broadly speaking, two types of studies can be discerned from available works: general mobility studies and studies of special groups.

General mobility studies refer to the ones which obtain their information from a sample of the general population either nationwide or of a region, a province, or a city. Studies of special groups are those studies of elite and poverty groups. Some of these special group studies do not specify occupations; rather, certain occupations are implied. Both types of studies have similar objectives: the extent and basis of social mobility in Canadian society and, in some cases, comparisons are made with other industrial societies, particularly the United States. In the following pages the major mobility patterns that have emerged from these studies are discussed.

(a) Educational Attainment

In general, the findings of the few studies of social inheritence conducted in Canada are consistent with our common knowledge. That is, individuals[4] whose fathers are well-educated and/or who have high status jobs with high educational requirements obtain more education (years of schooling) than do persons whose fathers are less well-educated and/or who have lower status jobs. For example, Ornstein reported that about 40 percent of the men in Ontario with fathers in the two lowest occupational categories (Blishen scores 20-39)[5] did not attend high school, compared to about nine percent with fathers in the 40-50 range and less than one percent with fathers scoring 60 or more. More than 50 percent of the sons of fathers with the highest status jobs graduated from university, compared to only 4.1 percent of the sons of fathers in the lowest categories (Ornstein:1981:190). This finding is in agreement with those of several previous studies (Turrittin, 1974; Cuneo and Curtis, 1975; McRoberts et al., 1976; Tepperman, 1975). In summarizing the results of these studies Hunter states that "anywhere from about one-sixth to about one-quarter of the differences among men in their levels of educational attainment can be shown to derive from differences among them in their socioeconomic backgrounds" (1981:143). These studies of course differ from one another in terms of size of sample and number and kinds of variables used as indicators of socioeconomic background, which make it difficult sometimes to compare the results, but the pattern is unmistakable.

(b) Intergenerational Mobility

In terms of occupational mobility between generations, again there is a fair amount of social inheritance. Ornstein reported that fathers with high status occupations tend to have higher status sons (in terms of their present occupations). As it is shown in Table 6-6, only 2.4 percent of the sons with fathers in the lowest occupational category (scores 20-29) obtain occupations in the highest category (70 to 79); 35.4 percent of the sons of men in the highest category have occupations in the highest group. At the other end of the spectrum, few of the sons with fathers in the top category had very poor jobs. The gamma value for this table is .359. It indicates that if one knows the occupation of a father, the chances of predicting the respondent's occupation increases about one-third, compared with a guess without that knowledge (Ornstein, 1981:187).

The findings presented above are also consistent with the frequently observed patterns reported in those mobility studies men-

Table 6-6
Intergenerational Mobility in Ontario

Father's Occupation (Blishen score)	Respondent's occupation (Blishen score)							Mean	Standard Deviation	Number of Cases
	Percentage distribution									
	20-29	30-39	40-49	50-59	60-69	70-79	Total			
20-29	19.8	36.0	22.3	12.7	6.5	2.7	100.0	40.7	12.0	404
30-39	15.7	45.8	19.6	7.2	7.4	4.3	100.0	40.4	12.4	1121
40-49	7.3	22.0	27.9	14.2	17.6	11.0	100.0	49.1	14.4	342
50-59	5.0	23.9	13.0	21.0	19.7	17.4	100.0	52.6	15.4	117
60-69	2.7	2.7	10.8	21.7	41.2	20.9	100.0	60.7	11.2	62
70-79	2.4	14.2	8.0	20.7	19.3	35.4	100.0	58.8	15.0	71
Total	13.7	36.5	20.5	11.0	11.0	7.3	100.0	43.8	14.1	2117

For Intergenerational mobility: $\gamma = .357$; E^2 for ANOVA=.163

Source: Adapted from Ornstein, 1981:186, top panel of Table 1. Reprinted from the Canadian Review of Sociology and Anthropology, Vol. 18:2(81), p. 186 by permission of author and publisher.

tioned above. However, the magnitude of intergenerational movement is not large. Ornstein's computations show that 36 percent of
the sons have jobs scoring within four points of their fathers (p. 187).
For his entire sample, 24.0 percent of the men make gains of 15 points
or more, and only 4.8 percent experience the same downward
mobility; 8.0 percent have jobs 30 points above their fathers, and
only 0.9 percent experience so great a decline. Apparently, there is far
more upward than downward mobility. However, much of it is
because of the changing composition of the labour force, mainly the
growth of the white-collar sector and the decline of farming (Ornstein, 1981:187; Turrittin, 1974:171).

(c) First Job and the Present Occupation

In regard to a person's first job the most important single
influencing factor is the person's own education, which also has the
strongest effect on his or her present occupation (Turrittin, 1974;
Cuneo and Curtis, 1975; McRoberts et al., 1976; Ornstein, 1981).
Superficially, these findings may be used as basis for the argument
that individual achievement is much more pervasive than ascription.
However, further analysis shows that this is not the case. The father's
education is indirectly related to a person's first job. That is, men
whose fathers are well-educated tend to be better educated themselves and, as a consequence, tend to move into the labour market in
higher-status jobs. The influence of the father's occupation on a
person's present job is both direct and indirect through its effect upon
the individual's level of educational attainment. Thus, while a person's own education has the strongest effect on his or her occupational status, education itself is to a great extent influenced by family
background.

In summary, as it is shown in the studies mentioned above, the
combined effect of father's occupational status, father's education,
and the person's own education amounts to between one-quarter and
one-half of the difference among men in the status of their first jobs.
When the effect of the first job is added to the above-mentioned
three, together they explain anywhere from one-third to nearly two-
thirds of the variation in present occupational status (Hunter,
1981:144).

While educational and occupational inheritance in Canada are
undeniable and are likely underestimated in existing studies,[6] the
duration of family influence appears to be in dispute among
researchers. Goyder and Curtis (1977) find in their four-generation
occupational-mobility study that family influence is strongest

between adjacent generations and it tends to weaken in subsequent ones. In other words, one undoubtedly benefits a great deal from a well-placed father. A well-placed grandfather is still of help. But the advantage of having a great-grandfather of high status is rather marginal. Some other writers, however, indicated that Canada is not a mobility-oriented society (Porter, 1965; Clement, 1975:72-269; Gonick, 1970; Puxley, 1971; Croll, 1971). In other words, in Canada, the rich remain rich and the poor stay poor through generations. Upon closer examination of the works of these writers, one finds that their research effort is mainly devoted to studying either the elite or poverty. It is to these studies that we turn now.

Strictly speaking, studies of elite and poverty groups are not "occupational mobility" studies because they do not always specify occupations involved in those groups. However, the occupational categories to which members of these groups may belong can be identified without many difficulties, particularly the elite groups studied by Porter and Clement. They studied the very rich and the most highly placed people in Canada. Occupationally, most of these people are the top-level executives or officials. Let us briefly introduce their work. By using the 1951 census data, John Porter (1965) studied five elite groups in Canada. He found members of the Canadian economic and other elites tended to be drawn in disproportionate numbers from among sons of upper class families, indicating that inherited advantage is important in Canada. Porter's data in Table 6-7 illustrates this point. Based on the 1971 census data and using the same approach, Clement (1975) studied the economic elite in Canada. Findings of this study show that among the elite, family influence not only remains important but even more so. This trend is shown in Table 6-8.

Occupations of poverty groups are more difficult to identify. This is partially because of the lack of precise information. Nonetheless, fragments of information are available. For example, the Special Senate Committee on Poverty in Canada mentions, in its report (Croll, 1971), the following occupations which paid less than the minimum wage: laundries, cleaners, pressers. A sizable portion of workers in industries such as leather, cotton, yarn, woollen mills, knitting mills, clothing, wood, retail trade and personal services also were earning less than the minimum wage (p. 24). In a more recent publication, Clairmont *et al.* reported that there were 27 low wage industries employing 436,025 workers in the Maritimes. A low wage industry is defined as one which, in 1970, had more than 60 percent of their full-time workers earning less than $120.00 per week. These industries range from knitting mills (93.2% low wage workers) to fishing (83.1%) and logging (78.7%) to forestry services (60.7%)

Table 6-7
Class Origins of 611 Canadian-born Members of the Economic Elite

Class Indicator*	No.	Cumulative No.	%	% of top 100**
Upper				
Father in economic elite	135	135	22.0	30.3
Father in other elite groups	13	148	24.0	37.0
Wife from elite family	41	189	31.0	46.6
Father in substantial business	42	231	37.8	54.5
Middle or higher				
Attended private school	75	306	50.0	67.0
Middle				
Father in middle class occupation and/or attended university	197	503	82.0	85.2
Possibly lower than middle class	108	611	100	100

*Some persons could, of course, be put into more than one category.
**The percentages in this column are of the 88 Canadian-born who have been classed in the top 100.
Source: Porter (1965: 292, Table XXVIII).

Table 6-8
Class Origins of Members of Economic Elite
Lasting Over Twenty Years

Class	Core Group*	Elite 1951	Elite 1972
Upper class	68.5%	50%	59.4%
Middle Class	28.9	32	34.8
Working Class	2.6	18	5.8
Total	100%	100%	100%
N	(76)	(611)	(673)

*The core Group are the 76 members who have survived over twenty years. They appear in both the 1951 and 1972 economic elites.
Source: Clement (1975:194, Table 22.).

(1980:266-87). One can infer occupational groups from the list of low-wage industries.

In general, researchers in this field maintain that poverty is being perpetuated in Canada. Because of the structural feature of the capitalist system, the marginal population (*i.e.,* the infirmed, the aged, the uneducated, the Natives) and the working poor are trapped in a state of impoverishment. Because they are generally poorly educated and unorganized, they are unable to sway the political and economic processes to their benefit. Because of their own low occupational positions, it is less likely that their children will obtain better education and better jobs. The possibility for them to be upwardly mobile is, therefore, very limited. Thus, in spite of the existence of a complex social security system in Canada, the economic and class factors in our society have the effect over time of keeping the rich rich, and the poor poor.[7]

Comparing the findings of the studies of the elite and poverty groups and those of the general mobility studies, two points can be made. First, the facts of the intergenerational inheritance of advantage or disadvantage in Canada are unmistakable. The difference between the bulk of the population and the two extreme levels of the society is only a matter of degree. Second, in light of the findings of the Goyder and Curtis occupational study over four generations, and the results of studies of elite and poverty groups, it might be concluded that the "achievement" interpretation is more applicable to the social structure of the bulk of the Canadian population, while the "ascriptive" interpretation is more applicable to the very upper and very low ends of Canadian society (*cf.* Goyder and Curtis, 1977:316).

No discussion of occupational mobility in Canada is complete without involving the factor of ethnicity. Not only is Canada largely populated by descendents of immigrants, but the rate of immigration continued at a high level during post-war years. Ethnicity as an important characteristic of the Canadian social structure has, therefore, received a great deal of attention from social scientists. However, researchers do not agree among themselves about the role of ethnicity in affecting occupational stratification. Porter emphasizes the extent of ethnic differences (1965: 73-98). The reason that he characterizes Canada as a "vertical mosaic" is partly derived from his analysis of the relations between ethnicity and occupations based on the 1931, 1951 and 1961 census data. Pineo (1976:120) finds "no more than two percent of the current occupational status of the Canadian male labour force can be said to derive from ethnic origin."

The two pictures of Canada painted by Porter and Pineo are apparently inconsistent with each other. Findings of more recent studies tend to be more in agreement with Pineo. For example, a study on the differences between Anglophones and Francophones in mobility and status-attainment processes has been reported by McRoberts *et al.* (1976). They have found that there were measurable differences between Anglophones and Francophones. However, the differences in mobility are primarily the result of differential changes in the labour force distributions affecting the two populations. Their cohort analysis provides strong evidence of convergence in mobility patterns between the two groups, especially for the youngest members in the labour force. Darroch reviewed a number of mobility studies and came to the conclusion that "in Canada as a whole it is an exaggeration of any data available to date to suggest that ethnic affiliations can be counted as a primary factor sustaining structures of class or status" (1979:22). Most recently, in a study of the occupational mobility of men in Ontario, Ornstein (1981) also finds that ethnicity is less important than place of birth, education and mother tongue in explaining occupational differences. He concludes: "if the amount of immigration to Canada is significantly curtailed, it is likely that the net ethnic differences in occupations and income will decline dramatically, as larger proportions of the members of all the groups come to be native born and educated and to use English in the home" (p. 211). Similarly, one of the major findings of the national Canadian survey referred to earlier is that ethnic status does not have much influence on occupational attainment for men born in Canada. The study found that there is little correlation between a native-born Canadian male's ethnic standing and his first job, his current job and his father's occupation (Boyd *et al.*, 1981:667).

While the centrality of ethnicity as a factor in occupational mobility in Canada seems to be diminishing (as it is shown in some recent studies), whether this is true for all ethnic groups remains to be tested. The problem is the operationalization of the concept of ethnicity. In some studies the dimension of ethnicity means a comparison between the Anglophones and the Francophones (*e.g.*, McRoberts *et al.*, 1976; Turrittin, 1974). In others, while more ethnic groups are compared, still the emphasis is on European groups. For example, Ornstein divided his sample into nine ethnic groups of which eight are European. All the rest were put in one category: "Other" (1981: 196-98). This "other" group includes, at least, the Jews, Russians, the Native groups, the Blacks and the various Asian groups. This is a conglomeration of vastly diverse groups. They are not one ethnic group. Furthermore, most of them are visible minorities. Historically, socially and perceptually, their environment is different from that of the European groups. The methodological problems created by the small size of these groups in a macro-analysis is understandable. However, given the reasons pointed out above, whether ethnicity is no longer significantly affecting the mobility opportunities of these minorities is at best unknown.

IV. SUMMARY

This chapter is concerned with occupational mobility between generations. It starts with a discussion of a series of theoretical issues as to why occupations occupy different positions within the stratification system, why occupation has become a major indicator of people's placement in the social structure, and what are the determinants of the status of an occupation.

Functional and conflict theories are introduced to illustrate different theoretical interpretations of the phenomenon where occupations have differential positions in society. While social stratification is universal, the fact that occupation has become a major indicator of a person's social status is a relatively recent phenomenon in human history. It is argued that industrialization which necessitates occupational specialization leads to the displacement of status-fixing attributes such as ancestry, political affiliation, and personal character by occupation.

Next, we proceed to introduce various occupational ranking scales which serve as frameworks for explaining vertical mobility in many studies. Finally, intergenerational mobility patterns in Canada are discussed. A great number of conceptual and methodological problems are encountered in studies of social mobility over generations. The problem of accuracy in historical data, and the difficulties of evaluating relative statuses of occupations in historical context are particularly difficult to overcome. Given these problems, the existing findings can best be treated as hypotheses. One general conclusion that can be drawn from our discussion is the varying degrees of social inheritance that exist in all levels of Canadian society. However, in general, Canada is probably no more ascriptive or no less achievement-oriented than most other industrial capitalist societies.

Notes

1. There are other explanations of social stratification such as Max Weber's theory, the convergence theories, the embourgeoisement thesis, the post-industrial society theories, and so on. However, structural-functionalism and Marxism remain "the major contenders doing battle

in the regions of social inequality." For an introduction to these theories, see Alfred A. Hunter (1981), Chapter 4.

2. A collection of articles of the debate as well as the original statements can be found in Bendix and Lipset (1967).

3. Hall disputes this point. He argues that this may not be the case, depending on one's values in regard to the family and housewifing. He suggests, though, that this area requires additional research (1975: 254). Similarly, Samson and Rossi (1975) suggest that the wife's race, occupation and education do have an effect on family social status, though it is not to the same extent as the effect of the same characteristics of the husband. Finally, Guppy and Siltanen's recent work (1977) outlined above indicated that the ranking of occupational prestige differs according to the sex of the incumbent.

4. All published studies except one (Cuneo and Curtis, 1975) excluded women from their analysis.

5. Ornstein used Blishen's 1967 scale which was presented in Table 6-5 in this chapter.

6. Hunter suggests that because of a number of conceptual and measurement problems the intergenerational determination of social inequality is likely underestimated. These problems include, for example, failure of inclusion of some socioeconomic factors (mother's education, occupation, and income) and non-socioeconomic family variables (birth order, family size, parental values, etc.) in the analytical models, and failure of taking into consideration of qualitative variables (type of education, location of a person's occupation in the technical division of labour; and measurement errors inherent in the various occupation ranking scales). For a detailed discussion, see Hunter, 1981:144-45.

7. In addition to the works referred to previously, Harp and Hofley's recent publication, *Structural Inequality in Canada* (1980), is particularly useful in understanding the issues of poverty.

Suggested Readings

Bendix, Reinhard and Seymour Martin Lipset (eds.)
    1966. *Class, Status and Power: Social Stratification in Comparative Perspective*, 2nd ed. N.Y.: The Free Press.
Boyd, Monica, J. Goyder, F. Jones, H. McRoberts, R. Pineo, and J. Porter
    1981. "Status Attainment in Canada: Findings of the Canadian Mobility Study." *The Canadian Review of Sociology and Anthropology, 18(5)* 657-73.

Clairmont, Donald H., Martha MacDonald and Fred C. Wein
1980. "A Segmentation Approach to Poverty and Low-wage Work in the Maritimes," in John Harp and John R. Hofley (eds.): *Structural Inequality in Canada*. Scarborough: Prentice-Hall of Canada.

Clement, Wallace
1975. *The Canadian Corporate Elite: An Analysis of Economic Power*. Toronto: McClelland and Stewart.

Cuneo, Carl J. and James E. Curtis
1975. "Social Ascription in the Educational and Occupational Attainment of Urban Canadians." *The Canadian Review of Sociology and Anthropology, 12(1)*: 6-24

Darroch, A. Gordon
1979. "Another Look at Ethnicity, Stratification and Social Mobility in Canada." *The Canadian Journal of Sociology 4*:1.

Davis, Kingsley and Wilbert Moore
1945. "Some Principles of Stratification." *American Sociological Review, 10(2)*: 242-49.

Goyder, J.C. and J.E. Curtis
1977. "Occupational Mobility in Canada Over Four Generations." *The Canadian Review of Sociology and Anthropology, 14(3)*: 303-19.

Hunter, Alfred A.
1981. *Class Tells: On Social Inequality in Canada*. Toronto: Butterworths.

Jones, Frank E.
1976. "Social Origins in Four Professions: A Comparative Study." *International Journal of Comparative Sociology, 12(3-4)*: 143-63.

Pineo, Peter C.
1976. "Social Mobility in Canada: The Current Picture." *Sociological Focus, 9(2)*: 109-23.

Porter, John
1965. *The Vertical Mosaic: An Analysis of Social Class and Power in Canada*. Toronto: University of Toronto Press.

Chapter 7

Disadvantaged Groups in the Work Context

I. INTRODUCTION

It is commonly accepted by many Canadians that their society is egalitarian. Contrary to this general image, sociological analysis has made it abundantly clear that this is not the case. Men and women, the rich and the poor, the Natives and the non-Natives are in different structural positions, enter into different occupations, receive different levels of incomes, and in sum, have different life styles and life chances. In this chapter we attempt to deal with the positions of some disadvantaged groups and the treatments they receive in the work context. While a number of groups can be considered as disadvantaged, we shall limit ourselves to the discussion of sexual and ethnic groups only.

Traditionally, a woman's place was in the home. Times have changed, however. For a variety of reasons more and more women are seeking paid employment outside of the home. We have touched upon the phenomenon of women's increasing participation in the labour force and raised a number of related issues in Chapter 2. We shall now return to those issues. In addition, a more detailed analysis of women's participation will be presented.

Canada is a society composed of a multitude of ethnic groups. Depending on the time of entry, the immigration policy at the time of entry and the attitudinal climate of the receiving society—particularly the attitude of the dominant groups toward various ethnic groups—entering immigrants are given different jobs in different regions of the country. The power relationship between the dominant and the lesser groups to a large extent determines the contour of the ethnic distribution in the occupational structure. We shall analyze this distribution and trace its change over time. Particular attention is paid to the Native people, a group which has been treated most poorly in the work context. The barriers they are confronted with in employment are analyzed.

II. GENDER INEQUALITY IN THE WORK CONTEXT

As we have pointed out in Chapter 2, one of the most striking changes in the Canadian economy has been the increasing number of women entering the labour market. From the turn of the century to 1951, the change was relatively small and characterized with fluctuations during and immediately after the war years (Marsden, 1975:13). Since 1951 up to now, the change has been both steady and dramatic (Table 7-1). In terms of females' labour force participation rates, the pattern is equally impressive. As it is shown in Table 7-2, while the participation rates for men have slowly declined, the rates for women have risen continuously.

In 1961, less than 30 percent of women 15 years of age and older were working or seeking employment outside of the home. By 1981, over half of the women were doing so. Despite the facts that the rate of enrollment of working-age women in educational institutions more than doubled during the period 1941-71, and there was a higher proportion of women 65 or over, the female participation rate in the labour force in 1981 was more than three times larger than that of 1901 (Table 7-2).

To put it in a different way, in the 10-year period 1966-1976, while the female population increased by 29.3 percent, the female labour force increased by 73.4 percent. The increases for men were 28.7 and 25.0 percent respectively (Women's Bureau, 1978:11, Table 2). A longer stay in school and earlier retirement were responsible for the slow but steady decline of the male participation rate. The

Table 7-1
Percentage of Females in the Labour Force, 1901-1981

	Labour Force (in '000)	Females (in '000)	Females/L.F.
1901	1,783	238	13.3%
1911	2,724	356	13.4
1921	3,173	490	15.4
1931	3,927	666	17.0
1941	4,196	833	19.9
1951	5,179	1,147	22.1
1961	6,455	1,764	27.3
1971	8,631	2,831	32.8
1981	12,267	5,000	40.8

Source: Censuses of Canada of respective years.

Table 7-2
Male and Female Labour Force Participation, 1901-1981

Year	Both Sexes	Male	Female
1901	53.0%	87.8%	16.1%
1911	57.4	90.6	18.6
1921	56.2	89.8	19.9
1931	55.9	87.2	21.8
1941	55.2	85.6	22.9
1951*	54.3	84.1	24.2
1961	55.1	80.8	29.1
1971	58.0	75.4	39.9
1976	60.0	75.5	45.0
1981	64.8	78.3	51.8

*Includes Newfoundland.
Sources: 1901-1961, from Ostry, 1971:18; 1971, 1976, and 1981 from Censuses Canada.
Reproduced by permission of the Minister of Supply and Services Canada.

overall result has been a relatively slow increase in the percentage of working-age Canadians in the job market in the twentieth century. Of course, all women do not participate in the labour force at the same rate. Their participation varies, among other things, with age, marital status, and level of education. In Chapter 2, we have already shown (Table 2-2) the patterns of participation rates of women in different age groups. The most noticeable changes were in the participation rates of the 25-34 and the 35-64 age groups. Take the younger group—the most active period of childcare—for an example. In 1951, about a quarter of women in this age bracket were in the labour force; in 1971, the proportion jumped to almost 44 percent. By 1981, it stood at more than 60 percent. The older group had the same pattern, although the percentages were somewhat smaller. These patterns mean that, in the last decade or so, women not only participate more, but they also stay in the labour force longer.

Table 7-3 shows the women's participation rates in terms of marital statuses. While the increases of single persons, the divorced and the widowed were steady, the increase of married women was dramatic. Since 1951, the number of married women entering into the labour market has been increasing at a pace which has never been witnessed in Canadian history. A further analysis (Table 7-4) also shows that in 1971, more married women, who had husbands absent and the divorced worked, than married women who had husbands at home. Women's participation also varies with their level of education. As may be expected, better educated women were more likely to

Table 7-3
Female Labour Force Participation by Marital Status, 1931-1971*

	Participation Rates				Married Women as a Percentage of Total Women
Year	Married	Single	Other	Total	in the L.F.
1931	3.5%	43.8%	21.3%	19.3%**	10.0%
1941	4.5	47.2	17.3	20.3	12.7
1951	11.2	58.3	19.3	24.1	30.0
1961	22.0	54.1	22.9	29.5	49.8
1971	37.0	53.5	26.5	39.9	59.1

*Statistics from the 1931 census are for the age groups 10 and over. Statistics from 1941-51 census are for the age group 14 and over. Statistics 1961 and 1971 census are for the age group 15 and over. Figures exclude those of active military service. Newfoundland is included, from 1951 on. The Yukon and the Northwest Territories are not included.
**The figures for 1931-1961 are slightly different from the corresponding percentages which appear in Table 7-2. Those were based on male and female populations 14 years of age and over respectively. But these slight variations do not change the patterns.
Sources: 1931-1961 figures are from Spencer and Featherstone, 1970:12; 1971 Census Vol. IV, Cat. 94-706, Table 14; Cat. 94-774, Table 8.

Table 7-4
Participation Rates of Females by Marital Status and Level of Schooling, 1971

	Less than Grade 9	9-11	12-13	Some University	University Degree	Total
Single	38.2%	42.9%	68.8%	76.0%	82.5%	53.4%
Married with Husband	25.3	37.1	46.6	50.8	53.9	36.2
Married with Husband Absent*	32.9	54.5	67.2	72.3	77.7	48.7
Divorced	47.8	68.9	78.1	77.8	87.4	67.2
Widowed	14.0	29.1	30.9	40.0	48.3	21.0

*Including the separated.
Source: Derived from Canada Census, 1971. Vol. III-7, Table 8. Cat. 94-774.

work outside of the home than those who were less educated (Table 7-4).

Since the participation of married women in the labour force has shown the most rapid growth, Gunderson analyzed separately the various factors influencing their decision to work (1976:99-102). Table 7-5 presents data of this analysis. As it is consistent with the

Table 7-5
**Labour Force Participation Rates of Married Women, Husband
Present, by Age, Education, School Level of Children, Income,
Employment Status of Husband, and Residence, Canada, 1971**
(percentages)

	Age				
Variable	15-24	25-34	35-44	45-64	15-64
Education:					
Incomplete high school	40	34	38	35	36
Complete high school	64	46	47	47	50
Complete university	78	55	46	49	55
Children:					
No children	76	78	62	39	57
Pre-school children only	30	30	27	25	30
School children only	50	47	45	37	42
Both pre-school and school children	24	26	25	23	25
Family income less own wage:					
$3,000 or less	50	47	48	45	47
$3,000 - 5,999	52	43	44	40	44
$6,000 - 8,999	52	42	45	40	44
$9,000 - 11,999	44	35	39	37	38
$12,000 - 14,999	40	29	34	33	33
$15,000 or over	42	26	27	26	27
Husband's employment status					
Employed	51	39	41	38	41
Unemployed	41	37	38	36	38
Residence:					
Urban	53	40	41	38	41
Rural non-farm	35	32	38	36	35

Source: Special 1971 Census tabulation from Statistics Canada.
Table from Gunderson (1976:100-01). Reproduced by Permission of the Minister of Supply and Services Canada.

general pattern, the more highly educated among married women
are much more likely to participate in the labour force obviously
because of their greater earning power. Those who have children,
particularly preschoolers, tend to participate less. Economic necessity is clearly a strong influencing factor of women's participation in
the labour market. Data in Table 7-5 show that the lower the family
income (less own wage) is, the higher the rate of the married women's
participation. Forty-seven percent of the women whose family
income (less own wage) is less than $3,000.00 would be working
outside of the home or seeking such employment. The fact that a fair
number of women whose family income is at higher levels may
suggest that economic pressures for married women to work can
continue into higher-income categories. It is also likely that more
women in higher income levels undertake paid employment for
reasons other than economic ones—such as self development and self
actualization.[1]

Gunderson offers a number of interpretations of the lower
participation rate among women with unemployed husbands. He
suggests that a husband's unemployment may not result in a decline
in family income. His unemployment may be seasonal and compen-
sated for by higher wages for seasonal work. It may be temporary and
its impact may be mitigated by unemployment benefits. In these
cases, family income does not decline and there is little incentive for
the wife to enter into the labour force.

However, the lower participation rate of women with unemployed husbands may also be because they themselves have low
potential for being employed and thus may be discouraged from
entering the labour force to seek employment. They may also be
working outside the officially defined labour force and, therefore, are
not covered by the statistics.

While women's participation in the labour force has been
increasing remarkably fast in recent decades, they do not enter into
the occupational structure evenly. When an occupation is dominated
by one sex or the other, it is labelled as a man's or woman's job. This
has considerable implications for that occupation. Furthermore, the
knowledge of the sex composition of occupation may add to our
understanding of the social structure in terms of gender. We shall
analyze the sex composition of occupations first by presenting data of
the proportions of women in various occupational categories, then
the occupational distribution of the female labour force and finally
the concentration of women in some specific occupations.

Table 7-6 shows the proportion of women in broad occupational
categories for every other census year, 1901-1961. Because the occupational categories used in the 1971 census are different from previous

Table 7-6
Women as a Percentage of the Labour Force[a],
by Occupation Division, Canada,[b] 1901-1961.

	Percentage				Difference
	1901[a]	1921	1941[c]	1961	1901–1961
White Collar	20.1	29.5	35.1	41.3	+21.2
Proprietary and managerial	3.6	4.3	7.2	10.3	+ 6.7
Professional	42.5	54.1	46.1	43.2	+ 0.7
Clerical	22.1	41.8	50.1	61.5	+39.4
Commercial, financial	10.4	25.6	32.1	40.3	+29.9
Blue-Collar	14.4	10.7	12.3	11.4	− 3.0
Manufacturing and mechanical	24.8	24.1	19.0	16.8	− 8.0
Construction	0.0[e]	0.0[e]	0.1	0.2	+ 0.2
Labourers[d]	1.0	0.2	4.4	6.1	+ 5.1
Primary	1.1	1.6	1.5	9.2	+ 8.1
Agricultural	1.2	1.7	1.7	11.7	+10.5
Fishing, hunting, trapping	0.0[e]	0.0[e]	0.6	1.1	+ 1.1
Logging	[f]	[f]	[f]	0.2	+ 0.2
Mining and quarrying	0.0[e]	0.0[e]	0.0[e]	0.0[e]	+ 0.0[e]
Transportation and communication	1.4	8.3	5.3	7.9	+ 6.5
Service	68.7	58.6	65.0	50.0	−18.7

[a] 10 years and over in 1901
[b] Excluding Yukon and Northwest Territories; including Newfoundland in 1961.
[c] Excluding those on active service, June 1941.
[d] Except those in Primary
[e] Less than 0.05% but not empty category.
[f] Empty category
Source: Computed by Hunter (1981:114) from Ostry (1971: Table 3). Reproduced by permission of the Minister of Supply and Services Canada.

years, the data presented in Table 7-7 are not directly comparable with those in Table 7-6. The trend is nevertheless clear.

The most noticeable trend as shown by these data is the rapid movement of women into clerical and commercial occupations. They also moved more quickly than men into agricultural, proprietary-managerial, transportation-communication, and labouring jobs, albeit to a much lesser extent. The only occupational categories

Table 7-7
**Women as a Percentage of the Labour Force,
by Occupation Division, Canada, 1971, 1981.**

	Percentage	
	1971	*1981*
Managerial, administrative, and related	16.0	24.7
Natural science, engineering and mathematics	7.3	13.9
Social Sciences and related	37.3	52.5
Religion	15.7	28.7
Teaching and related	60.4	59.7
Medicine and Health	74.3	77.7
Artistic, literary, recreational and related	27.2	39.4
Clerical and related	68.4	77.7
Sales	30.4	42.2
Service	46.2	52.7
Farming, horticultural, and animal husbandry	20.9	22.0
Fishing, hunting, trapping and related	[a]	5.5
Forestry and logging	2.1	6.1
Mining and Quarrying	[a]	2.1
Processing	17.8	22.2
Machining and related	5.7	6.8
Product fabricating, assembling, and repairing	23.7	24.6
Construction trades	1.0	1.9
Transport equipment operating	2.4	6.4
Materials handling and related	19.7	22.5
Other crafts and equipment operating	12.4	21.1

[a]Too few women for reliable calculations.
Source: Derived from 1971 Census of Canada, Cat. 94-723; 1981 Census of Canada, Cat. 92-920, Table 1. Reproduced by Permission of the Minister of Supply and Services Canada.

into which men moved more rapidly than women were manufacturing-mechanical and service. These trends of movement of the labour have coincided with the tremendous growth of tertiary industries in Canada during the last few decades. Clearly, the massive influx of women into the labour force has basically been channelled into the lower level of white-collar jobs. An exception of this is the movement of women into agricultural occupations, while this category experienced drastic decline during the same period. In 1971, 20.9 percent of agricultural workers were women. It increased to 22 percent in 1981.

To what extent have these patterns of sex composition of occupations changed since 1971? The 1981 figures are presented in Table 7-7 to show the changes. As can be seen from these figures, the general contour of the sex composition of occupations shows little change in the last decade. However, the proportion of women has increased in all but one category of occupations. The most noticeable trend is the sharp increase of women in those traditionally male-dominated occupations such as natural science and engineering, transport-equipment operating, and crafts and equipment operating. The proportions of females in these occupational categories are still small, but their sizes have increased. The increase ranged from about 100 percent for some occupations to more than 200 percent for others in one decade. The only category which has shown a slight decline is teaching and related occupations.

Since the majority of women have entered into occupations where the demand has been high, these occupations tend to be sex-typed as "women's work." However, the categories used in Table 7-6 and Table 7-7 are too broad to reveal the extent of concentration of women in specific occupations. In some cases they even give distorted impressions. For example, Table 7-7 shows that more than three quarters of workers in medicine and health were female. This figure gives the impression that the great majority of women are in the prestigious, high paying medical profession. It obscures the fact that this category includes many different jobs ranging from physicians to dentist's office helpers. Some of the occupations are almost entirely female, such as nurse and nurse's aide, and some of them, such as physician and surgeon, for the most part are male. Similarly, in the sales category, about two-thirds of all sales clerks are female, while five-sixth of all sales supervisors are male. In 1971, about 60 percent of employed women worked in some 50 occupations in which at least 60 percent were female. A decade later, these patterns changed little. Table 7-8 lists only those occupations 80 percent or more of whose members were female in 1981. They alone consist of more than 40 percent of the female labour force. These statistics demonstrate clearly that a very large proportion of female workers are concentrated in a small number of jobs.

Table 7-8
Leading Female Occupations, 1981

	Female % of Occupation	% of all Female Workers
Elementary and Kindergarten Teachers	80.4	2.9
Supervisor, Nursing Occupations	91.3	0.4
Nurses, Graduate and Nurses-in-training	95.4	3.5
Nursing Assistants	91.5	0.8
Physio- and Occupational Therapists	84.5	0.2
Supervisors, Stenographic and Typing	92.3	0.1
Secretaries and Stenographers	98.9	7.6
Typists and Clerk Typists	97.8	2.1
General Office Clerks	80.5	0.1
Tellers and Cashiers	93.0	4.7
Bookkeepers & Accounting Clerks	81.9	6.8
Receptionists and Information Clerks	94.6	1.8
Telephone Operators	94.8	0.7
Library File Clerks	87.7	0.8
Waiters, Hostesses and Stewards, Food and Beverage	85.7	4.1
Chambermaids	91.0	0.5
Babysitters	96.6	0.9
Personal Service Occupations	89.1	0.8
Sewing Machine Operators	94.8	1.9
Total		40.7

Source: Calculated from 1981 Census of Canada, Cat. 92-920, Table 1

From the above analysis, it is clear that occupations tend to be dominated by one sex or the other. As a consequence, they tend to be sex-typed as "male" or "female" jobs. Has this tendency changed over the years? The evidence seems to be that it has slowly but steadily decreased since the turn of the century (Lautard, 1977:9; cited by Hunter, 1981:116). The tendency of change, however, generally involves "the movement of women into relatively low-paying 'male' jobs (as in the case of clerical category generally, and those of agricultural and other labourers) and of men into relatively high-paying 'female' jobs (such as school teacher)" (Hunter, 1981:116). It can be concluded that, although there has been some decline of occupational sex segregation in the last few decades, it has not been sufficient to produce appreciable improvement of women's positions in the occupational structure.

Looking into the future, there may be some hope. It has been reported that enrollments of female students in law schools and medical schools have been increasing. For example, in 1958-59, eight percent of enrollment in Canadian medical schools were women and six percent female graduates. By 1978-79 these figures were 33 and 31 percent respectively. In 1979-80, six of the sixteen Canadian medical schools reported that 40 percent or more of their first-year students were female (Association of Canadian Medical Colleges, 1980). The enrollment of female students in law schools is equally encouraging (Table 7-9). In 1971-72, 14.9 percent of full-time students in law schools in Canada were female; by 1981-82 this proportion increased to almost 40 percent. If the increase of enrollment remains high and a high percentage of the enrolled complete their training, it should not take too long for women to form a significant proportion of these professions.

Another way of examining equality or inequality between the two sexes is to compare their incomes. Equal pay for equal work is both an ideal and the manifest purpose of legislation in recent years. Various studies comparing incomes of men and women have revealed that this goal is far from being reached.

Gunderson (1976) examined the changes that took place between 1961 and 1971 (Table 7-10). On the whole, women who worked full-time during that period earned about 60 percent as much as male full-time workers. When all wage earners were taken into consideration, the wage gap appeared increased. McDonald (1975) studied the period 1967-1972 and reached the same conclusion that the gap between men's and women's income was widening. Women's Bureau (1978) compared full-year female and male workers' average earnings in 1972 and 1977 (Table 7-11). Although there was some improvement, still the highest ratio of female earnings to that of men was only 63.7 percent (clerical).

What are the reasons for sex differences in earnings? They might arise because of differences in labour market productivity or because of discrimination (Gunderson, 1976). Early socialization, educational background, household activities, absenteeism, and turnover are all productivity-related factors. These factors, in turn, may be interrelated with discrimination. Parents tend to encourage their daughters to participate in household work rather than labour market activity. School's tendency of channelling females into educational streams would affect their "choices" when they enter the labour market. Because women might leave the labour force to raise children, many employers, sometimes women themselves, are reluc-

Table 7-9
Percentage of Enrollment and Graduates of Female Law Students
in Canada, 1971–82

Year	71–72	72–73	73–74	74–75	75–76	76–77	77–78	78–79	79–80	80–81	81–82
Enrollment	14.9	18.0	20.3	23.7	26.7	29.7	32.1	33.9	36.4	38.2	39.9
Graduates	12.1	13.8	16.8	20.8	22.1	27.6	27.7	31.8	35.0	35.8	a

Note: a. data not available.
Source: Calculated from Statistics Canada: Education in Canada, 1975: Table 36;
1979; Table 3 and Table 8; 1982: Table 3 and Table 35, Cat. 81-229.

tant to make substantial investments in occupational training on female workers.

Whether there is higher turnover and absenteeism among women than among men is difficult to determine. But one thing is

Table 7-10
Ratio of Female Earnings to Male Earnings[a], All and Full-time
Wage Earners, by Occupation, Canada, 1961 and 1971

Occupation	1961 Census[b] All Wage Earners	1961 Census[b] Full-Year,[c] Full-time	1971 Census All Wage Earners	1971 Census Full-Year,[c] Full-time
Manager/Professional[d]	.46	.56	.49	.56
Clerical	.61	.74	.59	.67
Sales	.35	.45	.34	.49
Service	.47	.47	.37	.50
Primary	.43	.60	.38	.47
Blue-Collar[e]	.53	.59	.47	.53
Other	—	—	.47	.55
All Occupations	.54	.59	.50	.59

[a]Earnings figures are for wage and salary earners and exclude self employed in unincorporated business. 1961 and 1971 ratios are not strictly comparable. In 1961, wage and salary data were collected, with fine breakdowns to the income level of $12,000, with an open-end class of $15,000 or more. For calculating averages, all incomes of $15,000 or more were given the value of $15,000. This means that, for occupations that had any incomes of $15,000 or more, the averages are too low. The groups most likely to be affected are the managerial and professional. In 1971, actual earnings were collected, so that the same bias does not exist in 1971 data.

[b]1961 occupational groupings are based on the 1951 Census categories and are not directly comparable with the 1971 figures, which are based on the Canadian Classification and Dictionary of Occupations groupings.

[c]Worked 49-52 weeks for 35 or more hours per week.

[d]1961 figures are an unweighted average of the ratios for managers and professional and technical, used because the two groups had approximately equal numbers in 1961.

[e]1961 ratios are a weighted average of the ratios for transportation and communication with craft, production, and related workers. The latter ratio was weighted by three to reflect the fact that there were approximately three times as many craft, production, and related workers as transportation and communication workers. 1971 figures consist of CCDO occupations 81-95, which include crafts, production, transportation, communication, and construction workers.

Sources: 1961 data are derived from Sylvia Ostry, *The Female Worker In Canada*, Table 16 (Ottawa: Queen's Printer, 1968). 1971 data are from special 1971 Census tabulations from Statistics Canada. Table from Gunderson (1976: Table 4.9). Reproduced by permission of the Minister of Supply and Services Canada.

Table 7-11
Ratio of Female to Male Average Earnings, Full-year Workers
by Occupation, 1972 and 1977

	1972	1977	Difference
Managerial	51.6%	58.1%	+6.5%
Professional	58.2	60.8	+2.6
Clerical	63.9	63.7	−0.2
Sales	39.4	46.9	+7.5
Service	39.0	48.3	+9.3
Processing and Machining	71.0	59.3	−11.7
Product fabrication	52.2	54.2	+2.0
Transportation and communication, etc.	53.6	58.0	+4.4

Source: Labour Canada, Women's Bureau, 1979, II:Table 8B (Women in the Labour Force). Reproduced by permission of the Minister of Supply and Services Canada.

clear; that is, turnover tends to lower women's wages because many of them participate in the labour force intermittently.

Depending on the interpretation of the productivity-related factors discussed above, the estimate of the wage gap between female and male workers may vary. According to Gunderson, females typically earn 50-80 percent of male earnings, and when adjustments are made for productivity differences, they typically earn 80-90 percent of male earnings.

> If one argues that current productivity differences are due to past discrimination, then all of the unadjusted wage gap can be attributed to discrimination. Alternatively, if one argues that current productivity differences reflect rational choices, especially with respect to household responsibilities, then only a small portion of the wage gap can be attributed to discrimination (Gunderson, 1976:120).

Even if we use Gunderson's latter interpretation, there is still a 10 percent difference which cannot be explained away.

In a more recent analysis of female and male workers in terms of the technical division of labour, Hunter (1981:123) discovered that an overall difference of $5,873 (or 54.6%) was in favour of men over women in annual earnings among a sample of Canadians employed full-time in 1977. When men and women were compared as if the women had occupations identical in skills to those of the men, the income difference between them was only reduced to $4,144 (or 47.8% male advantage). In other words only a small portion (*i.e.*, $5,873 − 5,144 = $729) of the annual earnings differential between men and women occurred from their having occupations with different skill requirements, while the rest derived from the fact that "equal skills did not always command equal pay."

Women's bureau analyzed men's and women's average weekly earnings in a variety of "similarly described occupations" (*e.g.*, junior clerk, order clerk, meat packager) in 1977, although the ratio of women's to men's earnings appeared higher than those based on 1971 census data,[2] only in a few cases (*e.g.*, in all twenty office occupations; in one of the 22 sales and service occupations; in four of the 52 blue-collar occupations) were the wage rates for women not lower than the rates for men (1979: Tables 1, 3, 5).

From the discussion presented above, only one conclusion can be reached. That is, in spite of legislation specifically requiring equal pay for equal work, there is still a wage gap between women and men. The only points for disagreement seem to be how wide that gap is and whether there has been improvement through the years. In the following paragraphs we shall discuss the nature of the equal pay legislation and some more recent developments in this area.

Equal pay for equal work legislation has been enacted since the early 1950s.[3] Most provinces now have equal opportunity provisions that apply to women. They have been enacted since the 1960s. From our discussion earlier, these laws obviously have not been effective. A number of reasons can be attributed to their ineffectiveness. For example, equal pay legislation emphasizes the "sameness" or "similarity" of work by men and women in the same establishment. Only when employers pay lower wages to women than to men who perform the same jobs, can they be charged of discrimination. The legislation does not concern itself with the employer's behaviour towards women in areas such as recruitment, training, promotion, and job assignment, all of which might affect wages. This emphasis is both narrow and easy to evade. All the employer has to do to escape the equal pay legislation is either to segregate jobs into "male" and "female" categories or to introduce variations in job requirements so that the jobs will no longer be the same or substantially similar. In places where virtually no men work, the legislation is largely irrelevant for the women who do work there.

An attractive alternative to the narrow "equal work" policy is the "work of equal value" concept which is endorsed in Convention 100 (or Rome Convention) of the International Labour Organization (Cook and Eberts, 1976:177). The "equal value" approach does not depend on the fact that there are men and women working at the same or similar jobs. Rather, it depends on the evaluation of jobs, taking effort, skills, and responsibility and working conditions into consideration.[4] If the value of the work of a senior secretary (most likely a woman) and a company truck driver (most likely a man) are assessed to be the same, they should be paid equally. Job evaluation to determine the "value" of the work is by no means simple and easy. However, a legislation based on this concept would be more difficult for the employers to escape by segregating jobs. So far, only the province of Quebec and the federal government have enacted equal-value legislation in their jurisdictions; but it is too soon to see any results (Grass, 1980).

Both as an alternative and a complement to equal pay legislation is the equal opportunity legislation. The purpose of equal opportunity legislation is to combat discrimination in hiring, promotion and conditions of employment. The provisions available for women in Canada vary from province to province. In general, they provide protection against discrimination on the basis of sex or both sex and marital status by employers and trade unions. Because of the diversity of the provisions, an evaluation of the overall effectiveness of equal opportunity legislation is difficult. Cook and Eberts (1976:180) reported that women are using this legislation more often than they have used equal pay legislation in the past. No evaluation of its "success" is available.

In addition to the narrow scope of equal pay and equal opportunity legislation, the adversary method—a process that involves a contest between parties—adopted for enforcing these laws and the exceptions contained in the legislation are significant reasons for their lack of effectiveness. Exceptions in these antidiscriminatory measures could lead to abuse, or at least to prolonging the investigation and enforcement process. The adversary method of enforcement necessitates individual action by an affected person. In other words, unless there is an actual case and complaint to set it in motion, the legal mechanism cannot be in operation. Therefore, to take advantage of the protection these laws provide requires knowledge, ability, resources, motivation, and determination on the part of the affected individual. After a complaint is made, from investigation to settlement (if it reaches this stage) it often is a long drawn out process. Relatively few female workers (or any workers, for that matter) have sufficient knowledge of these provisions, even fewer have the ability and resources to sustain such a long process. In order to remove the inequities between men and women in the workplace, not only more information about antidiscriminatory legislation should be made available to everyone concerned, particularly female workers, but more importantly, these provisions should be broadened and improved.

A future directed and more comprehensive approach to equality in the work world is Affirmative Action initiated by the federal government of Canada. "Affirmative Action is a program for people who want to ensure that the desire to create equality of opportunity in the labour market has tangible results" (Employment and Immigration Canada, 1980:2). This is basically a voluntary measure. While there is a commitment at the governmental level, particularly the federal government, it appears that little action has taken place in the private sector.

> Federal experience with the promotion of voluntary affirmative action has demonstrated that while employers may be sympathetic to the objectives, they are reluctant to make corporate commitment unless they know their competitors are also moving in the same way. Other reasons may include the still-limited attention paid to human resource management in the corporate planning process, the failure to grasp the implications of labour market trends and educational profiles (especially of women) and continued traditional attitudes towards women's roles and biases against minorities. (Employment and Immigration Canada, 1981:108)

The federal government is now in the process of revising and/or designing policies that are directed at the removal of systematic barriers which exclude qualified females and workers of other disadvantaged groups from jobs and promotions. It also attempts to remedy the impact of these barriers on the distribution and utilization of members of these groups. Whatever the results of this process will be, one thing seems certain; that is, unless there is an overall change of attitude toward women and other disadvantaged groups, no legislation alone can achieve the objectives of equality.

Among the disadvantaged groups other than women are some ethnic groups. It is to the factor of ethnicity in the Canadian work context that we shall turn now.

III. WORK AND ETHNICITY IN THE CANADIAN CONTEXT

One of the distinctive dimensions of occupations in the Canadian context is ethnicity. It appears common for Canadians to associate Italians and Greeks with construction trades and the pizza business, Jews with commerce, Chinese with restaurants, West Indians with domestic services, Ukranians with farming and so on. Although these associations may have their factual basis, they have nothing to do with the occupational aptitude of these groups (Porter, 1965:74). Rather, the ethnic character of the occupational structure has its roots in the history of immigration in Canada. Two features stand out in this history. First, immigration patterns are closely, though not exclusively, related to the economic development of our society. Secondly, the ethnic composition of the Canadian population is, to a large extent, shaped by the dominant groups—mainly the

British and, to a lesser extent, the French—who select immigrants of different origins and channel them into different occupational levels. The analysis of these two factors is the burden of this section. Throughout the discussion, attention will be paid to disadvantaged ethnic groups.

The evolution of Canadian immigration policies is closely related to the development of the economy. Following Elliott's periodization, the management of immigration in Canada is reviewed in five eras (1983: 289-301): the Confederation through 1895, the beginning of selective immigration in 1896 up to World War I, the period between the wars when immigration ebbed, the post World War II era (1946-1961) and the current phase. Table 7-12 summarizes the major characteristics of each era.

Canada was, of course, not a "no man's land" when the Europeans started to enter about 300 years ago. The Indian, Métis and Inuit people were and are the Natives. The earliest groups of settlers were the French and the British. Other West Europeans were also among the early immigrants. A number of Blacks came to Canada and settled largely in the Maritimes during the American Revolution and, later, the war of 1812. If Canada was not a "no man's land," it certainly was an open land. The entry was free. Fur traders came to make a fortune. Farmers came to settle. Others came to exploit the sea. During the period of the construction of the railway, a great number of labourers poured in or were brought in. It was upon their entry that the less favourable immigrants were relegated to disadvantageous positions.

Although Canada's first *Immigration Act* was passed in 1869, it was not until Clifford Sifton was appointed Minister of the Interior that the immigration policy became selective (Elliott, 1983:294). After the completion of the Canadian Pacific Railway, the West was "opened" for immigrants. In his selective policy, Sifton put great emphasis on prior agricultural experience. The result was the population of the prairies with land-hungry peasants from central Europe. From the Confederation era to 1911, 41 percent of the total foreign born population of Canada was held in that part of the country. A historical irony, though, was that to make room for the newcomers, the Native Peoples were "cleared" from the land and their settlements were destroyed. The expansionist immigration policy was continued up until the outbreak of World War I. The all-time peak was reached in 1913 when over 400,000 people came to Canada.

During the war years and the Great Depression, immigration declined to a very low point. Promotional efforts stopped in 1930, and restrictive immigration measures were introduced. To control immigration at its source, visas were issued for the first time during this era. The most restrictive measure was the *Chinese Immigration*

Act in 1923, in which people of Chinese origin were barred from entering Canada as immigrants.

The gradual shift of the Canadian economic structure from a rural to an urban base started in the early part of the 20th century. The post-war industrialization quickened the pace of the transition. This change led to the need for a tremendous number of skilled, semiskilled, as well as unskilled workers. In 1947, Prime Minister MacKenzie King specifically advocated immigration as an avenue to population growth and economic development which Canada should pursue up to its "absorptive capacity" (Elliott, 1983:299). This view set the tone of the post-war immigration policy. More than two million immigrants entered Canada in the two decades between 1941 to 1961 (see Table 7-12). Most of them have concentrated in urban and industrial areas. East of Toronto, the greatest area of concentration was in Montreal. In Ontario, immigrants were heavily concentrated in Toronto, Hamilton, and Windsor in the south, and Sault Ste. Marie and the mining areas to the north. In the west, concentrations were to be found in the coal mining area of southwestern Alberta, in southeastern British Columbia and the mining area along the coast of Vancouver. With few exceptions, these were the areas that had experienced the greatest need for labourers, craftsmen, and other industrial workers associated with construction, heavy manufacturing, and mining activities (Kalbach and McVey, 1971:161).

The clearest mark of the current phase is the 1967 immigration policy. The "points system" was introduced. Discrimination on the basis of race or national origin was eliminated for all classes of immigrants. Admission to Canada is to be determined by points earned in nine areas: education, personal qualities, occupational demand, occupational skill, age, designated occupation or arranged employment, knowledge of English and/or French, relatives in Canada, and area of destination (Department of Manpower and Immigration, 1975: 59-60).

This fundamental change of the immigration policy greatly influenced the characteristics of the future immigrants to the extent that larger numbers of people were allowed to come from third world countries that were previously discouraged from applying. However, the emphasis on training, occupational demand and skills also coincides with the rapid development of tertiary industries in Canada in the last two decades. Thus, we see a greater number of new immigrants that come from the professional, managerial and technical occupations. For example, the proportion of immigrants that had intended to enter professional and technical occupations was only 10.3 percent in 1956; it increased to 19.2 percent in 1961, 23.8 percent in 1966 and peaked in 1969 to 31.9 percent. Since then it has levelled off somewhat (Parai, 1975:471:Table 4).

Table 7-12
Canadian Immigration Policy and Change (1861-1981)

Historical period	Decade	Population at start of decade (000's)	Immigration as a percentage of average decade population	Migration (000's)			Immigration policy	Primary destination and type of immigrant
				Immigration	Estimated Emigration	Net Migration		
Confederation 1861-1871 to 1895	1861-1871	3,090	7.5	183	375	-192	free entry (exception: first B.C. "head tax" on Chinese. 1885.)	Eastern Canada settled by immigrants from British Isles.
	1871-1881	3,689	8.8	353	440	-087		N.W. Europe and U.S.A.
	1881-1891	4,325	19.7	903	1,109	-206		
The Sifton era to W.W. I 1896-1914	1891-1901	4,833	6.4	250	380	-130	selective immigration. objective: land settlement	Prairies settled by farmers, many from Central Europe
	1901-1911	5,371	28.0	1,550	740	810		
War and economic depression (1914-1945)	1911-1921	7,207	20.2	1,400	1,090	310	restrictive measures.	Urban settlement as well as rural.
	1921-1931	8,788	12.6	1,203	974	229	Chinese Immigration Act. 1923.	War refugees. Jewish and other displaced persons.
	1931-1941	10,377	1.4	150	242	-092	visas first issued. "sponsorship" begins.	

Postwar era (1946-1961)	1941-1951	11,507	4.4	548	379	169	liberalization.	Urban areas in Central Canada. Southern European immigration begins many in manufacturing occupations.
	1951-1961	14,009[1]	9.6	1,543	462	1,081	1952 Immigration Act objective: population increase to "absorptive capacity".	
The Current phase	1961-1971	18,238	7.2	1,429	705	724	"points system" 1967, objective: universalistic criteria.	Urban settlement continues. Third World immigration begins. many professional and technical workers.
	1971-1979	21,568	—	1,297	—	—		

[1]Including Newfoundland.
Source: Elliot, 1983:292-93, reproduced from Kalbach and McVey, 1971, 1974: Tables 1.1, 1.2, 1.4 and 2.2.

The above is a very brief review of the evolution of the immigration policies primarily from the perspective of economic considerations. However, there is another salient dimension to the history of immigration policies. That is the dimension of racial and ethnic selectivity. Its influence is still evident in the current occupational structure. After his review of the immigration policies, Professor Elliott concluded this way:

> All in all, it would seem that MacKenzie King's concept of "absorptive capacity" has been retained in Canadian policy as it pertains to economics and rejected as it pertains to notions of ethnic or racial assimilability. (1983:297)

At least up until 1967, immigrants and potential immigrants were perceived to have three broad categories: the preferred (the British, the American, the French, northern and western European), the less preferred (the southern and eastern European), and the nonpreferred (the coloured). The attitudes towards immigrants are either "based on racial theories or on more respectable theories about the ease of assimilation (a not well-defined concept)" (Porter, 1965:68). Despite the unfoundedness of these theories, in Porter's term, the less preferred immigrants were given "entrance status" (1965:68). They came on sufferance and were funnelled into lower status jobs. The nonpreferred were either barred from entry entirely, as in the case of the *Chinese Immigration Act*, 1923, or only a small number were allowed in (without families or in the approximate sex ratio to form families) to work in menial jobs, such as domestic servants. The result of these practices is a kind of occupational segregation based on ethnicity. Porter's analysis of the census data convincingly documented this phenomenon (1965: 73-91). Table 7-13 presents his analysis of three censuses in terms of the over or underrepresentation of ethnic groups at various levels; that is, whether these groups appear in greater or smaller proportions than does the total labour force at these occupational levels.

For example, in 1931, the British and the Jewish were over represented in professional, financial and clerical occupations, and underrepresented in the rest of occupational levels; the Europeans were by and large overrepresented in agriculture (except the Italians) and primary and unskilled occupations; the Asians were over-represented in personal service and primary and unskilled occupations; the Native people were drastically overrepresented in primary and unskilled occupations and underrepresented in all other occupational categories. After a detailed analysis of the distribution of occupations, both male and female, Porter concluded that "a rank order of ethnic groups in the economic system of 1931 can be determined" (1965:81). The ethnic hierarchy was something like this: the British groups and the Jews ranked high, next would be the French, German and Dutch, followed by Scandinavian, East Euro-

Table 7-13
Ethnic Origin and Occupational Classes, Male Labour Force, Canada, 1931, 1951, and 1961,
Percentage of Over-Representation in Occupation by Ethnic Group

	British				French	German	Italian	Jewish	Dutch	Scand.	East Euro-pean	Other Euro-pean	Asian	Indian and Eskimo	Total male labour force
	British total	Eng-lish	Irish	Scot-tish											
1931															
Professional and financial	+1.6	+1.6	+1.0	+2.2	-.8	-2.2	-3.3	+2.2	-1.1	-2.9	-3.9	-4.4	-4.3	-4.5	4.8
Clerical	+1.5	+1.8	+1.0	+1.4	-.8	-2.2	-2.5	+.1	-1.9	-2.7	-3.4	-3.5	-3.2	-3.7	3.8
Personal service	-.3	0.0	-.5	-.7	-.3	-1.2	+2.1	-1.2	-1.5	-1.5	-1.1	-1.7	+27.8	-3.1	3.5
Primary and unskilled	-4.6	-4.4	-4.9	-4.8	+3.3	-5.3	+26.1	-14.5	-4.8	+1.4	+12.4	+35.8	+10.2	+45.3	17.7
Agriculture	-3.0	-6.1	+2.7	-1.5	+.1	+21.1	-27.6	-32.4	+18.5	+19.8	+14.5	-5.8	-20.9	-4.9	34.0
All others	+4.8	+7.1	+.7	+3.4	-1.5	-10.2	+5.2	+45.8	-9.2	-14.1	-18.5	-20.4	-9.6	-29.1	36.2
Total	0.0	0.0	0.0	0.0	0.0	0.0	0.0	0.0	0.0	0.0	0.0	0.0	0.0	0.0	100.0
1951															
Professional and financial	+1.6	+1.6	+.9	+2.5	-1.5	-2.2	-3.1	+4.2	-1.7	-2.1	-2.9	-2.4	-2.8	-5.2	5.9
Clerical	+1.6	+1.8	+1.3	+1.4	-.8	-2.5	-1.7	-0.0	-2.4	-2.8	-2.8	-2.5	-2.9	-5.2	5.9
Personal service	-.3	-.2	-.4	-.5	-.2	-1.2	+2.0	-1.4	-1.2	-1.0	+.6	+2.0	+23.9	-.6	3.4
Primary and unskilled	-2.2	-1.7	-2.2	-3.2	+3.0	-3.7	+9.6	-11.5	-1.7	+.5	+2.3	+5.7	-1.9	+47.0	13.3
Agriculture	-3.2	-5.5	+.5	-1.6	-.3	+19.1	-14.7	-18.7	+17.3	+14.7	+11.2	+3.4	-8.7	-7.8	19.4
All others	2.5	+4.0	-.1	+1.4	-.2	-9.5	+7.9	+27.4	-10.3	-9.3	-8.4	-6.2	-7.6	-28.2	52.1
Total	0.0	0.0	0.0	0.0	0.0	0.0	0.0	0.0	0.0	0.0	0.0	0.0	0.0	0.0	100.0
1961															
Professional and financial	+2.0	—	—	—	-1.9	-1.8	-5.2	+7.4	-.9	-1.9	-1.2	-1.1	+1.7	-7.5	8.6
Clerical	+1.3	—	—	—	-.2	-1.8	-3.2	-.1	-1.7	-2.4	-1.7	-2.0	-1.5	-5.9	6.9
Personal service	-.9	—	—	—	-.2	-.7	+2.9	-2.4	-.5	-1.1	+.9	+5.1	+19.1	+1.3	4.3
Primary and unskilled	-2.3	—	—	—	+2.8	-2.1	+11.5	-8.9	-2.0	-.2	0.0	+1.8	-3.6	+34.7	10.0
Agriculture	-1.5	—	—	—	-1.4	+8.8	-9.5	-11.7	+10.3	+10.6	+6.9	+.6	-6.5	+6.9	12.2
All others	+1.4	—	—	—	+.9	-2.4	+3.5	+15.7	-5.2	-5.0	-4.9	-4.4	-9.1	-29.5	58.0
Total	0.0				0.0	0.0	0.0	0.0	0.0	0.0	0.0	0.0	0.0	0.0	100.0

Source: Porter, 1965:87, Table 1.

pean, Italian, Japanese, "Other European," Chinese and the Natives. He admitted that this rank order of occupational status is rough. However, almost two-thirds of the 1931 labour force has been taken into account and this pattern of ranking stands out sharply. Furthermore, after a detailed analysis of the 1951 and 1961 census data, while there were increases and drops in their representation in the various occupations, Porter found that "the relative positions of the various groups had changed very little" (1965:86). Apparently, it is at least partially because of these results that he argues that the entrance status of ethnic groups tends to be perpetuated in the economic system (1965: 69).

How much change has there been in the decade of 1961-71? As it is shown in Table 7-14, the basic pattern has been maintained. In general, the Jews and the British are overrepresented in white-collar jobs, while other groups are underrepresented in varying degrees.

The ethnic nature of the Canadian economy is revealed by other data, too. For example, Briant's analysis of the construction industry provides a vivid illustration (P. Briant, cited in Hall, 1973: 52):

> The control and operation of large industrial engineering equipment is almost entirely in the hands of the Anglo-Saxon group in the country. The financing of construction is in the hands of this group and the Jewish group. Small scale contracting has become very much a special field for French-Canadians who employ Italians in substantial numbers. The organization of real-estate has fallen very largely into Jewish hands—they predominate heavily among the real-estate business.

While the basic pattern of ethnic ranking in the Canadian economy has been maintained over many decades, the historical trend seems to be in the direction of decreasing differences between groups (Pineo, 1976; Darroch, 1979). In general, the intergroup differences seem to be gradually narrowing. Some have even shown significant change. For example, the proportion of Asians in natural sciences and engineering and medicine have increased considerably in recent years (see Table 7-14). One group that is still lagging far behind is the Native people. In 1971, they were underrepresented in all but a few low level occupations. More serious is their high unemployment and unstable employment. The employment rate of the Native population and their individual income vary greatly from community to community, from year to year, and from season to season. But invariably throughout the country, there exists a substantial gap between the position of the Native people in the labour market and that of other ethnic groups.

A 1973 survey undertaken by the Department of Indian Affairs and Northern Development (DIAND) revealed that the general unemployment rate of reserves was 48 percent. In some Native communities, however, it is known to reach as high as 95 percent (Employment and Immigration Canada, 1979: 2). In urban centres, the Native unemployment rate currently is over 30 percent (Employment and Immigration Canada, 1981: 96). Not only are more Native people than members of any other group unemployed, the duration of unemployment is also very long. According to the Report of the Task Force on the Labour Market Development in the 1980s, released recently, the average length of each period of unemployment is over seven months (Employment and Immigration Canada, 1981: 96). For those who are employed, their income is usually very low. A 1971 survey conducted by DREE established that only 4 percent of the on-reserve work force in Manitoba earned $4,000 or more compared to 49.7 percent for the workers of that province as a whole (Employment and Immigration Canada, 1979: Table IV). In brief, existing studies repeatedly reveal the same pattern; that is, the Native people are concentrated in low-skill/low-wage occupations, they are faced with the barriers of mobility to more desirable jobs, they have frequent and lengthy unemployment, they have very low incomes and they depend heavily on social assistance.

What accounts for the less-favourable-ethnic-group position of the Native people? The Task Force Report on Manpower Services to Native People lists nine barriers to Native employment (Employment and Immigration Canada, 1979: 5-8) as follows:

(i) Information gap: while Native leaders have repeatedly expressed their desire to have manufacturing plants and other job-producing activities developed in or near their communities, government and business officials tend to hold on to the old notion which questions the ethics of involving Native people in industrial activities. In other words, the non-Native Canadians do not seem to take notice of the significant changes that have taken place in the Native way of life in the last 20 years. As with everyone else, most Native families take for granted that the money they need for their subsistence will have to come from wage employment. Although they prefer the implantation of economic activities in their own community, many of them have moved to urban centres where there is employment.

(ii) Cultural biases: Non-Natives tend to underrate Native peoples' abilities to perform well on the work site. Some businesses are located in the very heart of Native regions but hire very few Native workers.

Table 7-14

Ethnic Group by Occupational Group, 1971

	British Isles	French	German	Hungarian	Italian	Jewish	Netherlands
				per cent			
Managerial, administrative and related	5.2	3.7	3.6	2.8	1.8	10.7	3.5
Natural sciences, engineering and mathematics	3.1	1.8	2.7	4.7	1.3	2.6	3.3
Social sciences and related	1.0	0.9	0.6	0.6	0.3	3.3	0.7
Religion	0.3	0.4	0.3	0.2	0.1	0.2	0.4
Teaching and related	4.3	4.5	3.6	3.1	1.6	5.2	3.2
Medicine and related	4.1	3.6	3.5	3.4	1.1	4.9	3.6
Art, literature, performing arts and related	1.0	0.9	0.7	1.3	0.6	2.1	0.8
Clerical and related	18.5	14.7	13.4	11.5	9.7	18.8	11.9
Sales	10.4	8.7	8.7	6.7	6.7	24.2	8.8
Service	10.6	11.2	10.6	11.9	13.0	4.9	10.6
Farming, horticulture and animal-husbandry	5.4	4.4	12.5	9.4	1.8	0.4	14.2
Fishing, hunting, trapping and related	0.4	0.2	0.1		–	–	0.2
Forestry and logging	0.6	1.3	0.5	0.4	0.2	–	0.4
Mining, quarrying including oil and gas field	0.6	0.9	0.7	0.7	0.4	–	0.4
Processing	3.1	4.9	3.7	4.2	6.2	1.4	3.8
Machining	2.4	2.8	3.4	5.8	5.2	0.6	3.1
Production, fabrication, assembly and repair	5.9	8.2	7.6	9.7	15.6	6.4	6.9
Construction trades	5.6	6.9	7.9	7.2	15.3	1.7	8.1
Transport equipment operation	4.2	4.5	3.5	2.5	2.6	1.7	3.5
Material handling and related	2.4	2.2	2.3	2.4	3.4	0.8	2.3
Other crafts and equipment operation	1.4	1.3	1.1	1.0	0.7	0.6	1.1
Not stated and not elsewhere classified	9.5	12.0	9.0	10.5	12.4	9.5	9.2
TOTALS	100.0	100.0	100.0	100.0	100.0	100.0	100.0

Table 7-14—Continued

	Polish	Russian	Scandi-navian	Ukrai-nian	Asiatic	Native Indian	Other	Total
				per cent				
Managerial, administrative and related	2.8	3.0	3.8	2.9	3.1	1.5	2.6	4.3
Natural sciences, engineering and mathematics	3.2	3.1	3.0	2.5	7.1	1.1	3.3	2.7
Social sciences and related	0.6	0.6	0.7	0.6	1.0	1.3	0.7	0.9
Religion	0.1	0.2	0.2	0.1	0.1	0.1	0.1	0.3
Teaching and related	3.0	3.5	4.0	3.5	4.7	1.6	3.0	4.1
Medicine and related	3.2	3.2	3.7	3.0	8.5	2.2	3.8	3.8
Art, literature, performing arts and related	0.7	1.1	0.8	0.7	0.9	1.1	1.0	0.9
Clerical and related	14.2	13.7	13.7	14.8	14.7	6.9	12.2	15.9
Sales	7.2	7.7	9.1	8.4	9.1	2.7	6.3	9.5
Service	13.1	11.6	10.7	12.9	16.9	12.4	15.7	11.2
Farming, horticulture and animal-husbandry	8.0	10.4	12.6	11.6	2.2	5.9	5.0	5.9
Fishing, hunting, trapping and related	—	0.1	0.5	0.1	0.3	2.6	0.2	0.3
Forestry and logging	0.5	1.0	1.2	0.4	0.2	6.2	0.6	0.8
Mining, quarrying including oil and gas field	1.1	0.8	1.1	0.9	0.2	1.0	0.7	0.7
Processing	4.8	4.6	3.0	3.8	3.9	4.1	4.6	3.9
Machining	4.1	2.7	2.0	2.7	2.2	2.2	4.4	2.8
Production, fabrication, assembly and repair	8.9	6.4	5.2	6.9	8.0	4.4	11.0	7.4
Construction trades	6.7	7.4	8.0	6.5	2.0	9.8	7.4	6.5
Transport equipment operation	2.8	3.9	4.0	3.7	1.4	3.6	2.5	3.9
Material handling and related	2.9	3.0	2.6	2.8	2.0	3.1	2.5	2.4
Other crafts and equipment operation	1.0	1.1	1.2	1.1	0.8	0.7	1.0	1.3
Not stated and not elsewhere classified	11.1	10.9	8.9	10.1	10.7	25.5	11.4	10.5
TOTALS	100.0	100.0	100.0	100.0	100.0	100.0	100.0	100.0

Source: Perspective Canada, A Compendium of Social Statistics, Table 13:24; pp. 279-280. Reproduced by permission of the Minister of Supply and Services Canada.

(iii) Inexperience: This is a catch 22 situation for Native people. They are not employed because they lack experience; they cannot obtain experience, because they are not hired. Two reasons appear to be accountable for this situation: (a) inexperience is often equated with inability; (b) private entrepreneurs are not willing or not able to carry the cost of low productivity.

(iv) Low educational achievement: In general, Canada is a "credential-oriented" society. Great importance is attached to educational achievement by many employers. Since the attendance rate is low and the withdrawal rate is high among Native people,[5] a large number of them are perceived as lacking the necessary basic education to either obtain work or participate in training courses.

(v) Traditional training approaches: Since the level of formal schooling among Native people is low, traditional training approaches are often found inadequate. More creative ways, such as the use of Native community settings and Native instructors, have to be developed to attract or to retain Native adults in training programs.

(vi) Language: A large number of adult Indians, Inuit, and Métis are not fluent in either English or French. Their situation is similar to immigrants who speak only foreign tongues. The difference is that the federal government pays the cost for training in either of the official languages for the immigrants, whereas the Native adults do not have the benefit of such a policy.

(vii) Poor health: A result of poor housing, low income and the absence of public facilities. Suffering from a generally poor physical milieu, many working-age Native people do not have adequate physical fitness, mental activity and mental/body coordination required for work.

(viii) Fear of cultural genocide: Despite their desire and willingness for employment, Native people do not want to lose their identity and to disappear as a people. The suggested Native employment strategy is "to rely heavily on the Native Migration Policy of the Secretary of State with its network of Friendship Centres to provide a cultural continuum for reserves to urban areas to those who choose to settle in predominantly white communities" (Employment and Immigration Canada, 1979: 8). It remains to be seen whether or not this will be carried out, and if it is, whether it will work.

(ix) Different socioeconomic regimes: Canada is a vastly diversified society. "Regional disparities, widely differing opportunities, gradual levels of development and expectations will require that each Canada Manpower Centre become better acquainted with its own Native clientele and develop a program package tailored to the actual needs of the Native population within its jurisdiction" (p. 8).

Some of these barriers to Native employment appear to be a matter of knowledge, such as the information gap and the insufficient locally-tailored employment program package. Some others are derived from prejudices of individual employers, such as the underrating of Native peoples' working abilities. Most of these barriers seem to fall into what is known as "systemic discrimination." Systemic discrimination refers to the kind of discriminatory patterns and practices built in the employment institution. While equal in intent and in application, they have a disparate effect on certain groups (Employment and Immigration Canada, 1981: 92). The use of educational achievement as an arbitrary screening devise, the stress on experience, the lack of creative training programs, the requirement of language proficiency and the lack of (official) language training programs for the Native people, all seem to be employment patterns and practices residing in the employment system itself and are in nature, discriminatory against the Native groups. (Systemic discrimination against women and other disadvantaged groups apparently also exist.) This type of employment discrimination is a more complex and more pervasive phenomenon than was generally understood; and it is undoubtedly more difficult to deal with. It certainly would take the concerted effort of employment and training agencies, human rights commissions, courts at all levels, employers both in the public and private sectors and the Native groups themselves to overcome problems stemming from systemic discrimination. The Task Force on the Labour Market Development of 1980s has made a number of recommendations in its Report for improving opportunities for groups with special employment needs, of which people of Native ancestry is one (Employment and Immigration Canada, 1981). It is too early to know what recommendations will become policies and how effective they will be when they do become policies. The recognition and understanding of systemic discrimination against various minority groups, however, are indeed a very positive and significant departure from the past.

IV. SUMMARY

In this chapter, we have focused on the issues of gender and ethnicity in the work context in Canada. From the analysis in Section II we have seen Canadian women entering into the labour force in great numbers at a rapid pace in the last few decades.

However, the majority of female workers are concentrated in the lower levels of clerical, sales, and service occupations. There is a distinct pattern of occupational segregation. As Armstrong and Armstrong have put it forcefully: The work that women do tends "to be low in skill, low in pay, and low in prestige" (1978:44). Although some progress has been made, it has not been sufficient to change the structural position of women in the labour market. As recent as 1978 over 62 percent of working women support or help support a family, but 61 percent who work receive less than $6,000 a year, compared to 28 percent of men. Of sole support families headed by men, 8.5 percent have incomes below the poverty line; of sole support families with a woman as head, 44.1 percent have incomes below the poverty line (Canadian Human Rights Commission, 1981). The goal of gender equality in the work world is far from being reached.

In section III the distribution of ethnic groups in the occupational structure has been analyzed in a historical perspective. In general, the British and the Jewish have continually dominated the high status and high paying occupations, the other ethnic groups have been underrepresented in these highly desirable jobs at varying degrees. Porter's thesis of the vertical mosaic seems to stand the test of time. Clearly, the trend has been in the direction of decreasing ethnic inequalities over time. However, as Hunter (1981: 140) puts it, it would "take generations [as opposed to years and decades] for the system of ethnic inequalities in Canada to disappear, if ever it will."

Greater attention has been paid to Native Canadians. Including Metis, status and nonstatus Indians, and Inuit, this group consists of a population of no less than 600,000 people.[6] A significant proportion of them are residents of the resource rich northern and the arctic regions[7]. Yet they have fared the worst in the work context (and perhaps in every aspect) in Canada. It was pointed out that systemic discrimination is the most serious problem that they, along with other minority groups, are confronted with. The recognition and understanding of structurally rooted discrimination has just begun. Overcoming this discrimination will take the concerted effort of all involved.

Notes

1. Hall (1975:294) reported that twice as many middle and upper class married women stated that "need of mental stimulation" or "enjoy it" as the main reason for going out to work.

2. The ratios ranging from 65.1% for bindery workers to 99.5% for office girls (Women's Bureau, 1979: 5; 25).
3. This discussion follows Cook and Eberts' review of public policies pertinent to equal pay and equal opportunity for minorities in Canada (1976:174-185).
4. The *Canadian Human Rights Act*, Section II (1) and (2).
5. A 1969 Canadian Arctic Gas study found that 49% of the working age Native people of the MacKenzie district had never attended school. A 1974 Study of Yukon Native labour force established that 30% had never attended school and 14.6% had studied beyond grade 9. A 1971 study in northern Manitoba found 30% with less than grade 5 and 20% with more than grade 10. No comprehensive statistics exist for the total Native population. That a serious problem exists is nevertheless clear.
6. There are more than 3 1/2 million Canadians who could legitimately claim to be of Native ancestry. See Employment and Immigration Canada (1979:1).
7. For a geographic distribution of the Native people, see Employment and Immigration, Canada (1979, Table 1).

Suggested Readings

Armstrong, P. and H. Armstrong
   1978. *The Double Ghetto: Canadian Women and Their Segregated Work.* Toronto: McClelland and Stewart.
Canada
   1980. *Indian Conditions: A Survey.* Ottawa: Indian Affairs and Northern Development.
Canada
   1981. *Labour Market Development in the 1980s: A Report of the Task Force on Labour Market Development.* Ottawa: Employment and Immigration.
Connelly, P.
   1978. *Last Hired, First Fired.* Toronto: The Women's Press.
Jain, Harish C.
   1979. "Employment Problems of the Native People in Ontario," *Relations Industrielles, 34*:2.
Jain, Harish C.
   1981. "Discrimination Against Indians: Issues and Policies," in Katherina L. P. Lundy and Barbara D. Warme (eds.): *Work in the Canadian Context: Continuity Despite Change.* Toronto: Butterworths.

McDonald, L.
   1980. "Equal Pay—How Far Off?" *Canadian Dimension, 14, 6(May):*
   21-24.
Wilson, S. J.
   1982. *Women, The Family, and the Economy.* Toronto: McGraw-Hill
   Ryerson.

Chapter 8

Work Organizations

The types of work organizations that are the subject of this chapter are commonly called formal or bureaucratic. With the possible exceptions of the domestic activities performed by wives and husbands, the proportion of work in industrial societies that is not carried out in such organizations is negligible. Individual craft labour, subsistence agriculture, and to a lesser extent, self-employment are remnants of the past. Formal, bureaucratic organizations are everywhere. Canadians frequently encounter governmental agencies, retail stores, hospitals, schools, universities, manufacturing plants, restaurants and churches among the legion of such organizations that exist in this country.

What do all these organizations have in common? First, they all have a mission or as Perrow (1979:72) notes they are "designed to get some kind of work done." The mission of some organizations is oriented towards objects. Manufacturing industries represent a prime example of object missions with raw material such as iron or wood transformed into steel and paper. However, lending books to the public, repairing automobiles and forecasting the weather likewise fall into this category. Other organizations have a people mission. Humans are the raw material of hospitals, schools and employment agencies. They are transformed as they move through these health, education and social-welfare organizations.

The fulfillment of a mission entails the co-operative involvement of the many individuals who comprise the organization's membership. Co-operation is achieved because work is formally structured. Most members of an organization have a limited part to play in the pursuit of the mission. These numerous and disparate activities are typically parcelled out in a division of labour.

All organizations may share the attributes of mission and formal structure but the differences among them are more striking. Moreover, there is a divergence within sociology with respect to whether organizations are anything more than the individuals who come together to accomplish some mission. Some analysts claim that no organization can be understood apart from the people who comprise it (March and Simon, 1958; Simon, 1964; Strauss *et al.*, 1963; Blau,

1955). This socio-psychological perspective cautions against the reification of organization by viewing it as an entity that cannot be explained without reference to its members. In contrast, the structural perspective sees organizations, *per se*, as purposeful actors with distinctive characteristics (Hall, 1977; Perrow, 1970; Miller and Form, 1980). On the extreme, Perrow (1970:27) asserts that the knowledge that organizations are, after all, made up of people reveals little about their distinctive properties.

These two perspectives are not as antithetical as the last statement implies. Structural features do represent a meaningful and necessary level of analysis. The structure of an organization plays an important part in the determination of the conduct of its members. But the structure does not totally determine that conduct. It has differential effects depending on how the organization's members interpret and respond to it. In order to appreciate how organizations work we shall explore them from these two perspectives and hopefully capture the dynamic interdependence between structure and process.

I. THE ORGANIZATION AS A STRUCTURED ENTITY

Social structures are not directly observable. They are abstractions that describe the patterns and regularity of the interactions that occur within social groups. Following Hall (1977) we concentrate on three essential features of organizational structure, *viz.*, complexity, formality and centrality. We shall also relate these features to some other characteristics of organizations.

(a) Complexity

Complexity refers to the overall pattern of the division of labour within an organization. Work is commonly distributed along horizontal and vertical axes. Horizontal differentiation takes two forms: specialization of tasks and specialization of workers. In the specialization of tasks, work activity can often be minutely subdivided into discrete tasks that require little skill to perform. In this form of differentiation each worker performs only a few repetitive tasks. In contrast the specialization of workers is measured not by the number of discrete tasks performed but by the variety of specialized occupations involved. Perrow (1972) suggests that the critical difference between the two rests in the nature of the work performed. Nonroutine work is the reserve of specialists.

Supervisory authority is distributed vertically. Pugh *et al.* (1963)

believe that the simplest measure of vertical differentiation is to count the number of job positions between the chief executive and the employees who work on output. This belief assumes that authority is distributed according to the vertical levels of this axle. Hall (1977) notes that this may be a poor assumption. The proliferation of vertical positions may represent phenomena other than the distribution of authority. Some job titles are created to make allowances for increases in a given salary range and thus distort the true authority structure. Nevertheless, the Pugh method is commonly used.

Complexity presents organizations with problems of control, coordination and conflict resolution. This complexity develops particularly when organizations operate in multiple locations where they appear to be made of small, basic or unit organizations, each with its own vertical and horizontal axes. Problems of control and conflict increase with increased complexity.

(b) Formality

The essence of formality is aptly described in the expression, "there ought to be a rule." As a way of regulating and guiding human interaction, formality is:

> ...a process by which the informality of earlier social relationships is gradually replaced by varying degrees of rules, codes of conduct, laws and other means of regulation (White, 1980: 318).

While few areas of Canadian life escape the incursions of formality, many organizations assure the co-operative involvement of its members by regulating their behaviour from such simple activities as the time to report to work to exacting job descriptions and routines. Because work organizations outlive their individual members, their rules are codified and written down to ensure that they are consistent and enduring. Yet, formality is a variable. It varies from one organization to another and is conventionally measured by the proportion of codified jobs in an organization and the range of variation tolerated (Hage, 1965; Hage and Aiken, 1967; Pugh *et al.*, 1968).

(c) Centrality

Authority is the final key structural component of any organization. Centrality refers to the distribution of authority along the axes of an organization's division of labour. If the shape of this distribution resembles a pyramid, authority is centralized with the amount of power at any level being inversely related to the width of the pyramid.

The pyramid principle states that for every person there is one person above him or her, from whom he or she receives direction and to whom he or she reports. In other words, the crucial elements of centrality are who has the right to make decisions and evaluations.

Centralized organizations may exhibit tall or flat hierarchies. The number of subordinates whom a superior directly oversees, called the span of control, is the building block of an authority hierarchy. When the span of control is narrow, organizations tend to have tall hierarchies with many levels of authority. When it is wide the hierarchy is flat. An example of a flat, centralized authority structure is an organization with many divisions or departments. The head of each division is responsible for all members of that unit and in turn reports directly to a senior administrator, usually a vice-president. For almost thirty years analysts have debated what constitutes an optimal span of control.

Some organizations do not exhibit a pyramidal authority hierarchy. Many voluntary associations and professional societies have a decentralized power structure. The grass-roots or rank-and-file make most decisions and formulate policies for executive officers to carry out. Credit unions and co-operatives also operate within decentralized structures in that all members have the right to participate in decision making and no supervision is specified. Hall (1977) comments that the degree of centrality is an indicator as to what assumptions are made about an organization's members. A high degree of centrality implies that they need tight control. Low centrality implies that they can govern themselves.

(d) Bureaucracy

Complexity, formality and centrality can vary independently. Nonetheless, many social scientists believe that as organizations grow in complexity, the need for co-ordination and control engenders formality and centrality. This is the process of bureaucratization. Virtually all complex organizations are best classified as bureaucracies (Perrow, 1972; Ritzer, 1972; White, 1980).

Our understanding of bureaucracy owes much to the writings of Weber. He observed that organizational structures vary with particular forms of authority. He identified three types: charismatic, traditional and legal-rational authority. Charismatic authority depends on "devotion to the specific and exceptional sanctity, heroism or exemplary character of an individual person" (Weber, 1947: 328). Charismatic figures possess authority because their exceptional attributes inspire loyalty in their followers. Weber found this form of authority to be unstable and transitory. Many cult leaders possess it and it has been attributed to such political leaders as Ghandi and Nehru in India, Mao in China and Trudeau in Canada.

Traditional rule depends on "an established belief in the sanctity of immemorial traditions and the legitimacy of the status of those exercising authority" (Weber, 1947: 328). The monarchy and apostolic succession of bishops are contemporary examples. Legal-rational authority, on the other hand, rests on "a belief in the 'legality of patterns of normative rules' and the right of those elevated to authority under such rules to issue commands" (Weber, 1947: 328). Weber associated this type of legitimate power with industrial societies.

Weber further argued that organizations grounded in legal-rational authority have similarities which in their ultimate form resemble his ideal type of bureaucracy, having the following features:

1. A number of well defined offices with duties fixed by a comprehensive set of rules.
2. Offices arranged in a pyramidal hierarchy with clear lines of authority running down from the top.
3. Management based on written documents.
4. Impersonal selection and retention of personnel.
5. Personnel given the security of tenure.
6. Advancement based upon achievement.

Acknowledging that no organization would fully exhibit all of these features, he argued that those which do approach his conception of bureaucracy are the most likely to function efficiently and endure.

(e) Structure and its Correlates

Variation in the degree of complexity, formality and centrality are correlated with other organizational properties, especially size, technology and environment.

(i) Size

The evidence concerning the importance of size is somewhat conflicting. Blau and his associates present some compelling evidence that size is the major determinant of structure (Blau *et al.*, 1966, Blau, 1968; 1970; Blau and Schoenherr, 1971). These studies are primarily concerned with the relationship between size and complexity. They indicate that complexity increases with size, but that it also decreases with increasing size. Moreover, since the span of control increases with size, administrative overhead is lower in large organizations. In fact, large organizations can realize an economy of scale if close supervision is not deemed necessary, *i.e.*, where work is very routine or performed by professionals.

A series of studies conducted at Aston University found that the increased size of an organization is also related to its formality (Pugh *et al.*, 1963; 1968; 1969). These researchers conclude that an increase in formality is associated with large organizations. Strict adherence to these rules and procedures fosters the delegation or decentralization of power (Mansfield, 1973). Similar relationships among complexity, formality, centrality and size or organization are reported by Mahoney *et al.* (1972).

Conversely, some small organizations are characterized by very high levels of bureaucracy and some large ones exhibit low measures of complexity, formality and centrality (Hall and Tittle, 1966). Hall *et al.* (1967) report mixed findings with only a slight tendency for large organizations to be more formal and complex. Their analysis suggests that size is a consequence of bureaucratization, not a cause (Aldrich, 1972). These debates and inconsistent findings should not lead to the conclusion that size is unimportant. Rather, it should be considered in concert with other factors. A number of studies show that tendencies towards greater size, efficiency and, often, impersonality are influenced by an organization's technical system.

(ii) Technology

Woodward (1958; 1965;1970), Blauner (1964), and Perrow(1967; 1972) have constructed typologies that differentiate among organizations on the basis of technology. Woodward's classification is derived from a study of 203 British manufacturing companies. It consists of three categories which comprise a crude scale of technical complexity: small-batch (ship-building, custom suite); large-batch or mass production (automobiles, metal); and continuous process (petroleum, chemical). Although narrow in scope her typology does link technical features to structural attributes. She reports a clear relationship between technology and the shape of the authority pyramid with the number of management levels, the span of control, and the ratio of managers and supervisors to production workers all affected by the nature of the technology employed. She also reports that the social atmospheres of these firms were likewise affected by the nature of the technology employed. Zwerman (1970) has replicated her basic findings with American data.

Whereas Woodward is mainly interested in the structural correlates of various technologies, Blauner is concerned with the consequences for workers of different technologies. He identifies four
categories: craft, machine-minding, assembly-line and continuous.
Blauner argues that his typology articulates stages in the historical
trend towards increasing mechanization and he uses the printing,
textile, automative and chemical industries as representative examples of these four categories. He reports an inverted "U" curve
relationship between worker alienation and these four levels with
alienation lowest in the craft and continuous process industries and
highest on the automobile assembly line. Blauner's study is examined
in greater detail in Chapter 10. For the moment we simply wish to
note there is little dispute with his assertion that the historical
progression from craft to continuous process technologies has
resulted in greater complexity.

Perrow classifies organizations in terms of the kinds of tasks that
are performed in them. Their differences notwithstanding, he argues
that these tasks are applied to some raw material which an organization transforms into a marketable product and the nature of this raw
material determines the kinds of tasks which are performed on it. His
typology is based on two variables: the analyzability and variability of
the raw material.

A raw material is analyzable when no "search process" is needed
to discover how to treat it. If the material is readily analyzable, there
are known ways of treating it. A worker may respond automatically
or check an instruction manual or computer program for the optimal
process of transformation. If the raw material is not well understood,
manuals and computers do not have the requisite information and a
worker must rely on experience, judgement or intuition—processes
which Perrow labels unanalyzable search procedures.

Variability involves the number of exceptions an organization
encounters in the course of its business, *i.e.*, problems that may
necessitate search processes. In some research and development
undertakings, each assignment is novel with the exception being the
rule. Most manufacturing involves few or no exceptions to the rule.

By cross-classifying these two dimensions of technology, Perrow
develops four types of organizations: craft, non-routine, routine and
engineering. Craft and nonroutine organizations use unanalyzable
search procedures but differ on variability with craft organizations
experiencing few exceptions. Routine organizations encounter little
variability in raw material and use analyzable search methods.
Engineering organizations must conduct a search each time a new
order is placed (high on variability) but the treatment that is applied
to the raw material is known and understood (analyzable search).

This framework allows Perrow to posit some complex predictions about the structural correlates of these four technologies. While his predictions are not simply between routine and nonroutine or between bureaucratic and nonbureaucratic, he generally argues that routine technologies are most effectively exploited in organizations with high levels of bureaucracy. Hage and Aiken (1969) found a marked degree of variation in the routineness of sixteen welfare agencies. Even though these agencies fall on the nonroutine side of a continuum of routineness, they report finding a relationship between variations in routineness and formality.

Other research demonstrates how organizations adapt their structures to their technologies. Lawrence and Lorsch (1967) examined the effectiveness of three industries (plastics, packaged foods and standardized containers) marked by variations in task uncertainty. They found this dimension of routineness related to both complexity and centrality. The container industry was high on formality, low on complexity and heavily reliant on centralized authority. By contrast the plastics industry, and to a lesser extent, the packaged foods industry were more specialized and decentralized. Harvey's (1968) comparison of organizations in terms of their technical specificity yields similar results. Organizations making frequent product changes or variations tend to have flat authority hierarchies. All of these findings are generally consistent with Perrow's hypotheses.

Like Woodward and Blauner, Perrow is inclined towards technological determinism. The impact of technology is, however, not straightforward and the contention that technology is a major determinant of structure is the subject of considerable debate and disagreement. For example, the Aston researchers did not find strong relationships between technology and structure. They studied organizations which cluster more towards the routine side of the continuum. In these organizations technology has some impact but its effects vary considerably with size:

> The smaller the organization, the wider the structural effect of technology; the larger the organization, the more such effects are confined to particular variables, and size and dependence and similar factors make the greater overall impact. (Hickson *et al.*, 1969: 395).

Another group of British researchers, Trist and his colleagues at the Tavistock Institute, have demonstrated that there is no simple one-to-one relationship between technology and structure. Their observation that two rather different structures could operate efficiently mining the same coal seam and using identical technology led to their proposition that the technical and social systems are in mutual interaction and that all technical systems invariably offer some choice in the structuring of work relationships (Trist and Bamforth, 1951; Trist *et al.*, 1963). These Tavistock researchers have been very influential in conceptualizing organizations as open systems in which their structural features and social dimensions interact with each other and with the broader environment. They argue that these reciprocal interactions create a dynamic social field characterized by interdependence and continuous adjustments (Emery and Trist, 1965).

(iii) Environment

The argument thus far has been that organizational structure is contingent upon size and technology. The data which we have used to review this thesis generally stem from an image of organizations as relatively self-contained entities. An open systems perspective highlights the fact that they do not exist in a social vacuum but in a multi-faceted environment. Crozier (1964) has vividly demonstrated the tremendous impact of the general environment on the structure and process of two French organizations. Both the tobacco company and the clerical agency which he studied had fairly simple structures congruent with their respective technologies. Yet certain features of French society, such as civil service regulations combined with internal aspects of these organizations seriously limit their efficacy.

Arising from his concern with organizational strategies for coping with the contingencies posed by both technology and environment, Thompson (1967) developed a typology consisting of three categories: long-linked, mediating and intensive technologies. The long-linked type is characterized by a serial interdependence, such as the assembly line. A mediating technology brings together clients or customers who are or wish to be interdependent. He cites telephone companies, banks and post offices as organizations that employ this technology. Intensive technologies utilize a variety of techniques to change some object. Equally important, the selection, combination and order of application of these techniques is determined by the feedback received from the object itself. Hospitals and universities use this technology in their transformation of people. The construction industry uses it in the creation of buildings and bridges.

Thompson's typology has been used to analyze many organizations, ranging from the government and military to educational and medical. He observes that those organizations that use a long-linked technology can best exploit their environments when they deal with a single, standardized product. These organizations typically cope with the technical and environmental contingencies that affect their operations by adopting the strategy of vertical integration. The major American oil companies, for example, have integrated forward from refining to the control of marketing. They have also integrated backwards from refining to the control of exploration and shipping. This full integration allows the oil companies to resolve the uncertainties of supply and retail.

According to Thompson, organizations that operate mediating technologies need to reconcile the complexity of their clients' interests with a standardized processing procedure. An effective strategy for coping with environmental contingencies is increasing the size of the client population. Eastern Provincial Airlines demonstrated this strategy in a presentation to the Canadian Transportation Commission. It argued that in order to effectively serve its regional routes throughout the Maritimes, it needed to extend its extraregional routes beyond Montreal to Toronto.

Finally, Thompson notes that an intensive technology rests on the availability of an appropriate range of skills and resources in concert with a system for determining what combination is required. He suggests that these organizations counter uncertainties by placing their raw materials within boundaries of the organization. Hospitals, prisons and schools, for example, envelop the people on whom they work.

An organization may attempt to insulate itself as much as possible but it cannot avoid the dual influence of environment: it receives its inputs from the environment and its outputs return there where they are utilized and evaluated. Transnational studies have found that culture affects structure (Hickson, *et al.*, 1974; McMillan *et al.*, 1973). There is a greater reliance on written documents in Canada than in Britain. In the latter an emphasis on traditionalism appears to diminish the necessity for this aspect of formality. These studies also suggest that cultural environments have less impact on organizations with routine technologies. Where culture does influence structure the interrelationship among structural elements follow a common pattern. Indian organizations, for example, may exhibit less formality than Canadian ones but the positive relationship between size and formality occurs in both countries.

Political environments likewise affect organizations. Quebec's Bill 101 has accelerated the adoption of French in the conduct of corporate affairs. The fact that some firms have moved their headquarters elsewhere illustrates that they do not simply and passively react to political influence. They create strategies for dealing with it by in turn shaping the environment itself via lobbying, contributions to political parties and the like. Selznick's (1966) analysis of the early years of the Tennessee Valley Authority documents the ability of an organization to influence its environment.

Lipset (1950) shows how the Saskatchewan civil service resisted and blocked efforts by the Co-operative Commonwealth Federation (now the New Democratic Party) to initiate change. Lucas (1971) and Perry (1971) offer excellent Canadian examples of the impact of industrial organizations on their host communities. Lucas focuses on single industry towns. The pervasive influence of these industries on dependent towns that he observed is equally evident in stories about the future of Uranium City following upon the disclosure that its mine was to close. Perry recounts the problems that occur when Canadian managers of American subsidiaries are viewed by union and community officials as mere messenger-boys with no authority to make decisions that are of local interest.

Trist and his colleagues see organizations and environments as continuous with elements of each affecting organizational processes. They developed a field theory of organizational environments which posits four ideal typical environments with different "causal texturing," as the way in which elements of the environment are interrelated, thus making some courses of action more plausible than others. Moreover, they believe that those parts of the industrialized world that are drifting into a postindustrial era are entering a new "turbulent environment." These researchers conclude that successful organizational adaptation to rapid change and increasing interdependency of turbulent environments is likely to be the emergence of a more democratic structuring of work (Trist, 1969; Emery and Thorsrud, 1976).

Sociologists are only beginning to study the web of interorganizational relationships that comprise another aspect of the environment. Some believe that this interorganizational environment may hold the key to the distribution of power in the wider society. Porter (1965) noted a tendency for companies to be interlocked through common directors. Clement (1975; 1977) extends Porter's insights and adds to our knowledge of the nature of power in large Canadian corporations.

To date, the influence of environment has not been as well conceptualized as other features of organizations. Still, even the inadequate evidence that is available directs attention to the salience of sociocultural, political, interorganizational and physical environments. They directly and indirectly influence structure. This web of interdependencies exists "in a state of dynamic tension where the organization's role may be either proactive or reactive or both" (White, 1980: 341).

II. ORGANIZATIONAL CONTROL AND THE INDIVIDUAL

Our heretofore emphasis on structure ignores much of the fine texture of the social life within organizations. We now consider issues in organizational process, *i.e.*, the ways in which individuals and groups respond to the organizations of which they are members.

(a) Unintended Consequences

Studies of bureaucracies by Crozier (1964), Merton (1957), Thompson (1961) and many others contend that the unintended socio-psychological consequences for employees raise questions about the appropriateness of such organizations. Merton's discussion of bureaucratic structure and personality isolates the potential in organizations for individuals to become overly concerned with rules and regulations. The consequence is a very rigid, even ritualistic, mode of behaviour—an obsession with "doing it by the book." This response to a highly formal structure Merton labels as the bureaucratic personality syndrome.

Most studies of bureaucratic personality point to structural factors as the main causes. Blau (1955) argues that these ritualists and overconformers are motivated by their own insecurity and the ensuing fears about the attitudes and opinions of superiors. This conclusion is not at all strange since these individuals are evaluated on how well they follow the rules. Thompson's treatment of bureaupathic and bureaucratic behavioural patterns is a continuation of this theme.

All organizations rely on rules. When the rules become the most important structural source of security their intent is overlooked. In these situations conforming behaviour severely limits personal initiative. The real malady is not "red tape," *per se*, but the chronic underutilization of human resources (Crozier, 1964; Herzberg, 1966). Rebellion, resentment, sabotage, and wildcat strikes are among the manifestations of unintended socio-psychological responses to bureaucratic structure.

(b) Professionalism

The sociological literature on the employment of professionals in complex organizations points to some inherent strains and conflicts between the professional model and the tenets of organizational life. Professionals bring to organizations their own standards of authority and self-regulation. These professional norms frequently conflict with the official authority hierarchy and formality of complex organizations.

Daniels' (1969, 1970) study of military psychiatry is a good illustration. As a medical specialist, the psychiatrist is the ultimate professional authority on definitions of mental health and illness. While this authority is rarely questioned in civilian life, the military's emphasis on manpower needs overwhelms the psychiatrist's authority on these health matters. Instead of making definitive decisions on discharge, leave and special duties for soldiers, he or she is a mere advisor to the military hierarchy. Diagnoses are constrained by a variety of military rules and not made solely on the basis of professional judgement. For example, during a manpower crisis psychiatrists are under considerable pressure to be cautious in diagnosing soldiers as unfit for service. Daniels concludes that the organizational structure of the military channels psychiatrists whom it employs into providing a service to the military, not the patient.

The conflict between professional conduct and organizational control extends to questions of the structuring of work, leadership, the publication and direction of research, peer evaluation and recruitment (Kornhauser, 1962). These tensions rest in the implicit agreement that professionals must relinquish some of their autonomy in exchange for the resources of the organization. Engel (1969: 31) believes that these strains are not necessarily irreconcilable:

> It is not bureaucracy *per se* but the degree of bureaucracy that can limit professional autonomy.

She compared physicians in solo or small group practices with those employed in a large governmental organization. Her findings show a curvilinear pattern between bureaucratization and professional autonomy with the moderately bureaucratized organization offering these physicians the highest levels of autonomy. Studies of alienation among professionals in organizations show that expressions of alienation increase with the formality and centrality of their structures (Miller, 1967; Aiken and Hage, 1966).

These studies do not conclusively prove that high levels of bureaucracy inevitably create conflicts for professionals. Hall (1968) reports that centrality may not adversely affect the work of professionals if a superior's authority is viewed as legitimate. Moreover, he observes that as long as the rules are not unduly specific, formality does not appear to hinder their work. His findings caution against simply assuming that professionals employed in organizations always face conflict. Many organizations set broad limits for professionals and then allow them to function relatively autonomously. Moreover, it is incorrect to think that professionals must identify with either their organizations or their profession. Glaser (1963) has studied scientists who identify with both.

(c) Role and Role Conflict

Given the fact that professionals are becoming increasingly employed in organizations, our attention on conflicts specifically associated with this group is warranted. However, our treatment of the individual in the organization must include many who do not bring professional attributes to the workplace. The concepts of role and role conflict are other useful tools for exploring the interplay and interdependence between organizations and their members. Kahn *et al.* (1964) offer an insightful framework for an understanding of the nature of work roles and role conflict. Their analysis is based on structural, personal and interpersonal factors which they believe strongly influence the behaviour of individuals.

By now it should be evident that a person's location on the axes of the division of labour channels his or her behaviour. Despite the strength of structural elements, Kahn *et al.* argue that persons have some choice in their performances of work roles. The range of worker involvement is wide. In addition, superiors, subordinates and peers have differential expectations of how one should act. Because one works for or with these significant others, their attitudes, opinions and conduct affect one's own. Given that these social influences are not constant and equal, their model isolates five types of role conflict that occur when the mix among them generates incongruent demands on workers: role overload, intersender, intrasender, person role and interperson.

Role overload exists when one is confronted with incompatible expectations:

> [A worker] is likely to experience overload as a conflict of priorities; he must decide which pressure to comply with and which to hold off. If it is impossible to deny any of these pressures, he may be taxed beyond the limits of his abilities (*Kahn et al*. 1964: 20).

The potential for overload is a function of one's position in the division of labour. Executives and managers are particularly prone to it (Ritzer, 1972). Continuous overload can be disabling. For example, Sales (1969) found that persons in overloaded roles run the highest risk of coronary disease.

Kahn *et al.* call the significant others with whom one works "role senders." They list seven categories of them: management, direct superior, co-workers, subordinates, union officials, extraorganizational associates (clients), and a residual category including family and friends (1964: 56). Intersender conflicts exist when two or more of these significant others send incongruous messages of what they expect of a given individual. Intrasender conflict occurs when these contradictory messages come from the same person. For example, one superior may instruct one to cut personnel while another insists upon the implementation of an equal opportunity program. If the executive director issues both messages the conflict would be intrasender.

Everyone within an organization is faced with these various types of role conflict. Social service personnel frequently confront inter and intrasender conflict in their efforts to assist clients within the organizationally defined parameters of such assistance. Zald (1969) observes that members of boards of directors experience these conflicts when they are subjected to rather severe cross-pressures from internal and external sources. Within industry there is evidence supporting the proposition that intersender conflict is a basic dilemma of foremen. Their position exposes them to the strongest kind of employer-employee cleavages (Roethlisberger, 1945; Wray, 1949; Ritzer, 1972; Miller and Form, 1980).

Person-role conflict appears when the expectations associated with a work role violate personal values and aspirations. Much of our earlier discussion of professionals can be fruitfully examined in terms of person-role conflict. Business executives are called upon to perform many actions that improve their company's financial position. These activities range from illegalities such as misrepresentation of fiscal statements to controversial layoffs or closures (Mills, 1951). If one cannot reconcile one's personal morality with the morality of business, conflict occurs. In his seminal analysis of the vocabularies of motives, C. Wright Mills (1940) partially explains how we resolve such conflicts by compartmentalizing our lives. Foremen have been observed engaging in "double talk." Because of difficulties in identifying with either management or labour, they tell each group what they think it wants to hear.

All these types of conflict regard work as the focal role. When the expectations of the work-role conflict with the expectations of the same person in another role one experiences interrole conflict. This type of conflict is only conceptually distinct from intersender and person-role types when the work role is ascendant. If the messages sent from family members are incompatible with those from superiors or workmates, Kahn *et al.* (1964: 56) say that intersender conflict results. In fact this conflict is grounded in interrole conflict. Similarly, to the extent that one's values are linked to other, nonwork roles, person-role conflict is one expression of interrole conflict. While interrole conflict plagues all members of the organization, Ritzer (1972: 338) contends that it is most common at the management and supervisory levels.

(d) Informal Organization

Studies of role conflict encourage a wide-awake appreciation of both the taken-for-granted and recondite aspects of human social interaction. Much of the sociological study of organizations draws attention to the maligned informal structure which often comes into being along side the formal system. This literature is indeed rich with examples of the unofficial activities and informal arrangements which are so prominent in the daily operations of formal organizations. Blau and Scott (1962) observe than an informal organization emerges in response to the opportunities and problems created by the formal social structure. In a sense it comprises the underlife of organizations.

Participation in the informal structure constitutes important means of resolving the conflicts and contradictions created by the formal structure. Most of these difficulties stem from the organization's attempts to control the behaviour of its members. The informal organization operates as a counterforce with practices which not only protect individuals, but also redirect the organization's control of them. The formation of cliques, codes of conduct and ceremonies serve to either resolve or downplay conflict or generate satisfaction in otherwise alienative or meaningless worklives. Restriction of output is commonplace at almost all levels. It is an expression of a worker's definition of a fair day's work. These informal arrangements are typically sources of satisfaction (Gross, 1965; Roy, 1953; 1959; Zurcher *et al.*, 1966; Simpson and Simpson, 1959); or a means of beating the system (Harper and Emmert, 1963; Roy, 1952; 1954).

The recognition of the social dimension of organizations directs sociologists to examine how people in organizations cope with the working conditions created by various structural combinations. These studies, which comprise the most voluminous and substantial part of the literature on organizations, promulgates the view of individuals in organizations as reservoirs of untapped resources, who, if properly structured are creative and self-actualizing (Schein, 1970).

A most effective way for lower participants to maintain some control over their work and workplace is to obtain, maintain, and control access to persons, information, and instrumentalities which make higher ranking participants dependent upon them (Mechanic,

1962). Anselm Strauss and his associates argue that these dependencies can be used to renegotiate aspects of organizational structure (Bucher and Strauss, 1961; Strauss *et al.*, 1963: 1964; Bucher and Stelling, 1969; Bucher, 1970; Stelling and Bucher, 1972; Strauss, 1978). In their efforts to marry structural and process considerations in an analysis of organizations and professions, Strauss and his colleagues came to the realization that structural elements are continuously enacted in the interpersonal processes that go on in organizations:

> When individuals or groups or organizations of any size work together "to get things done" then agreement is required about such matters as what, when, where, and how much (Strauss, 1978: ix).

Their conception of organizations as negotiated orders avoids the structure versus process dichotomy by viewing structure as process. From their examinations of structural processes they conclude that no structural relationships exist without accompanying negotiation; that negotiations are not accidental but contingent upon specific structural conditions; and that all negotiated understandings have temporal limits requiring periodic review, re-evaluation, renewal or revision. Although an organization is a negotiated order, only a few items are under negotiation at a given point in time.

This insightful model of organizations as complex processes of constant negotiation and periodic appraisal links that consideration of the more formal and permanent structure with a microscopic analysis of how the work gets done. This linkage fosters an appreciation of how negotiation and appraisal "play into each other and into the rules, policies and other more stable elements of social order" (Strauss, 1978: 6).

III. THEORY AND APPLICATION IN HISTORICAL PERSPECTIVE

The development of organizational theory occurs over time and in concert with other events including but not limited to the implications of its application. What appears to us as self-evident now should not obscure the fact that it was not always so or that it may be seen differently at some later time. Here we outline three of the more influential schools of thought and their underlying assumptions about humans which have swayed both the design and study of organizations. These three schools are: scientific management, human relations and quality of working life. Weaving the theoretical strands of these three schools provides an historical perspective of the contemporary study of organizations.

(a) Scientific Management

The roots of organizational theory in North America can be traced to a turn-of-the-century movement concerned with how large-scale industrial companies might be made more efficient and productive. From the onset of the industrial revolution workers had to adapt themselves to machines which imposed their own rhythm and reduced the importance of human agency. Within this context the writings of Taylor (1911) and later Gulick and Lyndall (1937) inspired the school of scientific management or "Taylorism."

Briefly put, the goal of scientific management was to use systematic procedures to minutely analyze each job and the abilities of humans in order to isolate "the one best way" to match people to machines. With efficiency defined as the elimination of wasted movements causing fatigue and low productivity, Taylor's famous "time and motion" studies were conducted to determine the manner in which jobs could be redesigned to optimize the natural rhythm of machines. With the assimilation of workers to machines set by careful study, management could ensure productivity by establishing incentives and supervision that maintained homogenous machine-worker rhythms.

Taylorism was severely criticized for its implicit model of man as a mere appendage of machinery to be manipulated by management. Humanitarians becursed it as a source of human deprivation and feared that its emphasis on speed was potentially damaging to health. Unions denounced its promanagement orientation. From the standpoint of the labour movement Taylorism was a clear threat to its objectives. Nevertheless, its focus on the structural features of complex organizations, especially its central tenet that the division of labour be subdivided into discrete tasks, had profound effects on many practitioners and analysts. It introduced the belief that all organizations had basic similarities which could be exploited to maximize repetitiveness and minimize worker discretion.

From a sociological perspective the major limitations of scientific management lie in its assumptions about the individual in the organization. Firstly, it assumes that workers are solely motivated by economic gain. This assumption erroneously implies that worker-management conflict would diminish as long as earnings were directly related to productivity. Under this assumption scientific management benefited both groups by realizing higher wages for workers and higher profits for management. While it did promote undeniable economic advantages it also engendered boredom, absenteeism and turnover.

The proponents of scientific management also assumed that human feelings were irrational nuisances requiring careful and systematic control. This assumption heightened the latent hostility between management and labour for the former group was not only to reward productive activity but also sanction displays of irrational, unproductive behaviour. By their denial of human agency, both assumptions ignore the salience of the social dimension of work.

(b) Human Relations

Beginning in the 1920s a new movement emerged in reaction to Taylorism. Carnegie (1926) and Barnard (1938) espoused the importance of persuasion, cooperation and responsible leadership. Barnard, in particular, viewed organizations as co-operative systems with all members working towards common goals. When commensurate purposes did not exist, Barnard (1938: 87) saw the function of the executive as the indoctrination of lower participants even to the point of deception. His justifications for management authority and worker obedience strongly influenced the human relations movement.

A series of studies conducted by Mayo and his associates at the Hawthorne plant of the Western Electric Company gave rise to the human relations school (Mayo, 1945; Roethlisberger and Dickson, 1939). These researchers thoroughly documented the existence of informal groups and their abilities to control the behaviours of the organization's lower participants. They concluded that organizational behaviour was guided more by informal group norms and the sentiments of individuals than by formal rules and objective procedures. On the basis of this analysis, Mayo attacked what he called the "rabble hypothesis" of Taylorism that regarded workers as isolated, wage-maximizing beings. In contrast he emphasized the human desire to stand well with one's fellows and urged management to nurture human relation skills in order to create harmony and cooperation.

The human relations school applied to the day-to-day industrial life the knowledge acquired from the research of sociologists and psychologists. Miles (1965) suggests that the school can be separated into two branches which he labels human relations and human resources. The former is psychologically oriented and deals with the relationships among morale, leadership and productivity (Cummings and Scott: 1969). These studies are well designed and tell us a great deal about individuals and small groups. However, the findings are somewhat difficult to apply to organizational life because these researchers tended to relegate the formal structure to the status of an external variable. The human resources branch extends the analysis to the total organizational climate.

The better known members of the more socio-psychological, human resources branch are Maslow (1954; 1962), Argyris (1957; 1962), McGregor (1960), Likert (1961;1967) and Herzberg (1966). Building on the work of this approach Herzberg's "hygiene motivation" theory states that some aspects of work, such as company policy, administration, technical supervision and earnings are hygienic factors. They may decrease worker dissatisfaction but they cannot increase it. He goes on to specify five motivators (achievement, recognition, work itself, responsibility and advancement) which can actually increase work satisfaction. Accordingly, he asserts that companies should unlock their human resources by introducing these motivators into work situations.

Unlike the human relations' basic hypothesis that morale was the intervening variable between worker participation and productivity, the human resources approach offered the hypothesis that full worker participation directly improved productivity. These researchers saw morale as a by-product of an open and democratic organizational climate that allows workers to satisfy their higher-order needs for self-actualization and autonomy (Miles, 1965).

Real differences notwithstanding, both branches stressed the importance of communication and lower-echelon participation in decision making. Generally, owners and managers directed these insights towards the refinement of manipulative techniques designed to increase productivity and profit by making the work force content. In practice, if not in theory, the emphasis in human relations was on communicating what management wanted. Worker participation most often took the form of requesting advice with decisions remaining with senior management:

> As its extreme the human relations approach came to be known as "cow sociology": as long as the worker was content he would be productive (Ritzer, 1972: 245).

Human relations came about as a reaction to Taylorism. However, it shared a fundamental assumption of scientific management, namely, there are no irreconcilable differences between the interests of management and the interests of labour. This assumption obscured the realities of bureaucratic control and the vulnerable status of lower participants. Selznick (1969), for example, argues that there is a wide hiatus between fostering hygienic conditions and legitimate participation. The latter involves much more than rendering advice on matters with which one is familiar. Additionally, George Strauss (1963; 1969) questions the assumption of harmony and the reliance on Maslow's hierarchy of needs.

In opposition to the harmony view, contemporary structural views of organizations acknowledge the inevitable strains between structure and process (Etzioni, 1964; Perrow, 1972). Simon (1947; 1957) and March and Simon (1958) are among the precursors of this view. These works represent a strong continuity with the human relations school minus its central assumption of harmony. A pivotal element of their thesis concerns the environment of decision making, *i.e.*, the factors limiting the rationality of decisions. By moving back from the actual process of decision making to the premises upon which they are made, March and Simon demonstrate that structural aspects of organizations set these premises and consequently define the situations in which organizational members act and interact.

(c) Quality of Working Life

The quality of working life movement merges the contributions of Herzberg and others in the human resources tradition (Herzberg *et al.*, 1959; Herzberg, 1966; Seashore and Bowers, 1963; Salyes and Strauss, 1966; Marrow *et al.*, 1967) with the socio-technical approach of the Tavistock Institute (Trist and Bamforth, 1951; Emery and Trist, 1965). With the Tavistock evidence (discussed in the sections on technology and environment) that there are many innovative ways of restructuring work, this approach advocates restructuring in ways that meet both the motivational needs of people and the prerequisites of technology. To this end the quality of working life practitioners advocate the use of socio-technical concepts and principles:

> (1) for evaluating strengths and weaknesses of existing organizations from a socio-technical point of view and (2) for design or redesign of organizations so that technology complements rather than replaces the human component of enterprise (Johnston *et al.*, 1978: 3).

Intervention takes account of the environment of the organization in efforts to restructure work in ways that optimize the relationship between the structural and social dimensions of the organization.

The techniques of intervention most commonly used are job rotation, job enlargement, job enrichment and autonomous work groups. Each technique strives to reorganize work tasks so that the job comprises as many of Herzberg's motivating factors as possible (Robin, 1981). There are a variety of forms which the quality of working life has taken in Europe and North America. In Canada the emphasis has been on the shop floor and involves "work-linked democracy" with workers fully participating in the day-to-day decisions affecting their work and immediate work settings (Trist, 1981).

Much publicity has surrounded the quality of working life programs in Canada, the United States and Europe. It represents a renewed attack on the principles of scientific management that seeks to avoid the manipulative pitfalls of human relations. In redressing the errors of human relations it acknowledges the interdependency of the social and technical dimensions but holds to the harmony assumption. This affinity with human relations prompts criticism from structuralists. They contend that the movement still underestimates the structural determinates in failing to realize that organizations act as purposeful systems with an inner logic that is not fully apparent even to those who appear to control them (see Perrow, 1972). The validity of its empirical methods, especially with respect to Herzberg's contributions, has also been questioned (House and Wigdor, 1967).

At the level of practical implementation, the movement has been plagued with resistance from management and labour. Many companies reject its emphasis on worker democracy or give only qualified commitment to it. Many workers and unions perceive it as a threat. Some regard it as human relations in new clothes; others see it as an attempt to undercut collective bargaining. Compelling evidence in support of the movement is still wanting.

IV. SUMMARY

This chapter has examined the sociological literature on complex organizations. While there is no common denominator to the classifications of these organizations, sociologists do tend to concur that, like other kinds of social groups, they "have some properties that one can get to know without knowing anything about the properties of its [sic] members" (Eldridge and Crombie, 1974: 60). Viewing organizations as purposive social systems promotes attention to their structural or formal elements and the regulative effects of structure on individuals and groups. While emphasizing the salience of structure sociologists also employ a socio-psychological orientation to document the fact that organizational members are themselves purposeful. They creatively adapt to the regulative contingencies of structure. This concern with human agency opens awareness to the conception of organizations as dynamic systems located in multifaceted environments instead of closed systems operating in a vacuum.

The contemporary sociological study of organizations combines these structural, processural and environmental components. It goes without saying that organizations can be fruitfully viewed from a variety of perspectives—economics, political science, psychology and anthropology as well as sociology. Indeed each informs the other. The particular contribution of sociology is that it integrates to some extent, the formal component with the underlife and overlife of organizations—those contextual aspects which advance an understanding of organizations as purposive social systems.

Suggested Readings

Eldridge, J. E. T. and A. D. Crombie
  1974. *A Sociology of Organizations*. London: Allen & Unwin.
Hall, Richard H.
  1977. *Organizations: Structure and Process*. 2nd ed. Englewood Cliffs, N.J.: Prentice-Hall.
Kahn, Robert L., Donald M. Wolfe, Robert P. Quinn, J. Diedrick Snoek, and Robert A. Rosenthal
  1964. *Organizational Stress. Studies in Role Conflict and Ambiguity*. New York: Wiley.
Perrow, Charles
  1970. *Organizational Analysis: A Sociological View*. Belmont, Cal.: Wadsworth.
Strauss, Anselm L.
  1978. *Negotiations: Varieties, Contexts, Processes and Social Order*. San Francisco: Jossey-Boss.

Chapter 9

The Labour Unions

I. INTRODUCTION

In the days toward the twenty-first century, the labour union has become an organization that is much too familiar. While the degree of esteem accorded unions differs from situation to situation, and from person to person, organized labour is recognized in Canada as an integrated part of the social system. Through a state-guided collective bargaining framework, the Canadian industrial relations system provides a legitimate and significant role to labour unions in determining the web of rules of work. In this chapter, we attempt to expound two major themes: the labour union as a limited countervailing power to management in a capitalist society and the changes in work and their impact on the development of unions. However, before we explore these themes, a description of the current labour organizations in Canada and an introduction of types of labour organizations are necessary.

At the beginning of 1983, union membership in Canada was 3,562,799. This is a decrease of 1.5 percent from what it was a year earlier. Union members in 1983, represented 40.0 percent of nonagricultural paid workers and 30.6 percent of the civilian labour force. Table 9-1 presents the fluctuations of union membership since 1955. While the proportion of union members of the civilian labour force has been relatively stable in the last decade, their proportion among nonagricultural paid workers has had a noticeable increase.

Table 9-2 demonstrates the wide range in size of unions in Canada, both international and national, as indicated by membership. Six, or 2.7 percent of the international and national unions presented here are small organizations with less than 100 members. The smallest, International Association of Siderographers, had only four members in 1983. More than one-half (53.6%) of these unions had under 5,000 Canadian members. More than one-sixth (17.2%) of these unions were quite large with 20,000 or more members each. Five of these large unions had a membership over 100,000. As of the beginning of 1983, the five largest contained together almost one million members. These were the Canadian Union of Public

Table 9-1
Union Membership and Ratios of Union Membership
to the Civilian Labour Force and to
Non-Agricultural Paid Workers, 1955-1983

Year	Union Membership (Thousands)	Total Non-Agricultural Paid Workers (Thousands)	Union Membership as Percentage Civilian Labour Force	Union Membership as Percentage of Non-Agricultural Paid Workers
1955	1,268	3,767	23.6	33.7
1956	1,352	4,058	24.5	33.3
1957	1,386	4,282	24.3	32.4
1958	1,454	4,250	24.7	34.2
1959	1,459	4,375	24.0	33.3
1960	1,459	4,522	23.5	32.3
1961	1,447	4,578	22.6	31.6
1962	1,423	4,705	22.2	30.2
1963	1,449	4,867	22.3	29.8
1964	1,493	5,074	22.3	29.4
1965	1,589	5,343	23.2	29.7
1966	1,736	5,658	24.5	30.7
1967	1,921	5,953	26.1	32.3
1968	2,010	6,068	26.6	33.1
1969	2,075	6,380	26.3	32.5
1970	2,173	6,465	27.2	33.6
1971	2,231	6,637	26.8	33.6
1972	2,388	6,893	27.8	34.6
1973	2,591	7,181	29.2	36.1
1974	2,732	7,637	29.4	35.8
1975	2,884	7,817	29.8	36.9
1976	3,042	8,158	30.6	37.3
1977	3,149	8,243	31.0	38.2
1978	3,278	8,413	31.3	39.0
1980	3,397	9,027	30.5	37.6
1981	3,487	9,330	30.6	37.4
1982	3,617	9,264	31.4	39.0
1983	3,563	8,901	30.6	40.0

Note: The data for the years prior to 1955 are contained in the 1976-1977 report or previous editions. There was no survey conducted in 1979.
Source: Directory of Labour Organizations in Canada, 1983:18. Reproduced by permission of the Minister of Supply and Services Canada.

Table 9-2

International and National Unions by Size, 1983

Membership Range	International Unions		National Unions		Total	
	No. of Unions	Membership	No. of Unions	Membership	No. of Unions	Membership
Under 100	4	228	2	106	6	334
100- 199	5	657	5	683	10	1 340
200- 499	2	700	14	4 775	16	5 475
500- 999	3	2 214	14	10 436	17	12 650
1 000- 2 499	9	16 920	19	33 094	28	50 014
2 500- 4 999	7	22 955	34	117 575	41	140 530
5 000- 9 999	12	93 241	24	176 052	36	269 293
10 000-14 999	7	89 470	6	70 872	13	160 342
15 000-19 999	7	114 501	7	123 203	14	237 704
20 000-29 999	3	73 600	7	176 376	10	249 886
30 000-39 999	3	92 500	7	229 386	10	321 886
40 000-49 999	2	79 315	1	41 174	3	120 489
50 000-99 999	8	594 732	3	233 041	11	827 773
100 000 and over	2	289 400	3	683 209	5	972 609
TOTAL	74	1 470 433	146	1 899 982*	220	3 370 415

*Total of National Unions does not include 46,000 construction workers covered by the National Building Trades Department of the CLC.

Source: *Directory of Labour Organizations in Canada*, 1983: 22. Reproduced by permission of the Minister of Supply and Services Canada.

Employees, the National Union of Provincial Government Employees, the United Steelworkers of Canada, the Public Service Alliance
of Canada, and the United Food and Commercial Workers.

   In 1983, there were 826 unions in Canada. Of these, 240 (or 29%)
were independent local organizations. The rest of them were affiliates of various union congresses (see Table 9-3 in Section II). A more
detailed classification in terms of affiliation and related issues will be
discussed in the next section. It suffices to say here that the structure
of the Canadian labour movement is quite different from that of the
United States. Although Canada's labour force is only about one-
tenth that of the United States, proportionally more unions are active
in this country. In comparison, the structure of the Canadian labour
movement is relatively fragmented. This is strongly indicated both by
the large number of unions and by the small size of many of them.
This was true in the past (Kruger, 1971: 99) and is true now.

II. TYPES OF UNION ORGANIZATIONS

   Depending on the criteria used, unions may be classified in a
number of ways. Many researchers have attempted to develop typologies of union organizations. One classification is by affiliation.
Because of their unique historical background, unions in Canada
form a rather complicated picture of affiliations. Table 9-3 highlights
the total structure.

(a) International Unions

   International unions are unions whose headquarters are in the
United States but with locals both in that country and Canada. Most
of these locals are chartered by the American Federation of Labour-
Congress of Industrial Organization (AFL-CIO) through the Canadian Labour Congress (CLC). In 1983, 74 International unions
contained altogether 44.7 percent of the total membership.

(b) National Unions

   These are Canadian unions with regional and national organizations. The Canadian Labour Congress (CLC), the Confederation of
National Trade Unions (CNTU), Centrale des Sydicates Democra-
tiques (CSD), and the Confederation of Canadian Unions (CCU) are

Table 9-3
Union Membership by Type of Union and Affiliation, 1983

Type and Affiliations	No. of Unions	No. of Locals	Membership Number	Percent
International	74	3 943	1 470 433	44.7
AFL-CIO/CLC	46	2 855	851 341	23.9
AFL-CIO/CFL	10	406	213 301	6.0
CLC only	5	263	134 008	3.8
AFL-CIO only	7	257	167 515	4.7
Unaffiliated Unions	6	162	104 268	2.9
National Unions	146	11 321	1 945 982	54.6
**CLC	27	5 670	1 018 792	28.6
CNTU	10	1 620	212 646	6.0
CSD	3	204	21 826	0.6
CCU	20	120	38 684	1.1
Unaffiliated Unions	86	3 698	654 034	18.3
SUB-TOTAL	220	15 255	3 416 415	95.9
Directly Chartered Unions	366		44 633	1.2
CLC	74		8 909	0.2
CNTU	5		724	*
CSD	287		35 000	1.0
Independent Local Organizations	240		101 751	2.9
TOTAL	826		3 562 799	100.0

*Less than 0.1 percent.
**This table includes 46 000 construction workers who are members of organizations chartered by the National Building Trades Department of the CLC.
Source: *Directory of Labour Organizations in Canada,* 1983: 20. Reproduced by permission of the Minister of Supply and Services Canada.

national unions in Canada. Well over half of the total membership (54.6%) were in 146 national unions in 1983.

(c) Directly Chartered Unions

These are unions organized and directly chartered by a central labour body such as CLC, CNTU, or CSD.

(d) Independent Local Organizations

These are local union organizations. They are not affiliated with any national or international congresses. Nor do they have organizations at the national level.

Unions in the last two categories are of course Canadian unions. They amounted to 4.1 percent of the total membership. Together with the national unions, 58.7 percent of unions in this country, in 1983, were Canadian labour organizations. However, this was not the case in the past. The overwhelming majority used to be international affiliates. As a matter of fact, throughout the history of the labour movement in Canada, the identity of Canadian unions, many of which are part of an international congress, and the degree to which Canadian workers benefit from membership in international unions have been some of the major controversial issues. Despite their name, the so-called international unions are not world-wide organizations. Rather, they are mainly American based unions which have locals in Canada. For almost a century, the U.S. based unions have dominated the Canadian labour movement, both in terms of number and their philosophy. The conflict between the Canadian Congress of Labour (CCL—predecessor of the CLC) and the CIO during the 1940s is a pertinent example of nationalism versus internationalism. In terms of finances, the CIO-affiliated unions in Canada suffered losses of the flow of union funds to the United States. There is some evidence that the CIO headquarters actually subsidized the Canadian affiliates when they were first established. But since World War II the Canadians suffered net losses. This issue is still one of contention within the CLC today (Smucker, 1980:199).

With respect to political policies, CIO affiliates in Canada were often ordered by their American headquarters to take stands which were inappropriate for Canadian workers. For instance the CCL unions were asked to give a "solid labour vote to Roosevelt" and to "communicate to their senators their support of Henry Wallace as Secretary of Commerce." These are only some examples to illustrate the insensitivity of the international congress to its Canadian affiliates. What is more serious are the limitations the internationals imposed on the identity and autonomy of Canadian unions. The most striking example was, as cited by Smucker (1980:200), that in 1945 the CCL delegation had to fight hard to get itself seated in the World Labour Conference in London. With the support of the CIO, the conference attempted to deny the right of Canadian representation, arguing that "Canadian unions were merely affiliates of American organizations."[1]

Despite the ongoing contention of nationalism and internationalism within the Canadian labour movement, the balance between
the membership in the international and in the Canadian unions
shifted significantly during the 1970s. Membership growth rates of
the two forms of Canadian unionism in recent years are shown in
Table 9-4. As we can see, there have been more workers organized in
Canadian unions than in international affiliates. These trends persist

Table 9-4
Union Growth in Canada

Year	Union Membership as Percentage of all Non-Agricultural Paid Workers	Percentage of Total Membership in International Unions	Percentage of Total Membership in National Unions
1921	16.0	72.8	—
1931	15.3	69.5	—
1941	18.0	62.4	—
1951	28.4	70.5	—
1961	31.6	71.9	—
1971	33.6	62.0	34.9 (38.0)*
1972	34.6	59.6	37.7 (40.4)*
1973	36.1	55.3	42.1 (44.7)*
1974	35.8	53.2	43.6 (46.8)*
1975	36.9	51.4	46.1 (48.6)*
1976	37.3	49.6	46.8 (50.4)*
1977	38.2	49.0	47.4 (51.0)*
1978	39.0	47.4	50.0 (52.5)*
1979**	—	—	— —
1980	37.6	46.3	50.1 (53.7)*
1981	37.4	44.7	52.0 (55.3)*
1982	39.0	44.2	51.9 (55.8)*
1983	40.0	41.3	54.6 (58.7)*

*Percentage in parentheses include directly chartered unions and independent local
unions. All unions in these two categories are Canadian organizations.
**Not available
Sources: Compiled from Canada Department of Labour, Economics and Research
Branch, *Union Growth in Canada*, 1921-1967; Labour Canada, *Directory of Labour
Organizations in Canada*, 1972, 1973, 1974-75, 1976-77, 1978, 1980, 1981, 1982, and
1983.

in the 1980s. Several factors can be cited to explain the change. First, on the whole the Canadian unions have been growing much more rapidly than the internationals. Second, employees in the public sector have organized themselves to a greater extent in Canada than in the United States. Third, it is likely that a generally stronger nationalism among Canadian workers has also contributed to this phenomenon (Laxer, 1976, Ch. 18).

In the early part of the century Hoxie's classification was widely cited by labour economists (Hoxie, 1928; in Caplow, 1954). There are five types of unions:

1. Business unions are devoted primarily to the improvement of wages and working conditions.
2. Uplift unions seek to carry out benevolent activities, such as elaborate funerals, for their members.
3. Revolutionary unions attempt to subvert the existing government.
4. Reform unions endeavour to achieve social change through legislation.
5. Company unions are dominated openly or covertly by employers.

Examples of the last type would be the unions initiated by a number of firms in Winnipeg to co-opt their employees during the 1920s (Rinehart, 1975: 48). The initial stage of the Catholic union movement in Quebec during the 1920s was also attacked by other unions as being "little more than company unionism" (Williams, 1975: 144-45).

As ideal types, this classification may be useful in terms of identifying the major functions of unions. However, in reality few unions clearly fall in one or the other category. For example, most Canadian unions are business unions which also have reform motives (Smucker, 1980:176; Montgomery, 1977:116). Revolutionary unions of course also engage in "business" activities such as bargaining for wage increases.

In terms of the scope of their functions, Dubin suggests that there are three main types of unions: business unions, welfare unions, and life embracing unions (1958:71-81).

Business unions restrict their functions almost exclusively to issues relating directly to work. Thus, business unions affect the lives of the members to a limited degree. Their major activities focus on the members' bread-and-butter goals: wages, hours and working conditions. Such unions avoid matters beyond what is specifically covered in the collective agreement. As we have pointed out earlier, most unions in the Canadian labour movement are business unions.

Officials of business unions usually have relatively short and infrequent contact with the membership. The ties between members and the union are th more formal ones. Membership participation is usually minimal as long as the leaders can deliver a contract which improves their economic well-being. In the absence of a deep sense of fellow feeling among the members, business unions, except in special cases, do not serve to fulfill the psychological need as suggested by Tannenbaum (1951).

Welfare unions attempt to play an important part in the lives of their members in work-related issues and in the community as well. They are active to help solve community problems that workers face. Some unions have attempted to organize recreational programs for their membership. Some have entered the field of housing, selling food, household goods, and general merchandise through union-sponsored co-operative stores, personal and psychological counselling, banking, newspaper publications, and social-welfare work (Dubin, 1958:76). Since unions usually are not well staffed in offering this wide range of services, they are not in a strong position to compete with individual and community organizations which are specialized in such activities. As a consequence, only relatively large and wealthy unions can engage in welfare undertakings. The ex-CIO unions tended to be of this type (Miller and Form, 1980:424). As the governments have been expanding their functions, it appears that most unions have been focusing their effort on advocating and lobbying for legislations favourable to their members, though some of them still have a limited number of benefits and welfare programs.

A third type is the life embracing union. The scope of its function is the widest of all. Such unions perform major functions for their members on the job and in community life. This type of union is usually found in small one-industry towns where there are no adequate community organizations to provide services. Miners' unions are often life embracing unions.

Finally, according to Caplow (1964), the most familiar classification distinguishes craft, industrial, and white-collar unions. The craft union is limited to a single occupation. The industrial union is composed of workers in a single industry. While, in practice, there is not a clear-cut division between the two kinds of unions, they differ in several ways (Holley and Jennings, 1980:141-43).

Differences Between Craft Unions and Industrial Unions

(i) Differences in Membership

Craft unions are composed of members of a craft or skilled occupation, for example, bricklayers, carpenters, electricians, etc. Industrial unions have been organized on an industrial basis, for example, the steelworkers, auto workers, textile workers and so on. This, of course, does not mean that there are no skilled workers in steel, auto, or textile industries; but, it does mean that the electricians and carpenters in a steel plant or a mine operation would likely be members of the Canadian Steelworkers Union or the United Steelworkers of America or the International Union, United Mine Workers of America. On the other hand, many craft unions bring together a number of allied occupations in the same locals. International Brotherhood of Teamsters, Chauffeurs, Warehousemen and Helpers of America is a good example.

(ii) Differences in Philosophy

The leaders of craft unions tend to see their responsibility as a protection of the craft and the obtaining of periodic improvements in wages and working conditions. On the other hand, industrial unionists tend to regard the labour movement as a social force striving for the betterment of all workers, and indeed, all mankind (Williams, 1975:156).

The conflict, caused by philosophical differences, between craft and industrial unionism harked back to the early decades of this century. There were many bitter struggles between unions adhering to the two different positions. However, since the merger of the CIO and the AFL in the United States, and the creation of the Canadian Congress of Labour (CCL) in 1940, industrial unionists have exerted considerable influence on the course of the labour movement in Canada (Williams, 1975:164; Kruger, 1971:95). At the practical level, however, collective bargaining in Canada is still decentralized. Bargaining on a national industry wide basis has not developed in this country. Most collective agreements are between the employer and a union acting on behalf of the employees of a single establishment.

(iii) Differences in Skills

The craft members are highly skilled craftsmen who have had long periods of training. It is either in a formal apprenticeship program or a combination of vocational school education and apprenticeship. Many industrial workers, on the other hand, usually only require on-the-job training. The craftsmen, therefore, often enjoy higher status than industrial workers. Since their power and their interests are not the same, union behaviours of these occupational groups tend to differ from one another (Sayles, 1958).

In many cases, the training received by members of craft unions is jointly controlled and operated by the unions. Such arrangements allow the craft unions to control the entrance of new members and, thus, enable them to limit the numbers in their occupation.

(iv) Differences in Job Characteristics

Members of craft unions receive their work assignments from the union hiring hall, rather than from the employing company directly, particularly construction companies. Usually, the work assignments last only a short period. After the completion of their part of the project, the craftsmen return to the union hall for their next assignments. In this way, the union hiring hall serves as a clearing house or placement office for the employing companies and for the union members. In contrast, the typical member of an industrial union is hired by the company and will work for the same employer until employment is terminated.

Although there are dozens of books and articles entitled "White-Collar Unionism" or "White-Collar Unionization," the term is not precise. It includes a wide variety of union organizations, ranging from unions of government clerks to that of nurses, teachers, college professors and engineers. Perhaps the most obvious similarity that these unions share is that they are relative newcomers to the labour movement. Another unique feature of white-collar unions in Canada is that most of them are in the public sector. The increasingly strong trend toward unionization among clerical, technical and professional workers indicates significant changes in work. We shall analyze the relationships between changes in work and the development of unions at some length in the last section of the chapter.

Before the general theories of labour movements are introduced in the next section, let us discuss the contention over the basis upon which workers should be organized; namely, the conflict between craft unions and industrial unions in Canada. In many ways, this controversy is closely related with the conflict between nationalism and internationalism. In the early stages of the labour movement, most unions were craft unions. As more and more industries became huge, mass producing enterprises, the unions needed to change from craft-based organizations to industry-based organizations to meet the challenge. Many Canadian unionists saw this need and wanted to change. But their suggestions and actions were often met with strong opposition from powerful American, traditional trade unions. For example, as early as 1911, the Trades and Labour Congress of Canada (TLC) delegates endorsed the principle of industrial unionism (Smucker, 1980:197). But the AFL opposed this resolution and put pressure on the TLC to expel its industrial-oriented unions as they did in the U.S. It was not until the CIO gained popularity and power in the 1940s that industrial unions started to develop more rapidly.

After the merger of TLC and CCL on 1956, the industrial unions, joined by some public sector unions, came to dominate the CLC. The conflict between industrial and trade unions subsided somewhat, but never entirely disappeared. As a matter of fact, the American based building trade unions have had several fee boycotts (*i.e.*, they stopped paying per capita tax to the CLC) trying to bring the CLC down to their terms. The first fee boycott by the American construction unions was in 1971 to protest CLC's guidelines of Canadian autonomy. They were also opposed to the establishment of the National Council of Building Trades by Canadian Building Trades Unions (Canadian Dimension, 1981:17-20). The decisions were always made by the American leaders of these unions and the Canadian members were never consulted first. The last fee boycott occurred in May, 1980. Issues that triggered this last boycott included the decision by the Quebec Federation of Labour to affiliate a group of electricians who had broken away from the International Brotherhood of Electrical Workers, delegate representation at CLC conventions, and the organization of construction workers by CLC industrial unions. The CLC threatened to expel the boycotting unions if they did not comply with its directives. To counterattack, the Building Trades Unions declared, again without consultation with their Canadian membership, their intention to establish a new Canadian trade union centre, the Canadian Federation of Labour. The dispute was not successfully resolved. The unions of the building trades were consequently suspended from affiliation by the CLC in 1981. A year later, the Canadian Federation of Labour (CFL) with more than 200,000 members in ten unions of building trades was formally established (CCH, 1982: 553).

III. THEORIES OF LABOUR MOVEMENTS

While the history of the guilds as occupational organizations goes back to the medieval era, the first union in the modern sense was not founded until 1794 in the United States (Commons, 1909), and not until the early 1800s in Canada (Williams, 1975:1). Since then, the labour movements have developed into a significant social and economic force both in the United States and in this country. Although a general theory which takes into account the common factors responsible for the appearance of all types of employee organizations (unions, professional societies, foremen's associations, worker committees, and so on) is yet to be developed, many social scientists have sought to explain the rise of labour unions. From the perspective of the motivation of participation in unions, three theories may be identified: unions as economic instruments, as job protectors, and as communities (Schneider, 1969: 376-84).

(a) Unions as Economic Instruments

Sidney and Beatrice Webb regard workers as most directly concerned with immediate economic conditions of work: "wages, hours, health, safety, comfort" (1926:560). Workers are concerned with their individual powerless position in relation to employers. They realize that fierce competition among themselves can only result in poor conditions of work and lower wages. In order to be able to counter the power of their employers on equal terms and to reduce the negative effects of competition, workers turn to collective action. The most effective instrument of collective-labour action is the trade union. Thus, the immediate goal of the labour movement is "the deliberate regulation of the conditions of employment in such a way as to ward off from the manual-working producers the evil effects of industrial competitions" (Webb & Webb, 1926:807). To achieve this goal, the union has to have power. Therefore, the aim of the trade union is to further "democracy," which, in this case, means an equalization of power with management. Briefly, trade unionism has definite and far-reaching significance both for the industry and the society at large.

(b) Unions as Job Protectors

While allowing for unions' wage interests, Selig Perlman (1949) emphasizes the concerns with job control and job ownership. By examining the working rules, "customs and practices," about hiring and firing, discipline on the job, layoff, sharing of the job, hours of work, apprenticeship, and the introduction of new technology, Perlman concluded that these rules reflect a consciousness for scarcity of job opportunities. This consciousness for scarcity leads to a desire for control of the job. To organize a union is the best way to share job opportunities fairly. Perlman sees no evidence that the American union movement is interested in political goals—that is, to displace management, or to unite the working class to achieve these aims.

(c) Unions as Communities

Another theory of union movement is offered by Frank Tannenbaum. From his point of view, unionization is the workers' effort to create a meaningful community in which they can relate to one another and the job (1951). He reasons that industrialization and bureaucratization in the workplace have alienated workers from their work and the society. In order to minimize the loss of security, and to fulfill their psychological needs, workers strive to create a community—the union—of their own. As Tannenbaum puts it, "the union returns to the worker his society. It gives him a fellowship, a part in a drama that he can understand, and life takes on meaning once again because he shares the value system common to others" (1951:10). This drive for a meaningful community does not mean that workers ignore the economic side of their lives though. They, too, wish to maximize their economic returns, to have shorter hours of work, and better working conditions. However, these economic concerns, according to Tannenbaum, are secondary to their effort for achieving psychological and social security.

Even a brief consideration of these views will suggest that there are no conflicts among these different interpretations. It has been shown that workers join unions for different reasons (Seidman, 1951; Hagburg, 1966; Chen, 1968). In addition, unions mean different things in different historical epochs (Moore, 1960). The present functions of a union may not be the historical causes for its emergence. Thus, Perlman's theory, derived from examining the International Typographical Union—the oldest trade union in the United States—may be adequate to account for the rise of craft unions in a mature industrial society, while the Webbs may explain the development of class conscious (social rank) unions in an earlier era of industrialization. As for the view of unions as communities, it is simply out of date. Few, if any, Canadian workers today join a union with the major purpose of creating a community. We agree with

Moore (1960) that, although unions differ in their economic, social, and political characteristics, they are all concerned with a single goal of attempting to control the conditions of their work; in other words, to achieve worker autonomy.

However, workers' control is never complete. Their autonomy is always conditional because of a massive power imbalance between capital and labour. In a capitalistic society such as Canada, the economic power is dominated by a small minority of the population (Clement, 1975). Confronting this concentrated power, the workers who depend on their labour for a living are at an inevitable disadvantage. Given this context, they will continue to contribute to, and certainly not seriously obstruct, managerial goals of productivy and profitability (Hyman and Fryer, 1977; Hyman, 1980).

No rational union will go so far as to force its employer out of business, even when it has the power to obstruct crucial managerial decisions. Those who do go "too far" will likely suffer from retaliation. To this extent, "workers control" as exercised by the union is "necessarily partial and reactive" (Hyman, 1980: 318). As Hyman poignantly points out, "workers control" is a means of moderating the effects of subordination to capital dictates and management domination, not a means of enforcing different priorities (1980:318). The negotiated order at the workplace stands only so long as the employer is able to derive an acceptable level of profits.

Many factors can upset workers' autonomy in the work process, as limited as it is. Market conditions is one of the most powerful. For instance, during the economic recession in the early 1980s, the unions of auto workers both in Canada and the United States were asked to make concessions in their wages. Facing the possibility of even more massive unemployment, they could not but concede. Moreover, many alternatives are available to the employer to undermine, or to by-pass altogether the controls established by a powerful union. To displace a particular set of tasks by adopting a new technology, to close down a whole establishment, and to persuade the state to use coercive sanctions are only some of them.

What countervailing power does the union have to redress the imbalance? Objectively, the strength of a union can be affected by the density of organization among the potential membership, and the strategic importance of the workers covered (Hyman and Fryer, 1977: 155). Obviously, the more intensively a group of potential members are organized, the more pressure they can exert on the employer. Strategic importance enhances the probability that the union's demands are met; at least, it increases the impact of any forms of overt conflict in which they engage. Thus, a group of assembly-line workers can disrupt an entire production process.

Some groups such as the police and fire-fighters may be able to exert considerable pressure on the community and the government because of the nature of their services. Other groups like post workers, dock workers, and steel workers may have the power to oblige the government to intervene in any dispute to achieve terms in their favour, because their work is vital to a significant part, or even the entire economy.

Union power also depends on subjective factors such as "the manner in which workers perceive their situation and interests, and the solidarity and determination with which they pressure their objectives" (Hyman and Fryer, 1977: 155). Workers who are not ideologically committed to unionization are not likely to organize themselves; even if they do, their organization is unlikely to be effective. Worker groups in a specific area or a region with a low level of solidarity will not have a strong collective power to confront their employers, although local gains may be possible. A pertinent example is the collapse of the United Front for Free Collective Bargaining formed by eight public sector unions with the support of the Nova Scotia Federation of Labour in 1982. Facing the threat of wage increase restraints imposed by the provincial government, several individual unions defected from the Front to reach agreements with the government, instead of resisting the imposition as they originally alleged to do. Consequently, the solidarity of the Front was fatally eroded by internal contradiction between the general demands of the unions as a whole and the sectional interests of individual unions which composed the Front. Thus, they failed to achieve their goal of preventing government interference in the collective bargaining process (Thomson, 1984:26-36).

IV. CHANGES IN WORK AND THE LABOUR MOVEMENT

Unions, as we know them, are clearly by-products of the industrialization process. Whatever other reasons might have given rise to unions, the labour movement and the nature of work in an industrial society are inseparable.[2] In the early stages of Industrial Revolution in Britain, there was a great deal of human suffering among workers. To protect themselves, they turned to collective organization, despite the fact that union organizations were illegal. It was not until 1824 that the *Combination Acts*, which outlawed unions, were repealed (Williams, 1975:3). Since then union organization started to grow rapidly, although it was not without great difficulties and sacrifices.[3]

Throughout modern history, labour unrest and union movements are closely related to the change of work either at the factory level or at the industry level. They are, of course, also intimately related to the changes of the occupational structure. Factory workers often perceive (and rightly so) their livelihood as threatened by the introduction of new technologies. One group of English textile workers, known as the Luddites, smashed the machines which they thought jeopardized their jobs (Williams, 1975:3). The tailors in Toronto formed their union in 1852 aiming primarily at the removal of the Singer sewing machines from the shops (Williams, 1975:4). The militancy of the unions in the railway industry during the 1950s, which eventually led to the establishment of the Freedman Commission, was primarily a response to the increasing mechanization of the railways.

At a broader level, it was mainly the changing occupational structure during the late 1930s and the 1940s that sparked the bitter struggle between the craft unions and the industrial unions in Canada. These instances are only some examples cited to illustrate how closely the development of unions is related to changes in work. Unionization is certainly not the only response that workers have toward these changes. Some quit. However, since employment and income are almost synonymous in an industrial society, very few people can afford to do so. Some, particularly clerical workers, turn their attention inwardly and get satisfaction from informal relations with peers. But informal groups are hardly protection. They can not protect workers who are involved in these groups from the competition of other occupational groups. Nor can they protect workers from the threat posed by employers and machines. So, workers organize, strike, and bargain to protect their jobs, their livelihood and their human dignity.

But what do we mean by changes in work? Three changes may be identified: job content, work organization, and environment of work. Job content refers to the actual tasks that a worker is required to do; what skills are necessary; what tools are to be used; what work is to be done at what pace; and what is to be accomplished. One of the basic principles of industrialization is the rationalization of the work process (see Chapter 6). Rationalization affects both the individual and organizational levels. At the individual level, it changes the job content. For example, assembly line production is a form of rationalization. When the making of shirts is shifted from a tailor's shop to a mass producing factory, the tailor is reduced from a craftsman to a machine operator: from a skilled to a semi-skilled worker. The pace of work is changed from self-controlled to machine controlled. While tailors can use their skills and imagination to create a whole product —a shirt, in this case—machine operators are required to produce a standard item which is only a part of the whole product.

Rationalization also affects the content of the white-collar worker's job. Let us take for example the job of a claims examiner in an automated insurance company. Before computerization, when claims came in, claims examiners read the applications, reviewed the information against policy books and their own knowledge of contracts, and made decisions as to whether the claims were honoured or not. Now the criteria are programmed into the computer which decided on the basis of coded information whether or not to honour a claim. All she (almost all claims examiners are women) needs to do is to look up the information on an application in a code book, enter the codes on the appropriate form, which are then entered into the computer (Glenn and Feldberg, N.D.: 6). When the element of judgement is taken away from her, the claims examiner is deskilled to an attendant of the automated computer system.

Moreover, greater rationalization of work increases managerial control over workers. We have already mentioned that when craft production shifts to mass production, the pace of work is not controlled by the worker anymore. Rather, it is controlled by the machine whose speed is set by the industrial engineers. For an assembly line worker, even a biological function such as going to the washroom cannot be done when required unless a relief worker is dispatched by the foreman.

As for office work, managerial control is traditionally less stringent. This is primarily because of the difficulty involved in the quantification and standardization of paper work. However, there have been various attempts to rationalize office work by formulating more precise measurement standards. For instance, a manual with a title of *A Guide to Office Clerical Time Standards* was published in 1960 (Wallace, 1970). Time standards for various office "activities" are measured in fractions of a minute. For example, it should take .009 minute for a worker to turn in a swivel chair and .33 minute to get up from or sit down in a chair. Other organizations have developed time standards for clerical tasks. For example, in the insurance company cited above, the coding of each type A claim is allotted 4.0 minutes, type B claim 4.7 minutes. Each clerk keeps a continuous record of the work she does on a production sheet. Their production reports are analyzed and examined weekly (Glenn and Feldberg, N.D.:6).

The rise of new computer technology can increase managerial control even tighter. Let us go back to our extremely rationalized insurance company once more. The measurement of productivity of data entry clerks would be the most pertinent example. The job of these clerks involves entering information into the computer system from the coded forms by using electronic keyboards. While the information is keyed in, counts of keystrokes are made automatically, and the number of keystrokes is used as the measurement of productivity (Glenn and Feldberg, N.D.:9).

It has been well-established in the sociological literature that the lack of worker autonomy increases job dissatisfaction. One of the responses dissatisfied workers might have is to resort to unionization. It should be pointed out, however, that we are not suggesting a technological determinism, although most examples cited are related to technology. While machine technologies are physical, the creation and adoption of them are social (Bravermen, 1974).

Work organization refers to the form of division of labour. In other words, how work is organized in a unit: be it a crew, a department, a plant, or a whole establishment. A major determinant of how work is organized is the level of production technology (Faunce, 1981: 37). This statement can be clarified by some examples. The tailor's shop and the shirt factory are clearly two drastically different forms of division of labour. A recent development in wholesaling utilizes a direct telephone hookup to a computer system. The purchaser tells the computer what he or she wants and the computer then analyzes, sorts and routes the order to appropriate departments while checking the credit limit of the purchaser at the same time (Faunce, 1981:35). In this case, since several functions are synthesized in one single system, it obviously would affect redeployment, displacement, or unemployment of personnel.

A final example is the computerization of the insurance company cited earlier.[4] In order to utilize the automated systems, the work process in the firm has been reorganized. The largest units are the divisions which are based on types of policies. Within most divisions there are two major departments, one for claims processing and one for billing and collection. In addition, there are some special service departments such as work-processing, data entry, and so on. All activities have been subdivided and precisely defined; standards have been established. Standard formats for input and output records are required.

In this process of reorganization, some units were created, such as information coding and data entry. Some existing jobs were restructured. For instance, customer inquiry clerks used to have to call up different departments and talk to several people in order to get the information needed to answer a request; they now, are able to call up the records on the terminal without talking to anyone. Clearly, the utilization of automated computer systems in this company has drastically affected the organization of work. It is characterized by increasing rationalization and formalization. In addition to changing the job content of individual workers, interaction patterns between individuals and units are also affected.

The third change in work is the changing environment of work. Three aspects of the environment are discussed here:

(a) physical environment,
(b) relative occupational status (or other occupational groups as environment) and
(c) politico-legal environment.

One of the results of mechanization and automation of work is that the physical environments of factory work and office work are becoming more alike. While the plants in manufacturing industries are becoming cleaner and less noisy as the degree of mechanization increases, the automated offices are becoming more factory-like. An increasing number of office workers are now required to work with machines constantly. For these workers, their work is parallel with that of machine operators in factories. These changes have a much stronger impact on office workers than on blue-collar wage earners, because they have undermined part of the traditional bases upon which the prestige advantage is enjoyed by the former.

Changes in work have not only made the physical environment of some occupational groups less distinguishable, but have also narrowed or blurred the status difference between categories of occupations. Those groups whose statuses are threatened, often take collective action to protect themselves. For example, one of the things that traditionally defined clerical workers' superior status was their income. Now, this differential has been narrowed; unionized manual workers often earn higher wages than office employees. As for the professionals, while they still enjoy some economic advantages over other occupational groups, these advantages are gradually diminishing (Chen, 1979:7). Moreover, more and more offices become large and impersonal settings where face-to-face interaction with higher management does not exist; where professionals are no longer the privileged few; rather, they are part of the working masses.

Finally, we come to the politico-legal environment of work. Employment operates in a political and legal framework. Labour laws define the age a person can legally leave school for employment, the minimum wage, the maximum hours, and the rights and procedures of bargaining the conditions of work with the employer. Labour law also defines who has the right to strike and under what conditions. When government policies and laws change, the environment of work changes too.

Labour historian Jamieson (1973) states that government policies in Canada have put more emphasis on the prevention of strikes or lockouts than has been true of the United States. This emphasis tended to weaken the position of unions more than of employers in the previous decades. The policies of budget restraints and the cutback of services, which lead to the reduction of civil servants by various provincial governments, and the federal policy of restricting wage increases in the 1980s are pertinent examples. During the 1960s and 1970s, restrictions on the right to strike by employees in "essential services," such as transportation, communications, and the protection of life and property, had been reduced considerably. However, voices for reviving some of those restrictions are being heard again in the 1980s, although no legislative actions have been taken by any governments yet.

Most Canadians probably take for granted the right to collectively bargain with the employer. However, it is a right gained through bitter, sometimes violent, struggle. Thanks to their counterparts in Great Britain and other European countries, blue-collar workers in this country had their right to unionize almost from the very beginning. White-collar occupational groups gained their right much later. For instance, it was not until 1967 that federal employees, including some professional groups, were granted bargaining rights by the *Public Staff Relations Act* (Bairstow and Sayles, 1975:109; Chen, 1979; White, 1980). With the exception of Saskatchewan (where provincial employees have been covered by general labour legislation since 1944), all provincial governments also allowed collective bargaining in the 1960s with varying coverage and restrictions (White, 1980: 43-44). In the private sector, clerical workers in financial institutions, such as banks, have made moderate gains in organizing themselves in more recent years.

In brief, changes in work in recent years tend to stimulate the union movement in Canada. The momentum of white-collar unionization, to a large extent, can be accounted for by the changing physical, social and economic environments of these occupational groups. The expansion and frustration of public sector unions involve mainly the change of government policies.

V. SUMMARY

In this chapter, the nature of unions as a countervailing force and their development in relation to changes in work were discussed. We started with a simple description of labour organizations in contemporary Canada, and then proceeded with a presentation of typologies of union organizations. In this presentation, we discussed, wherever relevant, some major debates in the Canadian labour movement. In section III, some general theories of unions were introduced. It was pointed out that, within the framework of market economy and institutionalized collective bargaining, while some degree of worker control can be established, this control is always partial and reactive. Finally, the relationship between change in work and union development was analyzed. Three types of changes in work were identified: job content, work organization, and environment of work. Sometimes these changes lead to the expansion of unions; sometimes to stagnation or contraction of them.

Notes

1. For a more detailed treatment of the conflict between nationalism and internationalism, see Laxer, 1976, Parts II and VII and Abella, 1973.
2. Ivar Berg maintains that unions are more easily identified with (a) democratic impulses; (b) loosely defined equalitarian conceptions of the role of the state; and (c) the occupational and hierarchical characters of industrial and employer organization, respectively, than with physical technologies; *i.e.* tools, machines, assembly lines, factory methods and so on (Berg, 1979: 121).
3. For example, in 1834, a group of English agricultural workers were banished to Australia because they tried to form a union. They were known as the Tolpuddle Martyrs (Williams, 1975:3).
4. For general discussions of impact of mechanization and automation on office work, see Rico, 1967; Shepard, 1972; Hall, 1975:314-55; Glenn and Feldberg, 1977.

Suggested Readings

Baker, Maureen and Mary Ann Robeson
    1981. "Trade Union Reactions to Women Workers and Their Concerns." *The Canadian Journal of Sociology*, *6(1)*:19-32.
Crompton, Rosemary
    1979, "Trade Unionism and the Insurance Clerk." *British Journal of Sociology*, *13:3*:403-26.

Hyman, R. and R.H. Fryer
1977. "Trade Unions: Sociology and Political Economy," in Clarke and Clements (eds.): *Trade Unions Under Capitalism*, pp. 152-74. Glasgow: William Collins & Co. Ltd.

Hyman, R.
1980. "Trade Unions, Control and Resistance," in Esland and Salaman (eds.): 1980. *The Politics of Work and Occupations*, pp. 303-34. Toronto: University of Toronto Press.

McFarland, Joan
1979. "Women and Unions: Help or Hindrance?" *Atlantis*, 4:2.

Oppenheimer, Martin
1975. "The Unionization of the Professional." *Social Policy, 5(5):* 34-40.

Smucker, J.
1980. *Industrialization in Canada*. Scarborough, Ontario: Prentice-Hall. Chapters 8 and 9.

White, Julie
1980. *Women and the Unions*. The Canadian Advisory Council on the Status of Women, Chapters 1-5.

Chapter 10

Technology and Work

Humans are limited by their physical and biological environment. To overcome these limitations, they have invented and applied technologies of all sorts and are continuing to do so. The invention of the wheel increased human's physical mobility. The invention of the lever saved people a great deal of physical labour. The domestication of animals affected the life of the human race in more ways than one. That the contemporary world is characterized as a technological world, however, is because modern technology is qualitatively different from that in the past. Emmanuel G. Mesthene observes (1970: 25) that modern technology is much more powerful than any before. The rifle wiped out the buffalo, but nuclear weapons can wipe out the whole human race. Dust storms lay whole regions to waste, but too much radioactivity in the atmosphere could make the earth uninhabitable. The domestication of animals literally lifted the burden from our backs, but automation could free humans from all drudgery. Modern technology is so pervasive that it has become an important determinant of our lives and institutions. Major technological change almost invariably leads to major social change. For example, modern farming technology, which allows fewer people to produce more food, sets in motion throughout the world, population shifts from rural to urban areas. Our complex energy systems have given us a wide range of conveniences, but at a horrendous cost of the pollution of the air, water and land. Never before has there been such a wide-spread concern of the consequences of technology in our society. Never before has there been a greater need to understand technology. The purpose of this chapter is to examine the nature of technological change and its relations to some important aspects of work. We shall first analyze the impact of technological change on the occupational structure, then proceed to examine the reactions of the worker, and finally, consider technology and the future of work.

I. THE NATURE OF TECHNOLOGICAL CHANGE

Like many words in our language, technology is used with many shades of meanings. For many people, technology is a synonym of machine or hardware. For the understanding of work and the influences of technology upon it, this is too limited an approach because technology and technological change involve much more than simply machinery. In order to best see the extent and variety of the effects technology has on work, we follow Mesthene and Dorf to define technology as "the organization of knowledge for the achievement of practical purposes" (Mesthene, 1970: 25, Dorf, 1974: 1).[1]

"Technological change refers to alterations in technological systems" (Hall, 1975:315).[2] We use the terms "technical development" and "technical advancement" interchangeably with technological change in this chapter. No connotation of greater desirability, complexity or refinement is intended.

One of the most salient features of technological change is that it is continuous. From an anthropological point of view, the whole human history is one of technological change. For the present time, change is indeed the normal state of affairs. Innovations today are more intended rather than accidental. Perhaps two major reasons can be identified to account for this character of technology. First, Anderson implies in his discussion of technology that by nature humans always try to improve their way of doing things. He states (1964:125):

> Technical inventiveness is linked to man's work. It cannot cease unless man in his work ceases to be competitive and no longer tries to find easier and faster ways of performing his tasks.

Second, it has something to do with the nature of the scientific knowledge. With any given stock of knowledge, there are additional possibilities for further development. Thus, the combination of human desire for improvement and the self-multiplicability of scientific knowledge gives technology the continuous and inevitable momentum towards change. This leads us to the next major characteristic of technological development. That is, it not only has its own momentum but it also proceeds with an increasingly fast pace. There is little doubt that the pace of change varies from one technological sector to the next and from one time period to another in the same sector (Anderman, 1967:49-55). There are also some questions about the criteria used to evaluate the pace of advancement (Anderman, 1967: 56). Given these qualifications, the overall picture is still that technological change moves with an accelerating pace.[3] By using the span of time from development of a new technology to its practical application, this rapidity of change is effectively portrayed in Figure 10-1. As we can see, the time span (shown by a solid line) is constantly decreasing. While it took 33 years from the discovery of the vacuum tube to a practical radio, only three years elapsed between the development of the transitor and its application.

Figure 10-1
Time Spans of Technological Innovations
from Discovery to Practical Applications

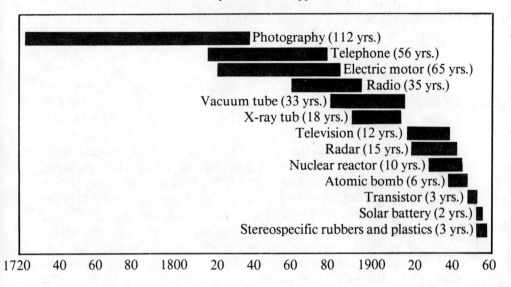

Source: From John McHale, *World Facts and Trends*, 1972.

The third feature of technological change is that it is "almost totally unidirectional. That is, the alteration in the system is toward less physical labour on the part of humans" (Hall, 1975: 317). The first step of the labour-saving process is the substitution of inanimate power for animate power and the mechanization of the processing operation. The electric powered moving assemble line, which replaces the effort of lifting materials from one work station to another, is an apt example.

The next step is automation where separate operations such as material handling and production control are linked into a continuous and automatic system. The clearest form of automation is oil refining where there is almost no direct contact with the product by humans. The worker-machine relationships are markedly different in these stages of technological change. While the workers are machine operators in mechanized production, they are machine monitors in automated production.

The fourth important feature of technology is discussed by John

K. Galbraith in his famous book *The New Industrial State.* He maintains that (1978:13):

> Nearly all of the consequences of technology, and much of the shape of modern industry, derive from this need to divide and subdivide tasks and from the further need to bring knowledge to bear on these fractions and from the final need to combine the finished elements of the task into the finished product as a whole.

These three needs are related to one another. Technology requires the division and subdivision of any practical task into its component parts because only in this way "can organized knowledge be brought to bear on performance: What is divided has to be put together again because the goal of technology is to systematically apply organized knowledge to practical tasks" (p. 12). For example, while metallurgical knowledge cannot be applied to the manufacturing of the whole car, it can be used to decide on the composition of the finish or trim (p. 13). The chassis, the engine, the crankshaft, the electrical system, the trim, and hundreds of other components have to be put together to have a finished product—in this case, a car.

All these characteristics of technology have their consequences. Continual change means unending adjustment at all levels of the society. The technological demand of division and subdivision of tasks and the advancement toward total automation produce both positive and negative effects. On the positive side, the division of tasks makes the application of knowledge to practical purposes possible; and in most cases it also increases productivity (Faunce, 1981: 55). Similarly, increasing mechanization and automation contribute to increased productivity and bring the rationalization to higher degrees. On the negative side, these features of technology create worker alienation and job dissatisfaction. We shall examine these important issues in some detail later in this chapter.

In this section we discussed the nature of technology and outlined some of the effects technological change has on work. Before we turn to the examination of the impact of technological change on the occupational structure, it should be pointed out that we do not take a technological deterministic point of view. The treatment of technological change as an independent variable is only for heuristic purposes.

II. THE IMPACT OF TECHNOLOGICAL CHANGE ON THE OCCUPATIONAL STRUCTURE

As has been indicated in the last section, technological change has consequences. One of these consequences is its impact on the occupational structure. Factors other than technology influence the distribution of workers among occupations, too. However, technology is a significant determinant of the patterns of the division of labour in a society. In this section, we shall first, discuss the impact of technological change on the occupational structure in general. Then the analysis will be focused on the effects of the so-called microelectronic revolution and the ensuing debate over what should be done about these effects.

(a) Technological Change and the Occupational Structure

Since we have analyzed the transformations of the Canadian occupational structure in Chapter 2, we need only to highlight the important patterns of change here. As it was shown, the greatest decline has been among farm workers. There is little doubt that this change is brought about by the vastly improved agricultural technology. The blue-collar sector has generally declined, but at a far more moderate rate. The long-term shift away from blue-collar and farming towards white-collar occupations is a clear and continuing trend. Within white-collar occupations, the growth of professional and technical occupations and clerical employment are particularly remarkable. These changes in the occupational structure over time are generally attributed to the changing technology.

In terms of industrial distribution of workers, one of the striking features of the Canadian economy in the past few decades, as it was pointed out in Chapter 2, has been the rapid expansion of service industries. In 1981, some 65 percent of the labour force was involved in various services. This means the employment in service industries has almost doubled what it was in 1941, while the manufacturing and construction sectors have remained about the same during this period. Similar sectoral shifts of occupations took place in most industrial countries (OECD, 1976). These changes, for the most part, represent a shift from more technologically developed industries (*e.g.*, manufacturing) to less technologically developed industries.

Peitchinis (1978: 26) points out that technological changes have impact on the structure in a variety of ways:

(a) the creation of new work functions;
(b) increases in the range of work functions of established occupations, requiring the separation and transference of some work functions to new occupations;
(c) the substitution of technological innovations for manpower; and
(d) the dilution of skills by technological innovations.

Thus, the functions of some existing occupations may be expanded, reduced, or entirely replaced.

Perhaps the most noticeable impact of technological changes on the occupational structure is functional differentiation. The proliferation of medical occupations is one example (United States Department of Labour, 1967: Peitchinis, 1970: Ch. 5); the array of occupations created by the introduction of the computer is another.

To the extent that a new technology is the substitute of an old one, it may mean the elimination of some occupations. Thus, one finds the old-time crotch sawyers (who split the hindquarters of cattle) are a dying species as the large meat-packing companies have turned increasingly to machines in processing the carcasses. In the post office, the skilled mail sorters have been replaced by coder operators and culler-facer-canceller attendants. In large financial institutions, the filing, posting and billing clerks have been displaced by data coding and data entry clerks.

(b) The Effect of Microelectronic Technology

The introduction of microelectronic technology has received a great deal of attention recently (*e.g.*, Science Council of Canada, 1980; Menzies, 1981a; 1981b; Humphreys, 1981; Zeman, 1979; Jenkins and Sherman, 1979; Neice *et al.*, 1982). Its effect is felt both in the manufacturing and the service sectors, but particularly in the latter. In the secondary sector, most empirical evidence of the impact of microprocessors is from industries where CAD/CAM (computer-aided design and computer-aided manufacturing) are applied. The CAD/CAM system is the realization of the concept of the automated factory. It integrates the entire manufacturing processes, from design to production and distribution. Robotics play a key role in CAD/CAM systems. Some examples of these systems include automated material handling, automated inspection and testing, automated packaging, automated inventory control, and automated warehousing (Science Council of Canada, 1980: 26).

The application of microprocessors has many economic advantages. First of all, it lowers costs. For example, microprocessors make the use of robots to replace as many human workers as possible. Since a robot does not require many benefits such as coffee breaks, vacation pay, and pension plans, the cost of operation is low. Allegedly, it is near or below minimum wage (Science Council of Canada, 1980: 26).

Another economic advantage is that microelectronics make possible the introduction of automated assembly techniques into areas of lower volume production. This possibility is particularly significant for Canada's small home market (Science Council of Canada, 1980, 26-27).

The structural impact of microelectronics is most felt in the form of job displacement in the information technology industries themselves. This is especially the case in the newspaper industry, where automation and work processors have radically changed the whole method of production. In a well-documented and well-researched book, Rogers and Freidman (1980) report that the printers—the "blue collar elite"—are losing their struggle to automation in New York City's dailies. This skilled craft will soon be in the graveyard of the history of occupations.

Its structural impact on manufacturing industries is not yet clear. There is some indication that the middle groups of the manufacturing force, "namely those that have had training and are at the centre of the distribution jobs" (Science Council of Canada, 1980: 29) are most affected. When the machine tools are displaced by electronic components and integrated into the production system, their jobs become redundant. However, this observation is preliminary. More research is needed.

As for the structural impact of microelectronics on white-collar occupations, Menzies' case studies on information work in Canadian industries are perhaps most indicative. She succinctly summarized the impact in her book *Women and the Chip* (1981a: 63): "In sum, then, the case studies indicate a radical upgrading of information work in Canadian industry, characterized by a diminishing demand for low-level clerical workers, an increasing demand for technical and professional workers, and a growing skills [*sic*], educational, and aptitude disparity between the occupational levels."[4] This situation is brought about by the application of informatics—a combination of computer and tele-communication technologies—into information processing. While this new way of information processing increases the productivity, it reduces the labour content of clerical functions and amalgamates formerly distinct clerical jobs; thus, there is a reduction in low level clerical workers. The banks offer an excellent example for this as indicated in Menzies: "With the teller now keying customer's transaction information directly into the bank's central computer, she not only saves herself a lot of paperwork, but also bypasses certain clerical functions in the data centre" (1981a: 57-58). Glenn and Feldberg's study (N.D.) cited in Chapter 9, reported similar consolidation of clerical functions in an insurance company.

On the other hand, automation of the office not only increases the skill content of the existing managerial staff, it also demands more professionals and technicians with training in computer science, engineering, business administration and other such technical fields. Since the skills that these specialists have, require more than on-the-job training, a new staff is almost entirely hired from outside (Menzies, 1981a: 28).

Another effect of office automation is centralization and the erosion of the authority of middle management. Traditionally, middle management ranks have been the backbone of administration because they get things done. Now the procedures and processes are automated and "the task of management is transformed from getting things done to knowing what to do next. As professionals are replacing company men and women in the senior ranks, traditional middle management is being eclipsed" (Menzies, 1981b: 10). One local bank manager's experience illustrates this point vividly:

> A Canadian local bank manager pointed out that his regional vice-president knows precisely the state of his branch at any point during the day by pressing the appropriate buttons. He can know the state of deposits of the bank, the state of withdrawals, the state of payments of loans, defaults on loans, everything that is put in the data bank, the bank's central place. So I asked the branch manager, "what is your role?" His response was "I'll be damned if I know." (Science Council of Canada, 1980: 11)

The redundancy of middle level managers can be clearly seen from this example. If the application of information technology becomes more diffused (there is every reason to believe that it will be), a shrinkage of middle management is foreseeable (Menzies, 1981b: 10).

In summary, then, while recent technological changes help to increase productivity, they also create job displacement and mobility barriers for clerical workers. Whether or not these changes will cause mass unemployment is, as always, an issue of controversy. We shall address ourselves to this issue at a later point.

(c) Debates over the Adjustments to the Effect of Microelectronic Technology

One of the frequently made suggestions is to retrain those who are displaced. But who is supposed to do the retraining? Private businesses, governments, educational institutions, or the individuals themselves?

Business firms' treatments of their dislocated personnel vary. They range from retraining, redeployment, reduction by attrition, to lay-off. In one study 48 percent of the firms responded to the enquiry reported using retraining programs (Peitchinis, 1979: 129).[5]

Most of these were on-the-job-training programs. The organizations studied by Menzies seemed to be in favour of the other methods. They reduce job openings by attrition. In some cases they transfer dislocated clerks to other departments, sometimes with demotion (Menzies, 1981a:61). "The high turnover rates among female clerks, sales, and service workers facilitate their job restructuring and consolidation efforts" (Menzies, 1981a: 60). In other cases, the displaced employees are simply asked to leave. One official in a large corporate office put it this way (Menzies, 1981b: 11): "They'll be sent to wherever redundant clerks go. I don't know. Unfortunately, that will be women. [But] its a question of social responsibility versus running a company. We may hold jobs for six months rather than lay someone off." So, firms like this one expect to "buy" the necessary talent; that is, to hire university-trained specialists and professionals with high salaries, instead of upgrading the skills of their current personnel.

At least three points can be made from the last example. First, since a large percentage of women are concentrated in a few clerical occupations, they are particularly vulnerable in the latest wave of technological change. Lateral transfers are still an option for rapidly dislocated clerks. As the office is rapidly being transformed by microelectronic technology that option may soon disappear. As a matter of fact, at least in insurance industry as a whole, clerical employment is declining. During the period from 1975 to 1980, 12 percent less women were employed in this industry (Statistics Canada, 1980, cited in Menzies, 1981a: 33).

Second, if the opinion voiced by the official in the corporation mentioned above is at all typical, then the private industry seems to be saying that: "Our primary job is to run our business. As for the social responsibility of not making the unemployment situation worse, our contribution would be very limited—such as holding vacancies for six months."

Third, the lack of effort of retraining the redundant clerks could mean that, from the point of view of the companies, these clerks are not retrainable. This is partially an attitude problem and partially true. Menzies (1981a: 61) summarized sharply the management's attitude toward upgrading their redundant clerical workers into the professional ranks: "You can't make a doctor out of a nurse."

Moreover, the skill gap between the clerical information work and the professional and technical information work is ever widening (Peitchinis, 1978:147; Menzies, 1981a: 61). The existing dual labour market[6] could be rigidified. Even if the companies are willing, the type of short-term, on-the-job training programs offered by most of them are probably inadequate. To bridge the gap, retraining or reeducation of a longer period would be required.

The government and educational institutions have the responsibility of providing training and educational programs. The "diagnoses" of a federal government Task Force on Labour Market Development in the 1980s (Employment and Immigration Canada, 1981) on the government training system and technical training at the post secondary level are generally negative. The Task Force reports that the existing programs are by and large not adequate in meeting the labour market demands in the 1980s. To make the training system with greater flexibility in order to meet projected skill requirements and to respond quickly to new and changing demands, the Task Force recommends, among other things, that the funding system be restructured by a smaller commitment of public resources (including the cut-back of federal funding at the post-secondary level) and a greater financial involvement of the private sector (both students and employers) (Employment and Immigration Canada, 1981: 176-77). Within the sector of post-secondary education, the Task Force also recommends that resources be "modestly reallocated from education, general arts and sciences and social work to engineering, business, economics and technology" (Employment and Immigration Canada, 1981: 154). These recommendations immediately spark debates and evoke concern among educators and students. The federal government is criticized for attempting to control the orientation of education, promoting elitism, and undermining general liberal education. It is quite conceivable that these debates will continue for some time.

III. TECHNOLOGY AND THE WORKER

In the last section our focus was to examine the impact of technology on the occupations structure. Clearly, the impact of technological change is not only on the structural level, but also on the individual level. In previous chapters we have touched upon how technological variations impinge upon the worker. The purpose of this section is to focus our attention on the relationship between work-related technology and the experiences of the worker in a more systematic manner.

There is a vast body of literature on this topic. Numerous books and articles dealing with job satisfaction, alienation, and physical and mental health of workers have been published. The following scheme[7] helps to summarize the major variables and their relationships. First, we discuss the relationship between technology and job characteristics. We then explore the effects of these job characteristics on alienation and job satisfaction.

Figure 10-2
Schematic Relationship Between Variables
and Their Relationships

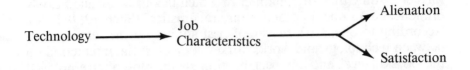

(a) The Impact of Technology on the Nature of Work

Industries vary by the nature of their technological production systems; each industry possesses a characteristic form of production technology. In order to systematically compare the differences between industries, either in organizational structures, work patterns, or job satisfaction, some typology of technologies is required. For instance, Blauner (1964) classified industries into three categories in terms of technology: craft, mass production and continuous processing. Similarly, Faunce (1965, 1968, 1981) formulates his classification scheme according to the three phases of technological evolution in the factory and office: craft production system; mechanized production system; and automated production system. Many other researchers (*e.g.*, Woodward, 1965; Perrow, 1967) have their formulations. However, studies in both the factory (Shepard, 1969, 1971; Form, 1972; Nichols and Armstrong, 1976; Nichols and Beymon, 1977) and the office (Shepard, 1971; Globerman, 1981) found that any given organization or industry may apply different types of technology to various aspects of the total work process. Let us take Riverside, a fertilizer plant of a large multinational corporation, as an example. Its major technology is continuous processing. In this plant there are "scientific workers" and "donkey workers" (Nichols and Armstrong, 1976; Nichols and Beynon, 1977—cited by Miller, 1981:77-79). While the "scientific workers" monitor the dials and adjust the various parts of the production process, the "donkey workers" use their physical labour to load bags of fertilizers. Similarly in some university libraries the serials and cataloguing department may be computerized; but circulation may still be employing manual and simple mechanical methods. We can see from these examples that there are significant internal differences within organizations. Thus, workers in the same organization can be differentially affected depending on the type of technology applied by the unit where they are employed.

One important assumption made by researchers regarding the impact of technology on the nature of work is that "the type of technology employed in the production of goods and services acts as a major determinant of the manner in which labour is divided." They further assume that "the manner in which labour is divided heavily influences a number of other job characteristics" (Shepard, 1977: 4). According to Shepard's survey of past studies on the relationships between technology and work, worker control, social interaction on the job, skill level, and job specialization are the most often employed job characteristics (Shepard, 1977: 4).

There seems to be a general agreement among researchers regarding the impact of technology on the four job characteristics mentioned above. The impact is best illustrated in five sketches by Meissner (1969: 6-10), based on existing case studies (Walker, 1922; Zaleznik, 1956; Walker and Guest, 1952; Popitz, 1957; Whyte, 1956) of widely different technical conditions and their effects on job characteristics. The five cases include:

(1) a maintenance crew of a steel plant in the 1920s;
(2) skilled workers in a machine shop of a small-instrument manu-facturer;
(3) the main assembly line of an automobile plant;
(4) a crew of workers on the blooming mill of a large and integrated steel plant;
(5) and three men working in the control room of a refinery producing aviation gasoline.

The levels of technology range from manual skills to machine opera-ting, to assembly line work, and to continuous processing. The following passage summarizes the relationships between technology and work in these situations (Meissner, 1969: 10):

> They vary by the extent to which work components are performed by men or machines and by the demands made on workers by the production process. They also suggest large differences in the opportunities workers have to participate in a network of relationships of their own making. The steel-plant maintenance men supply the muscle, work with hand tools, and control among themselves all of the work process. On routine operations in the refinery, nearly all the work components are built into the process, from the power of the engines and the integrated design to the monitoring and feedback controls. In the machine shop and on the assembly line, major parts of the work are done by both machines and men. On the assembly line, the work piece is moved automatically and the work is done by hand and hand-controlled tools. In the machine shop, work pieces are moved by hand, but much of the conversion of materials takes place in the machine. The job of the blooming-mill operators is control and coordination. The massive machinery

takes care of the movement and conversion of the work piece. These operators are confined to one position, with their hands on the controls. They communicate almost entirely through material objects, and cooperation is an unyielding technical demand. The auto assemblers move only with a short stretch of the line. Their possibilities for talking are quite limited. In the machine shop there is no technical necessity for cooperation, but plenty of occasion for the exchange of help and advice; on the assembly line there is neither. For the steel-plant maintenance gang and the refinery operators in the control room, technical necessity and voluntary cooperation appear merged. The maintenance men work together as a team. They communicate and coordinate their work directly. The refinery operators can talk to one another, but they are also linked and mutually influenced by the production process represented in the indicators on the wall. They have to keep an eye on the charts. Workers in the machine shop are technically independent. Their attention to the work is intermittent, but must be close. In the blooming mill, interdependence is high, and concentrated attention continuous. The work of an auto assembler is commonly independent of that of the next man, but they are both tied to the work flow on the line. The attention they must pay to the work is close but limited to the few repetitive bits of work assigned to them.

To sum up, regarding the relationship between technology and work in industrial production situations, some empirical generalizations can be made. The higher the level of technology, the greater the number of components of work performed by machines. The higher the degree of mechanization, the higher the degree of job specialization. These two tendencies, in turn, tend to reduce the skill level of workers and worker control.[8] As for the social interaction on the job, it is easier and may be continuous at the two extreme levels,–*i.e.,* craft or manual and automation, while machine operators and assembly line workers find it difficult to communicate or socialize with each other on the job, either because of noise level, distance, or attention requirements of machines. The only area which lacks agreement appears to be whether automation upgrades skill level or not. While some researchers (*e.g.*, Shepard, 1971; Rico, 1967) argue that fragmentation of work downgrades the skill level and is characteristic of mechanized rather than automated processing, others (*e.g.*, Montagna, 1977: 349) suspect that when the monitoring of the processing is replaced by electronic sensing devices, the skill level of workers at automated processing will also be downgraded.

Since the early 1960s, automation of the office has also attracted a great deal of research attention (Hoos, 1962; Baker, 1964; Rico, 1967; Crozier, 1973; Shepard, 1971; Glenn and Feldberg, 1977; Menzies, 1981; Science Council of Canada, 1980). Findings about the effects of EDP (Electronic Data Processing) on clerical work are not conclusive. However, the early argument that the introduction of EDP would upgrade skills, increase worker autonomy and job integration appears not to be supported by recent studies, particularly studies on the effect of microelectronic technology (Glenn and Feldberg, 1977; Menzies, 1981). We have documented how automated information processing systems have changed the content of the work of clerks in Chapter 9. It suffices to summarize the effect of the more sophisticated systems on office workers regarding the job characteristics examined above. "[T]he most striking features of 'paper work' in large organizations are the elaborate subdivision of tasks and the extreme specialization of workers" (Glenn and Feldberg, 1977: 55). The traditional all-round secretaries are disappearing from large offices. Instead, there are pools specializing in typing, telephone answering, appointment scheduling, duplicating, and so on. In addition, many new routine jobs such as transporting tape decks, key punching, data coding and data entry are created. This specialization has the effects of deskilling clerical work and increasing managerial control. Sophisticated microelectronic systems do require higher levels of knowledge and skill to operate. However, as we have pointed out earlier, clerks are rarely upgraded to fill the new jobs created by this requirement. Instead, professional and technical workers, who rank higher on the organizational hierarchy, are recruited from outside.

It should be pointed out that most of these studies were carried out in large offices. The findings cannot be generalized indiscriminately. Smaller offices and all-round clerks still exist in many organizations for sure. However, because of both economic (productivity, efficiency and competitiveness) and political reasons (environmental and energy issues), the diffusion of this new technology appears to be at a faster rate than any that has gone before. Its potential effect cannot be overemphasized.

(b) Alienation and Job Satisfaction

While there seems to be some agreement among researchers regarding the impact of technology upon the nature of work, there is considerable controversy surrounding the question of the effect of technology on alienation and work satisfaction. On the one hand, there are researchers who see technology and job characteristics as crucial to work satisfaction. On the other hand, there are those who think that the effect of technology has been grossly overemphasized.

Since Blauner's *Alienation and Freedom: The Factory Worker and His Industry* (1964) has been the single most influential study on technology, satisfaction and alienation in the recent past, we will start this part of our discussion by summarizing his work.

Blauner's study is based on two basic assumptions which are as follows:

(1) socio-technical systems vary in industries;
(2) socio-technical characteristics produce alienation and dissatis-faction.

If socio-technical characteristics are not present to the same degree or in the same form, then blue-collar workers must experience different degrees of alienation. While he isolated several factors[9] to distinguish industries, his major emphasis was on the impact of technology on the nature of work and the extent of alienation (Blauner, 1964:8). In order to empirically examine the relationship between technology and alienation, he transformed the ideological notion of worker alienation into a scientifically approachable concept. Four dimensions of alienation are differentiated:

(1) powerlessness: the worker cannot control the job activities;
(2) meaninglessness: the worker's contribution to the total product is fractional;
(3) social isolation: the worker does not belong to a close work group;
(4) self-estrangement: the worker has an instrumental orientation toward work.

Blauner selected four industries (printing, textiles, automobile manufacturing, and chemicals processing) to represent four evolutionary stages in the application of technology to industry. His major finding is that workers in craft industry are least alienated; workers are most alienated where mass production technology is employed; and those who work in automated industries also experience a low degree of alienation. To put it graphically, the relationship between alienation and technology is patterned as an inverted U-curve.

Blauner's *Alienation and Freedom* has stimulated considerable research and controversy. Some subsequent studies support his claim; some do not. Most noticeable are a series of studies carried out by Shepard (1969, 1971, 1973) to replicate Blauner's. Shepard interviewed 305 factory workers including craftsmen, assemblers in an automobile industry, and control-room operators in an oil refinery. He found, as Blauner, the same inverted U-curve pattern on all alienation scales. In a study in Israel by Tenne and Mannheim (1977), similar conclusions were reached.

However, the idea that reduced work alienation is always associated with automated technology is challenged in a comparative study of the most and the least automated plants by Susman (1972a,b). He reports an increase of powerlessness, meaningless, normlessness as the degree of automation reaches the highest levels. While not completely disagreeing with Blauner, Susman (1972b: 174) argues that "there is too great a reliance on technology as the sole explanation for worker attitudes towards alienation."

Shepard (1971) and Kirsch and Lengermann (1971) studied large numbers of office workers. Both studies supported Blauner's findings. However, more recent studies (Glenn and Feldberg, 1977; Menzies, 1981:62-63) found that automation of office work reduced the clerks' control over their job activities because the computer silently monitors every action and has the implicit pressure for greater output. Regarding the effects of information on the quality of work, Menzies comments (1981:62):

> The continuing standardization, streamlining, and fragmentation of work function, which was observed in all of the case studies, suggest that clerical work is becoming more like an assembly line. The monitoring feature is also symptomatic: it tends to place quantity of output over sophistication of input, and thereby subtly degrades the scope of the work involved.

Furthermore, job standardization and fragmentation affect interpersonal relations among the clerks. Glenn and Feldberg report: "Within units, external supervision and standardization of activities create contradictory forces. On the one hand, workers are tempted to ease strains through cooperation and solidarity. On the other hand, workers feel vulnerable, which decreases their desire for personal ties. Some women are fearful of being too open" (1967: 62). Although these studies are not specifically focused on alienation, it is not unreasonable to infer that office automation increases two forms of alienation: powerlessness, and social isolation.

If alienation is a rather difficult concept to deal with, job satisfaction is no less complicated. Here, too, there is a debate between those who claim that workers are generally dissatisfied with their jobs and those who say the opposite, although all studies or surveys do not necessarily use technology as an independent variable.

The "blue-collar blues" and the "white-collar woes" are well-known catchy phrases to reflect the dissatisfaction of workers. Numerous books, research reports, and magazine articles have been written on the subject of job boredom, worker frustration, and so on. Books such as *Where Have All the Robots Gone? Workers Dissatisfaction in the 70s* (Sheppard and Herrick, 1972), *The Job Revolution* (Gooding, 1972), *Work in America* (1973), *The Tyranny of Work* (Rinehart, 1975), *Working in Canada* (Johnson, 1975), and *Working: People Talk About What They Do All Day and How they Feel About*

What They Do (Terkel, 1974) have been especially important in bringing the issue of worker dissatisfaction into focus. A twenty-two-day strike by workers at the General Motors plant at Lordstown, Ohio, is perhaps the best illustration of job dissatisfaction produced by mass production technology (Dickson, 1977: 14). The issue of this strike was not pay, benefits, or any of the traditional reasons. The issue was dehumanizing, hard, repetitive and monotonous work. On average 101.6 Chevrolet Vegas were coming off the line every hour. That means each worker on the assembly line was allowed only 36 seconds to perform the same fragmented job 101.6 times per hour!

Absenteeism is generally seen as symptomatic of dissatisfaction with work. It has been estimated that over 282,000 persons, or 2.8 percent of the Canadian labour force do not show for work on any given day. The rates of absence vary depending on the type of work. It was found that production workers are absent more than office personnel, unskilled more than skilled labour and clerical personnel more than managerial and professional personnel (Department of Employment and Immigration, 1980: 63). While the specific focus of this information is not the impact of technology or associated job characteristics upon work satisfaction or dissatisfaction, it is somewhat indicative.

Labour turnover also has been used as an indirect indicator of work dissatisfaction. In a study of the effect of socio-technical systems, Fullan (1970) found continuous processing workers had the lowest rate of turnover; mass production workers, the highest. Fullan concludes that while technology is not the only determinant of worker integration (into the organization) and satisfaction, it is one of the most important facilitators or inhibitors.

In sum, there have been many studies which are directly or indirectly supportive of the basic ideas underlying Blauner's research: namely, job characteristics such as minute job specialization, repetitiveness, low skill requirements, predetermination of tools and techniques, and machine-controlled work pace tend to increase the level of alienation and work dissatisfaction.

However, in addition to studies cited earlier (Susman, 1972a,b; Menzies, 1981a; Glenn and Feldberg, 1977) there are other important studies which produced conflicting findings. The most widely cited ones are perhaps Goldthorpe's studies of auto workers (1966; Goldthorpe *et al.*, 1968). As a matter of fact, Goldthorpe's findings about car assemblers' work attitudes and behaviour are markedly similar to those of other studies (Goldthorpe, 1966: 228-29). The difference lies in his interpretation of these findings, particularly of the instrumental orientation of these workers toward work. In Blauner's perspective, instrumental orientation is the essential meaning of self-estrangement, a form of alienation, and is a result of the technologically associated job characteristics. Goldthorpe argues, however, that instrumental orientation to work is a cause rather than a consequence of the auto assemblers' employment (1966: 229). In other words, the unsatisfying and stressful work time is the price these workers are willing to pay for the higher economic benefits in return. Goldthorpe's evidence is that a sizable proportion of these workers had earlier held more highly skilled or higher status jobs than their present ones (Goldthorpe, 1966: 229-30).

Another critic of the technological explanation of alienation and job dissatisfaction is William Form (1972:1973:1976). He studied auto workers in the United States, Italy, Argentina and India. His findings support the view that "social life of the work situation is strongly conditioned by technology" (Form, 1976: 112). He also found that job satisfaction is relatively high among auto-workers in all of the four countries (ranging from 68 to 87 percent of workers reported as satisfied with their jobs), and it increases with skill level and degree of worker control over work operations (Form, 1976: 126, Table 6.6). While the latter finding is consistent with a long tradition of research, the finding that the majority of auto workers enjoy job satisfaction is drastically different from the results of many previous studies (Chinoy, 1955; Blauner, 1964; Kornhauser, 1965; Sheppard and Herick, 1972). Furthermore, he found that "assemblers complained little about job monotony, and the desire for change in work routines was quite limited." "Most found their jobs quite endurable. The skilled liked them for their interest, and the less skilled both interest and money. Whatever their reasons, auto-workers were not seeking to escape the factory" (Form, 1976: 136).

What conclusions can we draw from the above discussion? First of all, the technological explanation of alienation and satisfaction approximates to technological determinism. Form and Goldthorpe's studies move us away from this danger. As Hall (1975: 325-26) has pointed out, the technology utilized by an organization provides the social and physical parameters in which the worker interacts; but technology alone does not determine satisfaction or dissatisfaction. Many other factors may affect an individual's work satisfaction. Expectation is one of the crucial influential factors (Hall, 1975: 326). Many researchers have reported that an increasing number of workers expect interesting or challenging work (*Work in America*, 1973: 13; Burnstein, *et al.*, 1975: 29; Borow, 1973; Gottlieb, 1974). As there is a gap between what is expected and what is offered, we may expect more dissatisfied workers.[11]

In addition to worker expectations, age, education, income, unionization, occupation history, management policy, general conditions of the labour market, the social and cultural milieu from which the workers come[12] are all possible contributing factors to worker satisfaction or dissatisfaction.

Secondly, many of the studies in this area are flawed by theoretical and methodological problems. For example, Goldthorpe's contention that instrumental work orientation is the reason for individuals to seek employment in the high paying automobile industry is at best an association between past employment (more highly skilled jobs) and current employment. Methodologically, his research design did not allow him to test the direction of causation of the two factors (Shepard, 1977:10).

Many of the concepts (e.g., alienation and satisfaction) involved in this area of study are difficult to define and measure. Conflicting fidings are almost expected. Social sciences are still young in their development. Our knowledge will be enhanced as researchers are continually making efforts to improve their theoretical and methodological tools.

IV. TECHNOLOGY AND THE FUTURE OF WORK

At the outset it should be said that sociologists would do well not to predict the future. However, some insights and careful speculations on what may be in store for us are not entirely unwarranted. With this in mind, we shall, in this section, comment on the impact of technological change on (a) organizational authority; (b) quality of working life; and (c) the problem of employment. These comments lead to a discussion of possible new meanings of work and employment.

(a) Organizational Authority: Centralization and Decentralization

Early in this chapter we cited an example to show how centralization of information has eroded the authority of middle management in banks. The emergence of this structural change in organizations is one of the consequences of the development of the microprocessor. This new technology makes the transmission of information so fast and so inexpensive, much of the difficulty of centralization and communication within the organizational hierarchy is removed. Even more important for centralization to be more efficient is that "so much can be programmed in advance that the overload of decision-making at the centre can be radically reduced" (Cherns, 1980:708).[12]

Microelectronic technology is also able to facilitate decentralization because it makes the provision of information much easier. The problem in a centralized system is to know the needs and the difficulties that the local levels have; the problem of a decentralized system is to provide the periphery with information "about how decisions at local levels affect the attainment of over-all goals and how they affect the functioning of other points on the periphery" (Cherns, 1980:708). Again an automated system enabled by the microprocessor makes it possible to provide all who are involved with a total picture of the functioning mechanization if the whole system and the operations of each local point at the same time.

Further, Cherns argues that "the more uncertain the environment and the more it differs from point to point on the periphery, the greater the chance of the decentralized over the centralized approach" (p. 709). Besides, the microprocessor makes centralization less defensible because it makes the denial of information to the local level more difficult. Thus, the new technology offers possibilities. Whether decentralization will be a more prevalent approach or not, however, depends on the political will of the top management, the degree of opposition against central control, and the variability of the environment.

(b) The Quality of Working Life (QWL)

As we have discussed the Quality of Working Life Movement in Chapter 8, here we shall only deal with the relevance of microelectronic technology to the movement. As it has been pointed out, the philosophy of QWL is rooted in strong humanistic values.[13] While QWL does not deny economic imperatives, it "shifts the emphasis away from short-term efficiency and hierarchical accountability to one of long-term growth and widespread individual responsibility" (Johnston *et al.*, 1978: 1-2). Thus, its objectives focus on both the improvement of organizational effectiveness *and* the increase in job satisfaction. It seems only logical that quality of working life programs emphasize the decentralization of control and decision making to lower level, often autonomous or semiautonomous groups (Cherns, 1980: 707). It is apparent from the discussion earlier that the new technology can facilitate the realization of QWL programs, if organizations choose to adopt such programs. Unfortunately, empirical evidence seems to prove that a higher degree of centralized control is happening in organizations where office automation is most advanced (see Section III). If top management does not take the initiative to introduce quality of working life programs, the hope would have to lie in labour unions to apply pressure on the employer.

However, whether or not unions will wholeheartedly embrace the concept of quality of working life as a means of sharing the organizational resources of power remains to be seen. Currently, most Canadian unions seems to be more occupied with job retention and job creation than anything else.[14]

(c) Employment versus Unemployment

The debate on the impact of technological change on employment is not new. Since the beginning of the Industrial Revolution, with the widespread application of technology, there have been reactions to the process of change. The pessimistic view is that technology will lead to the permanent displacement of human labour. It is understandable that this view periodically attracts considerable attention. The optimistic view is that while there are definitely short-term job losses, a new technology will create more new jobs than it displaces in the long run. In the recent past, the debate was over the effect of automation during the 1950s and 1960s. The term generally referred to the installation of early generations of computers as well as extensions of mechanization and modernization programs. As history has it, the bleak predictions of technological unemployment did not come true. Thus, after commenting on the Freedman Report, an economist triumphantly concluded:

> If we can divide analysts of the relationship between technology and employment into "optimists" and "pessimists", it is clear that the optimists carried the day on the automation debates of the 1950s (Smith, 1980: 165).

We hear similar comments made elsewhere on how wrong previous predictions about technological unemployment were.[15]

In the current debate over the effect of the microelectronic revolution, again, there are two opposing lines of argument. On the one hand we hear the strong warning about "the collapse of work" (Jenkins and Sherman, 1979; Barron and Curnow, 1979; Norman, 1981). On the other hand, we have the cautious optimism as in the case of Professor Smith (1980) and the comforting assurance from Professor Peitchinis (1980, 1982), both economists. Smith's optimism comes from his claim that unemployment and technological change are unrelated. Many factors lead to unemployment, he claims, "but an autonomous increase in the rate of technological change is unlikely to be one of them" (Smith, 1980: 167).

Peitchinis' optimism, as he claims, is based on historical record. He takes the view that, in view of the respective social, economic and technostructures within which they were introduced, microelectronic technologies are not different in their impact for society and employment than were all previous major technologies (Peitchinis, 1982:6). Not only was there no massive unemployment subsequent to the first introduction of computer technology in the 1950s, instead, total employment increased in the following decades. The adoption of microelectronics, too, will have no negative effects on employment, even if this new technology has pervasive characteristics. However, Professor Peitchinis does recognize that the balance between the jobs displaced by the new technology and the new occupations and new jobs it creates would still be increasing involuntary unemployment (p. 29). What is the rescue then? The rescue lies in what he calls "the hours of work adjustment." Specifically, this means the decreasing number of hours that labour force participants actually work and the increasing number of employees, who opt for early retirement. Since those who have jobs work fewer hours in a week and fewer years in their lifetime, more individuals would be employed. He, therefore, optimistically concludes: "As long as production and total output continues to increase, and adjustments to hours worked and work-load continue to be effected, there is no reason not to expect a continuing capacity to provide full employment" (p. 30).

Indeed, the impact of technological change on employment is not easy to predict exactly, because many factors are involved. However, we disagree with the thesis that technological change and unemployment are unrelated. After all, technical innovations are labour-saving devices. Even if one concedes that changes caused by the introduction of microelectronics are not drastically different from those resulting from other technologies, there is still the difficult problem of adjustment in the transitional period. To say that more jobs will be created in the long run is small comfort for those who are caught in the transition. Society as a whole benefits from the high productivity induced by technological change, "but often at the expense of imposing transient costs on a few people" (Simon, 1977: 1188). This point cannot be overemphasized.

Further, it is true that while new technology such as microelectronics displaces labour, it also gives rise to new manufacturing and service industries which in turn create new jobs. However, being largely a branch-plant economy, we have high propensity to import hardware instead of producing them ourselves. The extent to which Canada could benefit from the new possibilities, therefore, is likely limited (Warskett, 1982:27).

Given these considerations, not only do we need continuing institutional arrangements which facilitate adjustment to technological change and a political will to transform our economy, some writers suggest that we also need to change our traditional meaning of work, a point to which we now turn.

A great mass of well-known research on Western societies has established that work is the most highly-valued activity. It not only symbolizes status and involves the satisfaction of an individual, one's value is virtually determined by one's work. Work is so important that people are reluctant to confess that they dislike their work, for to admit to hating one's job is almost to admit to hating one's life (Blauner, 1960; Goldthorpe, 1968:11; Anthony, 1977: 274). This view of work has served the industrial society with labour-intensive technologies well. It makes the high standard of living that is enjoyed by people in industrialized societies possible. Without it the goods and services that make up the standard of living could not have been produced. Now a new technology-microelectronics has been developed and its application is being introduced into increasingly wider areas of work. The difference in the new technology is that it allows for goods and services to be produced using a far lower level of labour and increases in their supply will not produce anything like the corresponding increases in employment. When the new, capital-intensive industry cannot absorb the displaced workers and new entrants, unemployment becomes a problem. Many remedies have been suggested. Expansion of employment is the most frequently—and also the traditionally—presented and demanded solution. Somewhat less frequently mentioned are the isolationist measures to avoid the export of jobs. In an increasingly competitive world market, expansion is not easy to achieve. Isolationist measures are only self-defeating. These traditional methods are, therefore, no solutions. Many writers suggest that what is needed is a fundamental change of the old notions underlying the work ethic (*e.g.*, Cherns, 1980: 712-16; Jenkins and Sherman, 1979: 158-73; Anthony, 1977: 300). Cherns argues that there should be a distinction between work and employment. He asks: "Is to be out of work the same thing as to be unemployed?" "Why is it so great to be employed? Work may be ennobling, but is not employment demeaning?" (Cherns, 1980:713). However, because in our societies we have confused work with employment and we rely on employment as a convenient means of distributing resources (material and moral), "we would rather see people idle on a payroll than busy without pay" (Cherns, 1980:713). There are only two categories of people in our society: workers and dependents. Workers are those who are employed and, thus, full citizens. Dependents are those who are preparing for employment (*e.g.*, students), and retired from employment (pensioners). This should not and cannot be the case in postindustrial societies.

However, Cherns does not suggest a utopia of leisure society. Nor does he provide us with a set of clearly-designed mechanisms to substitute employment as a resource-distributing device. One thing which seems certain is that in the future society Cherns envisages, the value of employment will be greatly weakened and organized employment drastically contracted. As for specific patterns, he expects that they will emerge in the process of transition. "Whether a period of employment will become a form of public service expected but not demanded from each citizen or whether it will become the lot of a new aristocracy of a new helotry depends upon the system of values which will emerge" (Cherns, 1980: 714).

Other suggestions include job-sharing (two or more persons share the same job), work-sharing (everyone works for a reduced number of hours but more people can have work), educational sabbaticals for all workers, and guaranteed annual income (Jenkins and Sherman, 1979: 163-72). Peter Watson's notion of "temporary work" is similar to Cherns' periodical employment. In his estimate, temporary work will occupy nearly two-thirds of the British work force by the year 2000 (cited in Anthony, 1977: 300). By temporary work Watson means people will have frequent intervals between jobs. "[A]t the moment we call it unemployment, but we shall probably need a new word. What we will have to get used to, however, is the fact that a person's job will no longer be the central factor in his or her life" (cited by Anthony, 1977: 300). This is not really entirely new. As far back as 1956, Dubin, in his study of "Central Life Interests," found that the great majority of industrial workers derived their major satisfaction in life off the job. The difference is that, in the microelectronic technology dominated society, more people will be further detached from work. Whether we will be able to benefit from the possibilities offered by the new technology will depend on how we manage it. Technology is a choice, not a determinant.

Notes

1. Most definitions of technology involve a material and nonmaterial dimension. The nonmaterial side of technology refers to the knowledge and technical skills involved in producing some product or service. The material dimension of technology refers to the mechanical devices (tools, machines, energy sources) used in changing "raw materials" into some goods or services (see Blauner, 1964:6; Perrow, 1967:195; Dubin, 1968:467; Smelser, 1976:96).

2. Professor Peitchinis uses two definitions for industrial and commercial enterprises respectively. For the former, technological change is defined as "change which involves the use of new and substitute products and services, new methods of materials handling, as well as new or modified production techniques and processes." For the latter, it is defined as "change which involves the use of new or more efficient information handling systems, the use of new and substitute products and services, new uses of computer control in transactions, as well as the mechanization of services previously provided mainly be personnel." (Peitchinis, 1978:10)
3. For a more comprehensive discussion of the rate of technological development, see Faunce, 1981: 46-57.
4. The discussion here is mainly based on information offered in Menzies, 1981a. She did four case studies in four different industries: transportation, insurance, banking and supermarket.
5. We should take notice, however, the return rate of Peitchinis' questionnaires was only 8.7% (1979:13).
6. For a discussion of dual labour market, see Doeringer and Piore, 1971; Bibb and Form, 1977.
7. This scheme is an adaptation of Jon Shepard's schematic summary of the relationships between technology, alienation, and job satisfaction. See Shepard, 1977:2.
8. It should be noted that some writers argue that technological changes upgrade skills (Parsons, 1968; Jaffe and Froomkin, 1968; and Bell, 1973). In simple form, this argument says that technological change increases productivity and in doing so requires a broader variety of skills and higher level of average skills from the work force. Furthermore, automation minimizes routined work, and increases worker control and responsibility. Proponets of the upgrading thesis cite the increase in educational levels and compositional changes in the occupational structure as supporting evidence. However, these studies used aggregate data to examine societal variations in skill. They tend to ignore variations at the micro level. For systematization of the literature on the effects of technology on skills, see Spenner, 1983.
9. Other factors are division of labour, social organization and economic structure (Blauner, 1964:8).
10. Even working in industries where continuous process technology is utilized can be boring for some workers, because the constant monitoring of dial panels is not all that interesting, even though when there is nothing else other than monitoring to do it means production is going on smoothly.
11. For example, Form found that work satisfaction (as opposed to survival) was a more salient expectation in more highly industrialized countries (1976: 117-21).

12. This discussion is based on Professor Cherns' analysis of impact of microelectronics technology on centralization and decentralization in organizations (1980: 708-10).

13. Cherns states that there has been a shift in values towards "post-materialism." The post-materialistic values represent a complex of attitudes towards economic, political, and social issues. The most prominent one is "an insistent humanitarianism and urge towards the exploration and fulfillment of self" (see Cherns, 1980: 706). Postmaterialistic values appear to be manifested among Canadian workers, too. In a national survey, respondents were forced to choose between interesting or challenging work and higher pay. Fully two-thirds of all respondents opted for interesting or challenging work (see Burnstein *et al.*, 1975: 29).

14. There are signs that some unions are quite concerned with QWL related issues such as involvement in decision making. Unions of postal workers, teachers, and hospital workers are pertinent examples. For the latter see Brunet (1981).

15. For example, UK government's Central Policy Review Staff commented in 1978 (cited by Cockcroft, 1980: 689):

> The predictions made...now...were being made 20 or so years ago about earlier generations of computers. The UK Civil Service has used computers for a number of years and a study of the employment effects show how wrong those predictions were!

Suggested Readings

Blauner, Robert
    1964. *Alienation and Freedom: The Factory Worker and His Industry.* Chicago: University of Chicago Press.

Burstein, M., N. Tienhaara, P. Hewson, and B. Warrander
    1975. *Canadian Work Values: Findings of a Work Ethic Survey and a Job Satisfaction Survey.* Ottawa: Department of Manpower and Immigration.

Cherns, A.B.
    1980. "Speculations on the Social Effects of New Microelectronics Technology." *International Labour Review, 119(6):* 705-21.

Cockroft, David
    1980. "New Office Technology and Employment." *International Labour Review, 119(6):* 689-704.

Faunce, William A.
1981. *Problems of An Industrial Society.* 2nd ed. New York: McGraw-Hill.

Form, William H.
1976. Blue-Collar Stratification: Autoworkers in Four Countries, Princeton, N.J.: Princeton University Press.

Goldthorpe, J.H., D. Lockwood, F. Beckhofer, and J. Platt
1968. *The Affluent Worker: Industrial Attitudes and Behaviour.* Cambridge, England: Cambridge University Press.

Johnston, Carl P., Mark Alexander, and Jacquelin Robin
1978. *Quality of Working Life: The Idea and its Application.* Labour Canada.

Menzies, Heather
1981a. *Women and the Chip: Case Studies of the Effects of Informatics on Employment in Canada.* Montreal: The Institute for Research on Public Policy.

Peitchinis, Stephen G.
1982. "Microelectronic Technology and Employment: Micro and Macro Effects," in David Neice, Laureen Snider, and Elia Zureik (eds.): *Workshop on Microelectronics—Information Technology and Canadian Society.* Kingston: Queen's University.

Shepard, Jon M.
1977. "Technology, Alienation and Job Satisfaction," in Alex Inkeles (ed.): *Annual Review of Sociology, Vol. 3*: 1-21.

Warskett, George
1982. "The Revolution in Microelectronics: Prospect for Social Transformation," in David Neice, Laureen Snider, and Elia Zureik (eds.): *Workshop on Microelectronics—Information Technology and Canadian Society.* Kingston.: Queen's University.

Chapter 11

Summary and Conclusions

The subject matter of sociology is the web of relationships which exist between people and the patterns of social organizations within which people work and live. It is from this general sociological perspective that work in Canada has been examined in this text. Analytically, we treated work from three points of view: that of the person as worker, that of the organization as the workplace, and that of technology which significantly affects both the worker and the workplace. These three areas have been analyzed with two specific theoretical approaches—social psychological and structural. Let us summarize the major themes under the following three headings: the worker, the workplace, and technology.

I. THE WORKER

Work looms large in life. Most people spend the majority of their lifetime at work. We learn to work by both formal (*e.g.*, schooling and apprenticeship) and informal ways (*e.g.*, in the family setting and on-the-job training). Through these processes, work attitudes are shaped, work motivations forged, work habits cultivated, and knowledge and skills acquired.

Most Canadians have been told at one time or another that "The occupational world is wide open. You can do whatever you want to do." This is more a myth than a reality. Canadians do have some freedom to choose their occupations. However, people with different individual and socio-economic characteristics have different degrees of freedom. In other words, opportunities are not randomly distributed, they are structured. Those who are from high socio-economic backgrounds not only have aspirations for high level occupations, they also have a high probability of realizing those aspirations.

Occupational careers have different paths or patterns. What factors contribute to the shaping of these patterns? Here, too, we see both the social psychological and structural forces that are at work.

Subjectively, the worker is an active participant in the shaping of his/her own career. Personal attributes and interpersonal dynamics serve as critical contingencies that may modify or redirect a person's career. Objectively, however, organizational and structural features of given occupations set the boundaries for individual efforts. The scope of opportunities and the criteria and sequence for advancement are closely associated with these features.

Ascending the level of analysis a notch higher, we examined what groups of workers fare better or worse in the world of work in Canada. Selectively, we have dealt with two topics: occupational mobility through generations and the status of women and the ethnic groups with a focus on the Natives. Methodological difficulties outstanding, some generalizations about status inheritance can be made. Canada is not a one class society. Nor does equality of opportunity exist in Canada. It is our ideal, but not yet a reality. The one general conclusion which emerged from our analysis of many studies of social mobility in Canada is that varying degrees of social inheritance exist in all levels of our society. However, Canada is probably no more ascriptive or no less achievement-orientated than most other industrial capitalist societies.

Despite the fact that half of the women of working age participate in the labour force and two-fifths of the members of the labour force are women, what Armstrong and Armstrong said remains true: the work that women do tends "to be low in skill, low in pay, and low in prestige" (1978). To be sure, women as a group have made some gains in a number of ways. The proportions of women in some professions (*e.g.*, managerial, etc.) are substantially higher now than a decade ago. An increasing number of women are enrolling in professional schools. More provinces are attempting to make "equal pay for work of equal value" laws. Pensions for part-time work have been proposed by the federal government. Most importantly, more women are aware of their rights and are prepared to struggle for equal treatment. However, more progress has to be made before the structural position of women in the labour market is changed.

As far as the status of ethnic groups in the world of work goes, John Porter's thesis of the vertical mosaic seems to stand the test of time. Among all ethnic groups, the Native groups fare the worst. Language barriers, cultural differences, educational gaps, and, most significant, systematic discrimination are the major issues. Some signs of change are present, although they are not analyzed in this volume. The most noticeable seems to be the emergence of competent and vocal leaders of these groups.

II. THE WORKPLACE

Most Canadian workers are employees of organizations. Two out of every five members of the labour force belong to labour unions. Organizations and unions are thus important settings of work in Canada. Complex organizations are purposive social systems. They are created to achieve specific goals of work. These large-scale organizations are perceived as dynamic systems located in a multifaceted environment instead of closed systems operating in a vacuum.

Two dimensions of organizations have been examined. The formal structure specifies the jurisdictions of each unit and regulates the behaviour of groups and individual participants. The informal structure constitutes the dynamics of the operation. The informal organization not only provides means of resolving the conflicts and contradictions created by the formal structure, but also serves as a counterforce which, to a certain extent, protects individuals from organizational control.

If the informal structure is a "natural" development in formal organizations and one of its functions is to resolve conflict or generate satisfaction in otherwise alienative or meaningless work lives, unions are purposively-formulated bodies to serve as a countervailing force to the employing organizations of their members. However, unions are reactive in nature. Because the imbalance of power between management and labour is so massive, unions can only redress part of it. Thus, the labour union is a limited countervailing force, although it is perhaps the best protection the workers have and sometimes it appears very powerful. The reactive nature of the union is also manifested in its patterns of change. When job content, work structure, and political and economic environments change, the labour union resists or adjusts to, but does not initiate, those changes.

III. TECHNOLOGY

The impact of technology and technological change is pervasive. We have discussed technology as it affects the total occupational structure throughout the process of industrialization in Canada. A dramatic case is the change of agricultural occupations. Between 1941 and 1981, the Canadian population increased almost three times, while the proportion of agricultural occupations in the labour force has shrunk dramatically. This proportion, in 1981, was only about one-seventh its size in 1941. The greatest contributor to this phenomenon is, of course, technology.

Since occupational structure is closely related to the social structure, stratification and mobility are affected as new occupations are created by technology and find their niche in the stratification system and as others become obsolete or decline in their market value. Specific research focusing on this topic is still meager in Canada.

Technological considerations are a major concern in our discussions of work satisfaction and dissatisfaction. Particular attention was given to the impact of microelectronic technology in our extensive review of relevant literature. A major conclusion which can be drawn from our discussion is that one of the most significant sources of work dissatisfaction is not so much physical technology (*i.e.*, machines) *per se* as the way it is used. Machines are often adopted with the purpose of increasing management control. This approach affords the majority of rank and file little scope for discretion, let alone self-actualization, in work. It gives rise to the issue of social technology—people's organization of other people. We suggest that more analytical attention on the part of social scientists be directed to this issue.

We have also posited some speculations on technology and the future of work. We shall not go so far as proclaiming that work will be collapsed because of the advancement of technology. However, along with many other writers, we do think that many signs indicating the requirement of a fundamental change of the meaning of work are present. The polarization of the occupational structure (*i.e.*, a highly specialized elite and a deskilled rank and file), structural unemployment and the increasing demand of leisure are some of the major ones. Exactly what might evolve, no one can predict for sure. However, the following scenario is not entirely beyond imagination: work and employment are differentiated. While employment becomes a public-orientated intermittent undertaking, work becomes a personal-orientated, lifelong pursuit.

Bibliography

Abella, Irving M.
1973. *Nationalism, Communism and Canadian Labour: The CIO, The Communist Party, and the Canadian Congress of Labour 1935-1956.* Toronto: University of Toronto Press.

Abu-Laban, Sharon and Baha Abu-Laban
1977. "Women and the Aged as Minority Groups: A Critique." *The Canadian Review of Sociology and Anthropology, 14(1)*:103-16.

Acker, Joan
1973. "Women and Social Stratification: A Case of Intellectual Sexism." *American Journal of Sociology, 78(January)* :936-45.

Aiken, Michael and Jerald Hage
1966. "Organizational Alienation: A Comparative Analysis." *American Sociological Review 31(August)*:497-507.

Aldrich, Howard E.
1972. "Technology and Organizational Structure: A Reexamination of the Findings of the Aston Group." *Administrative Science Quarterly, 17(March)*:26-43.

Anderman, S.D.(ed.)
1967. *Trade Unions and Technological Change: A Research Report Submitted to the 1966 of Congress the Swedish Confederation of Trade Unions.* London: Allen & Unwin.

Anderson, Nels
1964. *Dimensions of Work: The Sociology of a Work Culture.* New York: David McKay Co.

Anthony, P.D.
1977. *The Ideology of Work.* London: Tavistock Publications.

Argyris, Chris
1957. *Personality and Organization.* New York: Harper and Row.

Argyris, Chris
1962. *Interpersonal Competence and Organizational Effectiveness.* Homewood, Ill.: Dorsey Press.

Armstrong, Pat and Hugh Armstrong
1978. *The Double Ghetto: Canadian Women and Their Segregated Work.* Toronto: McClelland and Stewart.

Association of Canadian Medical Colleges
1980. *Canadian Medical Education Statistics.*

Astin, Helen S.
   1968. "Stability and Change in the Career Plans of Ninth Grade Girls."
   Personnel and Guidance Journal, 46 (June):961-66.
Atchley, Robert
   1976a. *The Sociology of Retirement*. Cambridge, Mass.: Schenkman.
Atchley, Robert
   1976b. "Selected Social and Psychological Differences Between Men
   and Women in Later Life." *Journal of Gerontology, 31(March)* :204-11.
Bairstow, Frances and Leonard Sayles
   1975. "Bargaining Over Work Standards by Professional Unions," in
   Collective Bargaining & Productivity. Madison, Wis.: Industrial Rela-
   tions Research Association.
Baker, E.F.
   1964. *Technology and Women's Work*. New York: Columbia University
   Press.
Baker, Maureen and Mary Ann Robeson
   1981. "Trade Union Reactions to Women Workers and Their Con-
   cerns." *The Canadian Journal of Sociology, 6(1)*:19-32.
Barnard, Chester
   1938. *The Functions of the Executive*. Cambridge, Mass.: Harvard
   University Press.
Barnes, Samuel H.
   1961. "The Evolution of Christian Trade Unions in Quebec," in Aranka
   Kovacs (ed.): *Readings in Canadian Labour*. Toronto: McGraw-Hill.
Barron, Iaan and Ray C. Curnow
   1979. *The Future with Microelectronics: Forecasting the Effects of
   Information Technology*. London: Frances Printer Ltd.
Baxter, E.H.
   1976. "Children's and Adolescents' Perceptions of Occupational Pres-
   tige." *Canadian Review of Sociology and Anthropology, 13(May)*:229-
   38.
Beattie, Christopher
   1975. *Minority Men in a Majority Setting*. Toronto: McClelland and
   Stewart.
Becker, Howard S.
   1952. "The Career of the Chicago Public School Teacher." *American
   Journal of Sociology, 57(March)* :470-77.
Becker, Howard S., Blanche Geer, Everett G. Hughes, and Anselm Strauss
   1961. *Boys in White: Student Culture in Medical School*. Chicago:
   University of Chicago Press.
Becker, Howard S., Blanche Geer, David Riesman and Robert S. Weiss (eds.)
   1968. *Institutions and the Person: Papers Presented to Everett C.
   Hughes*. Chicago: Aldine.
Bell, Daniel
   1973. *The Coming of Post-Industrial Society*. New York: Basic Books.

Bendix, Reinhard
 1956. *Work and Authority in Industry: Ideologies of Management in the Course of Industrialization*. New York: Wiley.
Bendix, Reinhard and Seymour Martin Lipset (eds.)
 1966. *Class, Status and Power: Social Stratification in Comparative Perspective*. 2nd ed. New York: The Free Press.
Bendix, Reinhard and Seymour Martin Lipset
 1967. *Class, Status, and Power*. New York: Free Press.
Bennis, W.G., K.D. Benne, and R. Chin (eds.)
 1976. *The Planning of Change*. New York: Holt, Rinehart, and Winston.
Berg, Ivar
 1979. *Industrial Sociology*. Englewood Cliffs, New Jersey: Prentice-Hall.
Berger, Peter
 1964. "Some General Observations of the Problem of Work," in Peter Berger (ed.): 1964. *The Human Shape of Work: Studies in the Sociology of Occupations.* Chicago: Henry Regnery.
Berger, Peter L. and Brigette Berger
 1972. *Sociology: A Biographical Approach*. New York: Basic Books.
Bernard, Paul
 1970. *Structures et Pouvoirs de la Federation des Travailleurs du Quebec*. Ottawa: Queen's Printer.
Bibb, Robert and William H. Form
 1977. "The Effects of Industrial, Occupational, and Sex Stratification on Wages in Blue-collar Markets." *Social Forces, 55*:974-96.
Blau, Peter M.
 1955. *The Dynamics of Bureaucracy: a Study of Interpersonal Relations in Two Government Agencies*. Chicago: University of Chicago Press.
Blau, Peter M.
 1968. "The Hierarchy of Authority in Organizations." *American Journal of Sociology, 73(January)*:453-67
Blau, Peter M.
 1970. "A Formal Theory of Differentiation in Organizations." *American Sociological Review, 35(April)*:201-18.
Blau, Peter M. and Otis Dudley Duncan
 1967. *The American Occupational Structure*. New York: John Wiley.
Blau, Peter M. and Richard A. Schoenherr
 1971. *The Structure of Organizations*. New York: Basic Books.
Blau, Peter M. and W. Richard Scott
 1962. *Formal Organizations: a Comparative Approach*. San Francisco: Chandler.
Blau, Peter M., Wolf V. Heydebrand, and Robert E. Stauffer
 1966. "The Structure of Small Bureaucracies." *American Sociological Review, 31(April)*:179-91.

Blau, Zena Smith
 1973. *Old Age in a Changing Society*. New York: New Viewpoints.
Blauner, Robert
 1960. "Work Satisfaction and Industrial Trends in Modern Society," in
 W. Galenson and S.M. Lipset (eds.): *Labour and Trade Unionism: An
 Interdisciplinary Reader.* New York: Wiley.
Blauner, Robert
 1964. *Alienation and Freedom: The Factory Worker and His Industry.*
 Chicago: University of Chicago Press.
Blishen, Bernard R.
 1958. "The Construction and Use of an Occupational Class Scale."
 Canadian Journal of Economics and Political Science 24(November)
 :519-31.
Blishen, Bernard R.
 1967. "A Socio-economic Index for Occupations in Canada." *Canadian Review of Sociology and Anthropology*, 4:41-53.
Blishen, Bernard R. and Hugh A. McRoberts
 1976. "A Revised Socioeconomic Index for Occupations in Canada."
 Canadian Review of Sociology and Anthropology, *13 (Feb.)*: 71-79.
Blishen, Bernard R. and William K. Carroll,
 1978. "Sex Differences in a Socioeconomic Index for Occupations in
 Canada." *Canadian Review of Sociology and Anthropology*, 15(3):352-
 71.
Bloom, S.W.
 1973. *Power and Dissent in the Medical School*. New York: The Free
 Press.
Borow, Henry
 1973. "Shifting Postures Toward Work: A Tracing." *American Vocational Journal*, *48(January)*:28-29, 108.
Boyd, M., J. Goyder, F. Jones, H. McRoberts, P. Pineo, and J. Porter
 1981. "Status Attainment in Canada: Findings of the Canadian Mobility Study." *The Canadian Review of Sociology and Anthropology*,
 18:(5):657-73.
Braude, Lee
 1975. *Work and Workers*. New York: Praeger.
Braverman, Harry
 1974. *Labour and Monopoly Capital: The Degradation of Work in the
 Twentieth Century*. New York: Monthly Review Press.
Breton, Raymond
 1972. *Social and Academic Factors in the Career Decision of Canadian
 Youth: A Study of Secondary School Students*. Ottawa: Manpower and
 Immigration.
Brim, O.G.
 1966. "Socialization Through the Life Cycle," in O. G. Brim and S.
 Wheeler (eds.): *Socialization After Childhood*. New York: Wiley.

Brim, O. G. and S. Wheeler
    1966. *Socialization After Childhood*. New York: Wiley.
Brinkerhoff, Merlin B. and David J. Corry
    1976. "Structural Prisons: Barriers to Occupational and Educational Goals in a Society of 'Equal' Opportunity," *International Journal of Comparative Sociology*, *17*:261-74.
Britton, John N.H. and James Gilmore
    1978. The Weakest Link: A Technological Perspective in Canadian Industrial Development. Ottawa: Science Council of Canada. Background Study 43. Supply and Services.
Brown, Martin
    1977. *Physicians in Nova Scotia: Growth, Change and Mobility, 1967-73*. Halifax: Dalhousie University.
Brueckel, Joyce E., *et al.*
    1955. "Effects on Morale of Infantry Team Replacement and Individual Replacement Systems." *Sociometry, 18 (December)*:331-41.
Brunet, Lucie
    1982. "Quality of Working Life in Hospitals," *Quality of Working Life, The Canadian Scene, 4(1)*:12-16.
Bucher, Rue
    1970. "Social Process and Power in a Medical School," in Mayer Zald (ed.): *Power and Organizations*. Nashville: Vanderbilt University Press.
Bucher, Rue and Joan Stelling
    1969. Characteristics of Professional Organizations." *Journal of Health and Social Behaviour, 10 (March)*:3-15.
Bucher, Rue and Joan Stelling
    1977. *Becoming Professional*. Beverly Hills: Sage Publications.
Bucher, Rue and Anselm L. Strauss
    1961. "Professions in Process." *American Journal of Sociology, 66(January)*:325-34.
Buhler, Charlotte
    1935. "The Curve of Life as Studied in Biographies." *Journal of Applied Psychology, 19*:405-09.
Burchinal, Lee G.
    1962. *Career Choices of Rural Youth in a Changing Society*. Minneapolis: Minnesota Agr. Exp. Sta. N.C.R.P. 142.
Burstein, M., N. Tienhaara, P. Hewson, and B. Warrander
    1975. *Canadian Work Values: Findings of a Work Ethic Survey and a Job Satisfaction Survey*. Ottawa: Department of Manpower and Immigration Canada.
Canada. Census Office
    1881. *Census of Canada, Vol. II*. Ottawa: MacLean, Roger and Company (Printer)*.
Canada. Census Office
    1891. *Census of Canada, Vols. I and II*. Ottawa: S.E. Dawson (Printer).

Canada. Census Office
   1901. *Fourth Census of Canada*. Ottawa: S.E. Dawson (Printer).
Canada. Department of Employment and Immigration
   1979. *The Development of an Employment Policy for Indian, Inuit and Metis People*. Ottawa: Employment and Immigration.
Canada. Department of Employment and Immigration
   1980. *Affirmative Action: What's It All About?* Ottawa: Employment and Immigration.
Canada. Department of Employment and Immigration
   1980. *The Work Importance Study in the Canadian Context*. Ottawa: Employment and Immigration.
Canada. Department of Employment and Immigration Canada
   1981. *Labour Market Development in the 1980s: A Report of the Task Force on Labour Market Development Prepared for the Minister of Employment and Immigration as a Contribution to a Process of Consultation with Provincial Governments and Organizations Representing Different Elements in the Private Sectors*. Ottawa: Employment and Immigration.
Canada. Department of Indian Affairs and Northern Development
   1980. *Indian Conditions: A Survey*. Ottawa: Indian Affairs and Northern Development.
Canada. Department of Industry, Trade and Commerce
   Annual Report of Corporations and Labour Unions Returns Act, Part II - Labour Unions. 1970, 1971, 1972, 1973, 1974, 1975, 1976, 1977, 1978, 1979. Ottawa: Statistics Canada.
Canada. Department of Labour, Economics and Research Branch
   1970. *Union Growth in Canada, 1921-1967*. Ottawa: Information Canada.
Canada. Department of Manpower and Immigration
   1975. *The Immigration Program*. (A Report of the Canadian Immigration and Population Study:2.) Ottawa: Manpower and Immigration.
Canada. Department of National Health and Welfare
   1979. *Retirement Ages*. Ottawa: Queen's Printer.
Canada. Department of National Health and Welfare
   1980. *Canada Health Manpower Inventory*. Ottawa: Queen's Printer.
Canada. Department of Trade and Commerce
   1962. *Annual Report of the Minister of Trade and Commerce—Corporations and Labour Unions Returns Act*. Ottawa: Statistics Canada.
Canada. Labour Canada
   1980. *Directory of Labour Organizations in Canada*. Ottawa: Labour Canada.
Canada. Labour Canada
   1981. *Directory of Labour Organizations in Canada*. Ottawa: Labour Canada.

Canada. Royal Commission on the Status of Women in Canada
1970. *The Report of the Royal Commission on the Status of Women.*
Ottawa: Information Canada.

Canada. Statistics Canada
1971. *Canadian Classification and Dictionary of Occupations.* Ottawa:
Statistics Canada.

Canada. Statistics Canada
1971. *Census of Canada, Vols. III and IV.* Ottawa: Statistics Canada

Canada. Statistics Canada
1974. Perspective Canada: *A Compendium of Social Statistics.* Ottawa:
Information Canada.

Canada. Statistics Canada
1976. *Census of Canada.* Ottawa: Statistics Canada.

Canada. Statistics Canada
1974. *Income Distributions by Size in Canada, 1972.* Ottawa: Statistics
Canada.

Canada. Statistics Canada
1979. *Income Distributions by Size in Canada, 1977.* Ottawa: Statistics
Canada.

Canada. Statistics Canada
1980. *Labour Force Survey, March.* Ottawa: Statistics Canada.

Canada. Statistics Canada
1983. *Federal Government Employment.* Ottawa: Statistics Canada.
Cat. 72-004

Canada. Statistics Canada
1983. *Provincial Government Employment.* Ottawa: Statistics Canada.
Cat. 72-007.

Canada. Statistics Canada
1983. *Local Government Employment.* Ottawa: Statistics Canada.
Cat. 72-009.

Canada. Unemployment Insurance Commission
1953. *An Explanation of the Principles and Main Provisions of the
Unemployment Insurance Act.* Ottawa: Edmond Cloutier, Queen's
Printer and Controller of Stationery.

Canada. Unemployment Insurance Commission
1977. *Comprehensive Review of the Unemployment Insurance in Canada.* Ottawa: Queen's Printer.

Canada. Women's Bureau
1978. *Women in the Labour Force: Facts and Figures, 1977.* Ottawa:
Department of Labour.

Canada. Women's Bureau
1979. *Women in the Labour Force: Facts and Figures, 1978.* Ottawa:
Department of Labour.

Canadian Dimension
1981. "The CLC and the Trades Go to the Mat." *Canadian Dimension*, *15 (6)*: 17-20.

Canadian Human Rights Commission
1981. *Methodology and Principles of Applying Section 11 of the Canadian Human Rights Act*. Ottawa: Canadian Human Rights Commission.

Caplow, Theodore
1954. *The Sociology of Work*. Minnesota: University of Minnesota Press.

Caplow, Theodore
1964. *Principles of Organization*. New York: Harcourt, Brace, and World.

Caplow, Theodore
1968. *Two Against One: Coalitions in Triads*. Englewood Cliffs, N.J.: Prentice-Hall.

Carnegie, Dale
1926. *Public Speaking and Influencing Men in Business*. (Retitled, How to Win Friends and Influence People.) Toronto: Musson.

CCH Canadian Ltd.
1982. *Canadian Industrial Relations and Personnel Developments*. Don Mills: CCH Canadian Ltd.

Centers, Richard and Daphne E. Bugental
1966. "Intrinsic and Extrinsic Motivations Among Different Segments of the Working Population." *Journal of Applied Psychology, 50(June)*: 193-97.

Chen, Mervin Y.T.
1968. *Correlates of Union Participation: A Study of Factors Affecting Membership Activity*. Unpublished M.A. Thesis, University of Guelph.

Chen, Mervin Y.T.
1979. *Unionization of Professional Workers: Some Interpretations*. Wolfville, N.S.: Mimeo

Cherns, A.B.
1980. "Speculations on the Social Effects of New Microelectronic Technology." *International Labour Review*, 119(6):705-21

Chinoy, E.
1955. *Automobile Workers and the American Dream*. Garden City, New York: Doubleday.

Chronicle-Herald (The)
1981. "Supreme Court of Canada Ruling." *The Chronicle-Herald*. Nova Scotia: October 22.

Clairmont, Donald H., Martha MacDonald and Fred C. Wein
1980. "A Segmentation Approach to Poverty and Low-Wage Work in

the Maritimes," in John Harp and John R. Hofley (eds.): *Structural Inequality in Canada*. Scarborough: Prentice-Hall of Canada.

Clark, Peter G.
1981. "The Stigma of Dirty Work: A Study of Building Cleaners." Presented at the sixteenth annual general meeting of the Atlantic Association of Sociologists and Anthropologists. Sackville, N.B.

Clarke, Tom and Laurie Clements (eds.)
1977. *Trade Unions Under Capitalism*. Glasgow: William Collins & Co. Ltd.

Clement, Wallace
1975. *The Canadian Corporate Elite: An Analysis of Economic Power*. Toronto: McClelland and Stewart.

Clement, Wallace
1977. *Continental Corporate Power*. Toronto: McClelland and Stewart.

Coburn, David, Carl D'Arcy, Peter New, and George Torrance (eds.)
1979. *Health and Canadian Society: Sociological Perspectives*. Don Mills, Ont.: Fitzhenry and Whiteside.

Coburn, David, George M. Torrance and Joseph M. Kaufert
1981. "Medical Dominance in Canada in Historical Perspectives: The Rise and Fall of Medicine." Paper presented at the annual general meeting of the Canadian Association of Anthropology and Sociology, Halifax, May 28-31. Subsequently published (1983), *Intl. J. of Health Services, 13*(3): 407-32.

Cockroft, David
1980. "New Office Technology and Employment." *International Labour Review, 119(6)*:689-704

Commons, John R.
1909. "American Shoemakers, 1648-1895." *Quarterly Journal of Economics, 24(November)*:39-84.

Connelly, Patricia
1978. "Female Labour Force Participation: Choice or Necessity?" *Atlantis, 3(1)*:40-53.

Connelly, Patricia
1978. *Last Hired, First Fired*. Toronto: The Women's Press.

Cook, Gail C.A. (ed.)
1976. *Opportunity for Choice: A Goal for Women in Canada*. Ottawa: Statistics Canada.

Cook, Gail C.A. and Mary Eberts
1976. "Politics Affecting Work," in Gail C.A. Cook (ed.): *Opportunity for Choice: A Goal for Women in Canada*. Ottawa: Statistics Canada.

Cornish, Blake M.
1981. "The Smart Machines of Tomorrow: Implications for Society." *The Futurist, 15(4)*:5-13.

Croll, D.A.
 1971. *Poverty in Canada. Report of the Special Senate Committee on Poverty*. Ottawa: Queen's Printer.
Crompton, Rosemary
 1979. "Trade Unionism and the Insurance Clerk." *British Journal of Sociology, 13(3)*:403-26.
C.R.O.P.
 1978. *Report 78-3*. Montreal: Centre de Recherches sur l'Opinion Publique.
Crozier, Michel
 1964. *The Bureaucratic Phenomenon*. Chicago: University of Chicago Press.
Crozier, Michel
 1973. *The Work of the Office Worker*. New York: Schocken.
Crysdale, Stewart
 1975. "Aspirations and Expectations of High School Youth." *International Journal of Comparative Sociology, 16(1-2)*:19-36.
Cull, John and Richard Hardy (eds.)
 1973. *The Neglected Older American*. Springfield, Ill.: Charles C. Thomas.
Cummings, L.L. and W.E. Scott, Jr.
 1969. *Readings in Organizational Behaviour and Human Performance*. Homewood, Ill.: R.D. Irwin.
Cuneo, Carl J. and James E. Curtis
 1975. "Social Ascription in the Educational and Occupational Attainment of Urban Canadians." *The Canadian Review of Sociology and Anthropology*, 12(1):6-24.
Curthoys, Ann, *et al.*
 1975. *Women at Work*. Canberra Australia: Australian Society for the Study of Labour History.
Curtis, J. and W. Scott, (eds.)
 1973. *Social Stratification: Canada*. Scarborough: Prentice-Hall of Canada.
Dalton, Melville
 1951. "Informal Factors in Careers Achievement." *American Journal of Sociology*, 56(March):407-15
Dalton, Melville
 1959. *Men Who Manage: Fusions of Feeling and Theory in Administration*. New York: Wiley.
Daniels, Arlene K.
 1969. "The Captive Professional: Bureaucratic Limitations in the Practice of Military Psychiatry." *Journal of Health and Social Behaviour*, 10(December):255-65.

Daniels, Arlene K.
1970. "The Social Construction of Military Psychiatric Diagnoses," in Hans P. Dreitzel (ed.): *Recent Sociology No.2*.

Darroch, A. Gordon
1979. "Another Look at Ethnicity, Stratification and Social Mobility in Canada." *The Canadian Journal of Sociology, 4(1)*:1-25.

Davidson, Percy E. and H. Dewey Anderson
1937. *Occupational Mobility in an American Community*. Stanford University Press.

Davis, Fred
1968. "Professional Socialization as Subjective Experience: the Process of Doctrinal Conversion Among Student Nurses," in Howard S. Becker, Blanche Geer, Davis Reisman, and Robert S. Weiss (eds.): *Institutions and the Person: Papers Presented to Everett C. Hughes*. Chicago: Aldine.

Davis, Kingsley
1953. "Reply to Tumin." *American Sociological Review, 18(August)*:394-97.

Davis, Kingsley and Wilbert Moore
1945. "Some Principles of Stratification." *American Sociological Review, 10(2)*:242-49.

Decker, David L.
1980. *Social Gerontology: An Introduction to the Dynamics of Aging*. Boston: Little, Brown and Company.

DeFleur, Melvin L. and Lois B. DeFleur
1967. "The Relative Contribution of Television as a Learning Source for Children's Occupational Knowledge." *American Sociological Review, 32(October)*:777-89.

Denton, Frank T. and Sylvia Ostry
1967. *Historical Estimates of the Canadian Labour Force*. Ottawa: Queen's Printer.

Denton, Frank T. and Byron G. Spencer
1980. "Canada's Population and Labour Force: Past, Present and Future," in Victor W. Marshall (ed.): *Aging in Canada: Social Perspectives*. Don Mills, Ont.: Fitzhenry and Whiteside.

Dickson, Paul
1977. *Work Revolution*. London: Allen and Unwin.

Dimick, D.E. and V.V. Murray
1978. "Career and Personal Characteristics of the Managerial Technostructure in Canadian Business." *Canadian Review of Sociology and Anthropology, 15(August)*:372-84.

Doeringer, Peter B. and Michael J. Piore
1971. *Internal Labour Markets and Manpower Analysis*. Lexington, Mass.: D.C. Heath Co.

Dorf, Richard C.
   1974. *Technology and Society*. San Francisco, Calif.: Boyd and Fraser Publishing Co.
Dorion, Raynald and Lucie Brunet (eds.)
   1981. *Adapting to a Changing World: A Reader on the Quality of Working Life*. Ottawa: Minister of Supply and Services.
Dreitzel, Hans P. (ed.)
   1970. *Recent Sociology No. 2*. London: Macmillan.
Drouin, Marie-Josee and B. Bruce-Briggs
   1978. *Canada Has a Future*. Toronto: McClelland and Stewart.
Dubin, Robert
   1956. "Industrial Workers' Worlds: A Study of 'Central Life Interests' of Industrial Workers." *Social Problems, 3(January)*:131-42.
Dubin, Robert
   1958. *Working, Union-Management Relations: The Sociology of Industrial Relations*. Englewood Cliffs, N.J.: Prentice-Hall.
Dubin, Robert
   1968. Human Relations in Administration. 3rd ed. Englewood Cliffs, N.J.: Prentice-Hall.
Dubin, Robert (ed.)
   1976. *Handbook of Work, Organization and Society*. Chicago: Rand McNally.
Dubin, Robert, R. Alan Hedley and Thomas Taveggia
   1976. "Attachment to work," in Robert Dubin (ed.): *Handbook of Work, Organization and Society*. Chicago: Rand McNally.
Duncan, Otis D.
   1961. "A Socioeconomic Index for All Occupations," in Albert J. Reiss, Jr. (ed.): *Occupations and Social Status*. New York: The Free Press.
Dunkerley, David
   1975. *Occupations and Society*. London: Routledge and Kegan Paul.
Durkheim, Emile
   1947. *The Division of Labor in Society*. Trans. George Simpson. New York: The Free Press.
Eichler, Margrit
   1973. "Women as Personal Dependants," in Marylee Stephenson (ed.): *Women in Canada*. Toronto: New Press.
Eldridge, J.E.T. and A.D. Crombie
   1974. *A Sociology of Organizations*. London: Allen and Unwin.
Elliot, Jean
   1971. *Immigrant Groups*. Toronto: Prentice-Hall.
Elliot, J.L.
   1983. "Canadian Immigration: A Historical Assessment," in Jean Leonard Elliott (ed.): *Two Nations, Many Cultures: Ethnic Groups in Canada*. 2nd ed. Scarborough, Ont.: Prentice-Hall of Canada.

Emery, Frederick Edmund and Einar Thorsrud
1964. Industrielt Demokrati: Reperesentasjon pa Styreplan i Dedriftene? Oslo: Universitet for laget. (English translation—Form and Content of Industrial Democracy, London: Tavistock, 1969.)

Emery, Frederick Edmund and Einar Thorsrud
1976. *Democracy at Work: The Report of the Norwegian Industrial Democracy Program*. Leiden: M. Nijhoff Social Sciences Division.

Emery, F.E. and E.L. Trist
1965. "The Causal Texture of Organizational Environments." *Human Relations, 18(February)*:21-32.

Engel, Gloria V.
1969. "The Effect of Bureaucracy on the Professional Authority of Physicians.." *Journal of Health and Social Behavior, 10(March):30-41*.

Esland, Geoff and Graeme Salaman (eds.)
1980. *The Politics of Work and Occupations*. Toronto: University of Toronto Press.

Esland, G., Graeme Salaman and Mary-Anne Speakman (eds.)
1975. *People and Work*. London: The Open University Press.

Etzioni, Amitai
1964. *Modern Organizations*. Englewood Cliffs, N.J.: Prentice-Hall.

Etzioni, Amitai
1975. *A Comparative Analysis of Complex Organizations. Revised and Enlarged Edition*. New York: The Free Press.

Evan, William M.
1963. "Peer-group Interaction and Organizational Socialization: A Study of Employee Turnover." *American Sociological Review, 28(June)*:436-40.

Faunce, William A.
1965. "Automation and the Division of Labor." *Social Problems, 13(Fall)*:149-60.

Faunce, William A.
1968. *Problems of an Industrial Society.* New York: McGraw-Hill.

Faunce, William A.
1981. *Problems of an Industrial Society*. 2nd ed. New York: McGraw-Hill.

Fillenbaum, Gerda
1971. "On the Relation Between Attitude to Work and Attitude to Retirement." *Journal of Gerontology, 26*: 244-48.

Flanagan, John
1973. "The First Fifteen Years of Project Talent: Implications for Career Guidance." *Vocational Guidance Quarterly, 22(September)*:8-12.

Foot, David K.
1979. *Public Employment in Canada: Statistics Series*. Institute for Research on Public Policy. Toronto: Butterworths.

Form, William H.
1972. "Technology and Social Behavior of Workers in Four Countries: A Sociotechnical Perspective." *American Sociological Review*, *37*:727-38.

Form, William H.
1973. "Auto Workers and Their Machines: A Study of Work, Factory, and Job Satisfaction in Four Countries." *Social Forces, 52*:1-15.

Form, William H.
1976. *Blue-Collar Stratification: Autoworkers in Four Countries.* Princeton, N.J.: Princeton University Press.

Fox, Bonnie (ed.)
1980. *Hidden in the Household: Women's Domestic Labour Under Capitalism.* Toronto: The Women's Press.

Fox, Renee
1957. "Training for Uncertainty," in Robert K. Merton, George G. Reader and Patricia L. Kendal (eds.): *The Student-Physician.* Harvard University Press.

Freidson, Elliot (ed.)
1963. *The Hospital in Modern Society.* New York: Free Press of Glencoe.

Fry, John Allan
1979. *Economy, Class, and Social Realities: Issues in Contemporary Canadian Society.* Toronto: Butterworths.

Fullan, Michael
1970. "Industrial Technology and Worker Integration in the Organization." *American Sociological Review*, *35(December)*:1028-39.

Galbraith, John K.
1978. *The New Industrial State.* 3rd ed. Boston: Houghton Mifflin Co.

Galenson, W. and S.M. Lipset (eds.)
1960. *Labor and Trade Unionism: An Interdisciplinary Reader.* New York: Wiley.

Gingrich, Paul
1978. "Unemployment: A Radical Analysis of Myth and Fact." *Our Generation, 12(3)*:16-31.

Ginzberg, E., S.W. Ginzberg, S. Axelrad and J.L. Herma
1951. Occupational Choice: An Approach to a General Theory. New York: Columbia University Press.

Ginzberg, Eli
1972. "Toward a Theory of Occupational Choice: A Restatement." *Vocational Guidance Quarterly, 20(3)*:169-76.

Glaser, Barney
1963. "The Local-Cosmopolitan Scientist." *American Journal of Sociology, 69(November)*:249-59.

Glaser, Barney G.
1964. *Organizational Scientists: Their Professional Careers*. Indianapolis: Bobbs-Merrill.

Glaser, Barney G.
1968. *Organizational Careers: A Sourcebook for Theory*. Chicago: Aldine.

Glaser, Barney and Anselm L. Strauss
1971. *Status Passage*. Chicago: Adline-Atherton.

Glasmer, Francis D.
1976. "Determinants of a Positive Attitude Toward Retirement." *Journal of Gerontology*, *31(January)*:104-07.

Glayson, J. Paul
1983. "Shutdown Canada," *Atkinson Review of Canadian Studies, 1 (1)*:21-24.

Glenn, Evelyn Nakano and Roslyn L. Feldberg
1977. "Degraded and Deskilled: The Proletarianization of Clerical Work." *Social Problems, 25(1)*: 52-64.

Glenn, Evelyn Nakano and Roslyn L. Feldberg
No Date. "The Clerical Labour Process and Worker Response." Mimeo.

Globerman, Steven
1981. *The Adoption of Computer Technology in Selected Canadian Service Industries*. Ottawa: Economic Council of Canada.

Goffman, Erving
1952. "On Cooling the Mark Out: Some Aspects of Adaptation to Failure." *Psychiatry*, *15(November)*:451-63.

Goffman, Erving
1961. *Asylums: Essays on the Social Situation of Mental Patients and Other Inmates*. New York: Doubleday.

Goldner, Fred H.
1965. "Demotion in Industrial Management." *American Sociological Review*, *30(October):714-24*.

Goldthorpe, J.H.
1966. "Attitudes and Behavior of Car Assembly Workers: A Deviant Case and a Theoretical Critique." *British Journal of Sociology*, *17*:227-44.

Goldthorpe, J.H., D. Lockwood, F. Beckhofer, and J. Platt
1968. *The Affluent Worker: Industrial Attitudes and Behaviour*. London, England: Cambridge University Press.

Gonick, C.W.
1970. "Poverty and Capitalism," in W.E. Mann (ed.): *Poverty and Social Policy in Canada*. Vancouver: Copp Clark Publishing Co.

Goode, William J.
1982. *The Family*. 2nd ed. Englewood Cliffs, N.J.: Prentice-Hall.

Gooding, Judson
  1972. *The Job Revolution.* New York: Collier Books.
Goodman, Leo A. and William H. Kyuskal
  1954. "Measures of Association for Cross Classification." *Journal of the American Statistical Association, 49*:749.
Goslin, David A. (ed.)
  1969. *Handbook of Socialization Theory and Research.* Chicago: Rand McNally and Co.
Gottleib, David
  1974. "Work and Families: Great Expectations for College Seniors." *Journal of Higher Education, 45(7)*:535-44.
Goudy, Willis, Edward Powers and Patricia Keith
  1975. "Work and Retirement: A Test of Attitudinal Relationships," *Journal of Gerontology, 30(March)*:193-98.
Gough, H. C. and W. B. Hall
  1977. "A Comparison of Medical Students from Medical and Non-medical Families." *Journal of Medical Education, 52*:541-47.
Gouldner, Alvin
  1954. *Patterns of Industrial Bureaucracy.* Glencoe, Ill.: The Free Press.
Gouldner, Alvin
  1957. "Cosmopolitans and Locals: Toward and Analysis of Latent Social Roles—I." *Administrative Science Quarterly, 2(December)*:281-306.
Goyder, John C. and James E. Curtis
  1977. "Occupational Mobility in Canada Over Four Generations." *The Canadian Review of Sociology and Anthropology, 14(3)*:303-19.
Grass, Jennifer
  1980. "No Agreement in Scrap to Close Pay Gap for Women." *Financial Post, February 2, 1980*:273.
Graves, B.
  1958. "Breaking Out: an Apprenticeship System Among Pipeline Construction Workers." *Human Organization, 17(Fall)*:9-13.
Gray, C.
  1980. "Women in Medicine." *Canadian Medical Association Journal, 123(8)*:798-804.
Green, Christopher
  1973. "The Impact of Unemployment Insurance on the Unemployment Rate." Paper Presented at the Meeting of the Canadian Economic Association, McGill (mimeo) cited in C. Green and J.M. Cousineau: *Unemployment in Canada: The Impact of Unemployment Insurance.* Ottawa: Economic Council of Canada.
Green, C. and J.M. Cousineau
  1976. *Unemployment in Canada: The Impact of Unemployment Insurance.* Ottawa: Economic Council of Canada.

Gross, Edward
1965. "Cliques in Office Organizations," in Neil Smelser (ed.): *Readings in Economic Sociology*. Englewood Cliffs, N.J., Prentice-Hall.

Grubel, Herbert G.Dennis Maki, and Shelley Sax
1975. "Real and Insurance-induced Unemployment in Canada." *Canadian Journal of Economics*, *8(2)*:174-91.

Gulick, Luthen and Lyndall Urwick
1937. *Papers on the Science of Administration*. New York: Columbia University Press.

Gunderson, Moreley
1976. "Work Patterns," in Gail Cook (ed.): *Opportunity for Choice: A Goal for Women in Canada*. Ottawa: Statistics Canada.

Guppy, L.N. and J.L. Siltanen
1977. "A Comparison of the Allocation of Male and Female Occupational Prestige." *Canadian Review of Sociology and Anthropology*, *14(3)*:320-30.

Gustad, John W.
1960. The Career Decisions of College Teachers. SREB Research Monograph series No. 2. Atlanta, Georgia: Southern Regional Education Board. Cited in Ronald M. Pavalko, *Sociology of Occupations and Professions*. Itasco, Ill.: F.E. Peacock.

Haas, Jack
1978. "Learning Real Feelings: A Study of High Steel Ironworkers' Reactions to Fear and Danger," in Jack Haas and William Shaffir (eds.): *Shaping Identity in Canadian Society*. Scarborough, Ont.: Prentice-Hall.

Haas, Jack and William Shaffir (eds.)
1978. *Shaping Identity in Canadian Society*. Scarborough: Prentice-Hall.

Haas, Jack and William Shaffir
1980. "Professionalizing Adaptations to Ritual Ordeals of Uncertainty." Presented to the fifteenth annual meeting of the Canadian Sociology and Anthropology Association. Montreal.

Haas, Jack and William Shaffir
1981. "The Professionalization of Medical Students: Developing Competence and a Cloak of Competence," in David Coburn, Carl D'Arcy, Peter New and George Torrance (eds.): *Health and Canadian Society: Sociological Perspectives*. Don Mills, Ont.: Fitzhenry and Whiteside.

Hacker, Helen Mayer
1951. "Women as a Minority Group." *Social Forces*, *30*:60-69.

Hackman, J. Richard
1969. "Nature of the Task as a Determiner of Job Behavior." *Personnel Psychology*, *22*:435-44.

Hackman, J. Richard and Edward E. Lawler
1971. "Employee Reactions to Job Characteristics." *Journal of Applied Psychology*, 55: 259-86.
Hackman, J. Richard and L.W. Porter
1968. "Expectancy Theory and Predictions of Work Effectiveness." *Organizational Behavior and Human Performance*, 3:417-26.
Hagburg, Eugene C.
1966. "Correlates of Organizational Participation: An Examination of Factors Affecting Union Membership Activity." *Pacific Sociological Review*, 9:15-21.
Hage, Jerald
1965. "An Axiomatic Theory of Organizations." *Administrative Science Quarterly*, 10(December):289-320.
Hage, Jerald and Michael Aiken
1967. "Relationship of Centralization to Other Structural Properties." *Administrative Science Quarterly*, 12(June):72-92.
Hage, Jerald and Michael Aiken
1969. "Routine Technology, Social Structure and Organizational Goals." *Administrative Science Quarterly*, 14(September):366-77.
Hagedorn, Robert (ed.)
1980. *Sociology*. Toronto: Holt, Rinehart and Winston.
Hall, Douglas T.
1976. *Careers in Organization*. Pacific Palisades, Calif.: Goodyear Publishing Company.
Hall, Oswald
1977. "The Informal Organization of the Medical Profession." *Canadian Journal of Economics and Political Science*, 12(February):30-44.
Hall, Oswald
1948. "The Stages of a Medical Career." *America Journal of Sociology*, 53(March):327-36.
Hall, Oswald
1973. "The Canadian Division of Labour Revisited," in J. Curtis and W. Scott (eds.): *Social Stratification: Canada* (pp.46-54). Scarborough: Prentice-Hall of Canada.
Hall, Oswald and Richard Carlton
1977. *Basic Skills at School and Work: The Study of Albertown, an Ontario Community*. Toronto: Ontario Economic Council, Occasional Paper 1.
Hall, Richard H.
1968. "Professionalization and Bureaucratization." *American Sociological Review*, 33(February):92-104.
Hall, Richard H.
1975. *Organizations: Structure and Process*. Englewood Cliffs, N.J., Prentice-Hall.

Hall, Richard H.
  1975. *Occupations and the Social Structure*. 2nd ed. Englewood Cliffs, N.J.: Prentice-Hall.
Hall, Richard H.
  1977. *Organizations: Structure and Process*. 2nd ed. Englewood Cliffs, N.J.: Prentice-Hall.
Hall, Richard H., J. Eugene Haas, and Norman J.Johnson
  1967. "Organizational Size, Complexity and Formalization."*American Sociological Review, 32(December)*:903-12.
Hall, Richard H. and Charles R.Tittle
  1966. "A Note on Bureaucracy and its 'Correlates'." *American Journal of Sociology, 72(November)*:267-72.
Harp, John and John R.Hofley
  1980. *Structural Inequality in Canada*. Scarborough, Ont.: Prentice-Hall of Canada.
Harper, Dean and Frederick Emmert
  1963. "Work Behavior in a Service Industry." *Social Forces, 42*:216-25.
Harvey, Edward B.
  1968. "Technology and the Structure of Organizations." *American Sociological Review, 33 (April)*:247-59.
Harvey, Edward B.
  1975. *Industrial Society: Structures, Roles and Relations*. Ill.: Dorsey.
Haug, Marie R.
  1973. "Social Class Measurement and Women's Occupational Roles." *Social Forces, 52*:86-98.
Haug, Marie R. and Jaques Dofny (eds.)
  1977. Work and Technology. Beverly Hills, Calif.: Sage.
Hayes, John and Peter Nutman
  1981. *Understanding the Unemployed*. London: Tavistock.
Hayner, N.
  1945. "Taming the Lumberjack." *American Sociological Review, 10(April)*:217-25.
Herzberg, Frederick
  1966. *Work and the Nature of Man*. Cleveland: World Publishing.
Herzberg, Frederick, B. Mausner, and B. Snyderman
  1959. *The Motivation to Work*. 2nd ed. New York: Wiley.
Hickson, David J., Derek S. Pugh, and Diana C.Pheysey
  1969. "Operations Technology and Organization Structure: an Empirical Reappraisal." *Administrative Science Quarterly, 14(September)*:378-97.
Hickson, David J. Christopher R. Hinings, Charles C. McMillan, and J.P. Schwitter
  1974. "The Culture-free Context of Organization Structure: a Tri-national Comparison." *Sociology, 8(January)*:59-80.

Himelfarb, Alexander and C.James Richardson
  1979. *People, Power and Process: Sociology for Canadians*. Toronto: McGraw-Hill Ryerson.
Hodge, Robert W., Donald J.Treiman, And Peter H.Rossi
  1966. "A Comparative Study of Occupational Prestige," in Bendix and Lipset (eds.): *Class, Status and Power: Social Stratification in Comparative Perspective*. 2nd ed. New York: The Free Press.
Holley, William H. and Kenneth M.Jennings
  1980. *The Labor Relations Process*. Hinsdale, Ill.: The Dryden Press.
Holmes, Jeffrey
  1974. "Demography Affects Employment/Promotion." *University Affairs (March)*:2-3.
Homall, Geraldine, Suzanne Juhasz, and Joseph Juhasz
  1975. "Differences in Self-Perception and Vocational Aspirations of College Women." *California Journal of Educational Research*, *26*:6-10.
Hoos, Ida Russakoff
  1960. "The Impact of Office Automation on Workers." *International Labour Review*, *82*:363-88.
Hoos, Ida R.
  1962. "When the Computer Takes Over the Office," in Sigmund Nosow and William Form (eds.): *Man, Work and Society: A Reader in the Sociology of Occupations*. New York: Basic Books.
House, J. Douglas
  1974. "Entrepreneurial Career Patterns of Residential Real Estate Agents in Montreal." *Canadian Review of Sociology and Anthropology*, *11(May)*:110-24.
House, Robert J. and Lawrence A.Wigdon
  1967. "Herzberg's Dual-factor Theory of Job Satisfaction and Motivation: A Review of the Evidence and a Criticism." *Personnel Psychology*, *20*:369-89.
Hoxie, Robert F.
  1928. *Trade Unionism in the United States*. New York: Appleton-Crofts.
Hughes, Everett Cherrington
  1943. *French Canada in Transition*. University of Chicago Press.
Hughes, Everett Cherrington
  1958. *Men and Their Work*. Glencoe, Ill.: The Free Press.
Hughes, Everett Cherrington
  1959. "The Study of Occupations," in Robert K. Merton, Leonard Broom and Leonard S. Cottree (eds.): *Sociology Today: Problems and Prospects*. New York: Basic Books.
Hughes, Everett Cherrington
  1978. "Work and the Self," in Jack Haas and William Shaffir (eds.):

Shaping Identity in Canadian Society. Scarborough, Ont.: Prentice-Hall.

Hum, Derek, P.J.
1981. *Unemployment Insurance and the Work Effort: Issues, Evidence and Policy Directions*. The Ontario Economic Council.

Humphreys, Elizabeth
1981. *Technological Change and the Office*. Technical Study 17 for the Labour Market Development Task Force.

Hunter, Alfred A.
1981. *Class Tells: On Social Inequality in Canada*. Toronto: Butterworths.

Hyman, R. and R.H.Fryer
1977. "Trade Unions: Sociology and Political Economy," in Tom Clarke and Laurie Clements (eds.): 1977. *Trade Unions Under Capitalism*. Glascow: William Collins and Co. Ltd.

Hyman, R.
1980. "Trade Unions, Control and Resistance," in Geoff Esland and Graeme Salaman (eds.): *The Politics of Work and Occupations*. Toronto: University of Toronto Press.

Industrial Relations Research Association
1975. *Collective Bargaining and Productivity*.: Madison, Wis.: Industrial Relations Research Association.

International Labour Review
1960. "Effects of Mechanization and Automation in Offices." Pts. I, II, III. *International Labour Review, 81 (February, March, April)*: 154-84, 255-83, 350-77.

Ireson, Carol
1978. "Girls' Socialization to Work," in Ann H.Stromberg and Shirley Harkess (eds.): *Women Working: Theories and Facts in Perspective*. Palo Alto, Calif.: Mayfield Publishing.

Isbester, Fraser
1971. "Quebec Labour in Perspective, 1949-1969," in Richard M. Miller and Fraser Isbester (eds.): *Canadian Labour in Transition*. Scarborough, Ont.: Prentice-Hall.

Jacques, Elliott
1965. "Death and the Mid-life Crisis." *International Journal of Psycho-Analysis, 46(4)*:502-14.

Jaffe, A.J. and Joseph Froomkin
1968. *Technology and Jobs, Automation in Perspective*. New York: Praeger.

Jain, Harish C.
1979. "Employment Problems of the Native People in Ontario," *Relations Industrielles, 34*:2.

Jain, Harish C.
   1981. "Discrimination Against Indians: Issues and Policies," in Katherine L.P. Lundy and Barbara D.Warme (eds.): *Work in the Canadian Context: Continuity Despite Change*. Toronto: Butterworths.
Jamieson, Stuart Marshall
   1973. *Industrial Relations in Canada*. 2nd ed. Toronto: Macmillan.
Jenkins, Clive and B.Sherman
   1979. *The Collapse of Work*. London: Eyre Methuen.
Johnson, Walter
   1975. *Working in Canada*. Montreal: Black Rose Books.
Johnson, Carl P., Mark Alexander, and Jacqueline Robin
   1978. *The Quality of Working Life: The Idea and Its Application*. Ottawa: Labour Canada.
Jones, Frank E.
   1976. "Social Origins in Four Professions: A Comparative Study." *International Journal of Comparative Sociology*, *17(3-4)*:143-63.
Judek, S.
   1964. *Medical Manpower in Canada: Royal Commission on Health Services*. Ottawa: Queen's Printer.
Kahn, Robert L., Donald M. Wolfe, Robert P. Quinn, J. Diedrick Snoek, and Robert A. Rosenthal
   1964. *Organizational Stress: Studies in Role Conflict and Ambiguity*. New York: Wiley.
Kalbach, Warren E. and Wayne M. McVey
   1971. *The Demographic Bases of Canadian Society*. Toronto: McGraw-Hill of Canada.
Katz, Daniel and Robert L. Khan
   1966. *Social Psychology of Organizations*. New York: Wiley.
Katz, Fred E. and Harry W. Martin
   1962. "Career Choice Processes." *Social Forces*, *41*: 149-54.
Kelner, Merrijoy
   1980. "The Transition From Student to Practitioner: The Making of a Chiropractor." Presented at the Fifteenth Annual Meeting of the Canadian Sociology and Anthropology Association, Montreal.
Kelner, Merrijoy, Oswald Hall, and Ian Coulter
   1980. *Chiropractors: Do They Help?: A Study of Their Education and Practice*. Toronto: Fitzhenry and Whiteside.
Kerr, C., J. T. Dunlop, F. Harbison, and C.A. Myers (eds.)
   1962. *Industrialization and Industrial Man* (reprinted 1973 by Harmondsworth, Penguin). London: Heineman.
Kirchner, E. and S. Vondracek
   1973. "What Do You Want to be When You Grow Up? Vocational Choice in Children aged 3-6." Paper Presented at the Meeting of the Society for Research in Child Development, Philadelphia, March, 1973. Cited by Carol Ireson (1978) as "Girls Socialization to Work," in

Ann H. Stromberg and Shirley Harnkess (eds.): *Women Working: Theories and Facts in Perspective*. Palo Alto, Calif.: Mayfield Publishing.

Kirsch, Barbara A. and Joseph J. Lengermann
1971. "An Empirical Test of Robert Blauner's Ideas on Alienation in Work as Applied to Different Type Jobs in a White-Collar Setting." *Sociology and Social Research, 56*: 180-94.

Klemmack, David and John N. Edwards
1973. "Women's Acquisition of Stereotyped Occupational Aspirations." *Sociology and Social Research, 57*: 510-25.

Kohn, Melvin
1969. *Class and Conformity: A Study in Values*. Homewood, Ill.: Dorsey.

Kornhauser, A.
1965. *Mental Health of the Industrial Worker: A Detroit Study*. New York: Wiley.

Kornhauser, William
1962. *Scientists in Industry: Conflict and Accommodation*. Berkley: University of California Press.

Kosa, John and Robert Coker, Jr.
1965. "The Female Physician in Public Health: Conflict and Reconciliation of the Sex and Professional Roles." *Sociology and Social Research, 49*: 294-305.

Kovacs, Aranka (ed.)
1961. *Readings in Canadian Labour*. Toronto: McGraw-Hill.

Krause, Elliott A.
1971. *The Sociology of Occupations*. New York: Little, Brown and Company.

Kronus, Carol L.
1976. "Occupational Versus Organizational Influences on Reference Group Identification: the Case of Pharmacy." *Sociology of Work and Occupations, 3(August)*: 303-30.

Kruger, Arthur M.
1971. "The Direction of Unionism in Canada," in Richard M. Miller and Fraser Isbester (eds.): *Canadian Labour In Transition* (pp.85-118). Scarborough, Ont.: Prentice-Hall.

Kuvlesky, W.P. and Robert Bealer
1966. "A Clarification of the Concept 'Occupational Choice'." *Rural Sociology, 31*: 265-76

Langner, Elinor
1970a. "The Women of the Telephone Company." *New York Review of Books, 14(March)*: 10-16.

Langner, Elinor
1970b. "Inside the New York Telephone Company." *New York Review of Books, 14(March)*: 16-24.

Lautard, Hugh
   1977. "Occupational Segregation by Sex and Industrialization in Canada: 1891-1971." Paper Presented at the Annual Meetings of the Canadian Sociology and Anthropology Association. Fredericton, N.B.
Lawrence, Paul R. and Jay W. Lorsch
   1967. *Organization and Environment: Managing Differentiation and Integration.* Boston: Harvard University.
Laxer, Robert
   1976. *Canada's Unions.* Toronto: James Lorimer and Co.
Lenski, Gerald and Jean Lenski
   1978. *Human Societies: An Introduction to Macrosociology.* N.Y.: McGraw-Hill.
Likert, Rensis
   1961. *New Patterns of Management.* New York: McGraw-Hill.
Likert, Rensis
   1967. *The Human Organization: Its Management and Value.* New York: McGraw-Hill.
Linton, R. (ed.)
   1945. *The Science of Man in the World Crisis.* New York: Columbia University Press.
Lipset, Seymour Martin
   1950. *Agrarian Socialism.* Berkeley: University of California Press.
Lipset, Seymour M. and Reinhard Bendix
   1952. "Social Mobility and Occupational Career Patterns." *American Journal of Sociology,* 57(March): 494-504.
Lockwood, David
   1958. *The Blackcoated Worker: a Study of Class Consciousness.* London: Allen and Unwin.
Lopata, Helena Znaniecki
   1971. *Occupation: Housewife.* New York: Oxford University Press.
Lopate, C.
   1974. "Women and Pay for Housework." *Liberation Magazine, June,* 8-11.
Lortie, Dan C.
   1968. "Shared Ordeal and Induction to Work," in Howard S. Becker, Blanche Geer, David Riesman, and Robert S. Weiss (eds.): *Institutions and the Person: Papers Presented to Everett C. Hughes.* Chicago: Aldine.
Lucas, Rex
   1969. *Men in Crisis: A Study of Mine Disaster.* New York: Basic Books.
Lucas, Rex
   1971. *Minetown, Milltown, Railtown: Life in Canadian Communities of Single Industry.* Toronto: University of Toronto Press.
Luxton, M.
   1980. *More Than a Labour of Love.* Toronto: The Women's Press.

Mackie, Marlene
1980. "Socialization," in Robert Hagedorn (ed.): *Sociology*. Toronto: Holt, Rinehart and Winston.

Maddox, George L.
1966. "Retirement as a Social Event in the United States," in John McKinney and Frank de Vyver (eds.): *Aging and Social Policy*. New York: Appleton-Century-Crofts.

Mahoney, Thomas A., Peter Frost, Norman F. Crandall and William Weitzel
1972. "The Conditioning Influence of Organization Size Upon Managerial Practice." *Organizational Behaviour and Human Performance, 8(October)*: 230-41.

Mann, W.E. (ed.)
1970. *Poverty and Social Policy in Canada*. Vancouver: Copp, Clark Publishing Company.

Mansfield, Roger
1973. "Bureaucracy and Centralization: An Examination of Organizational Structure." *Administrative Science Quarterly, 18(December)*: 477-88.

March, James G. and Herbert A. Simon
1958. *Organizations*. New York: Wiley.

Marchak, M. Patricia
1973. "Women Workers and White-Collar Unions." *Canadian Review of Sociology and Anthropology 10(2)*: 134-47.

Marrow, Alfred J., David B. Bowers, and Stanley E. Seashore
1967. *Management by Participation: Creating a Climate for Personal and Organizational Development*. New York: Harper and Row.

Marsden, Lorna R.
1975. "Why Now? The Mirage of Equality." *Canadian Forum 4*: 12-17.

Marshall, Victor W. (ed.)
1980. *Aging in Canada: Social Perspectives*. Don Mills, Ont.: Fitzhenry and Whiteside.

Martin, Norman H. and Anselm L. Strauss
1956. "Patterns of Mobility Within Industrial Organizations." *Journal of Business, 29(April)*: 101-10.

Martin, Norman H. and Anselm L. Strauss
1959. "Consequences of Failure in Organizations," in W. Lloyd Warner and Norman H. Martin (eds.): *Industrial Man*. New York: Harper.

Maslow, Abraham
1954. *Motivation and Personality*. New York: Harper and Row.

Maslow, Abraham
1962. *Towards a Psychology of Being*. Princeton, N.J.: Van Nostrand.

Matheson, Gwen (ed.)
1976. *Women in the Canadian Mosaic*. Toronto: Peter Martin Associates, Ltd.

Mayo, Elton
　　1945. *The Social Problems of an Industrial Civilization*. Boston: Harvard University Press.
McCready, Gerald B.
　　1977. *Profile Canada: Social and Economic Projections*. Georgetown, Ont.: Irwin-Dorsey Limited.
McDonald, Lynn
　　1980. "Equal Pay—How Far Off? "*Canadian Dimension, 14 (May)*: 21-24.
McDonald, Lynne
　　1975. "Wages of Work: A Widening Gap Between Women and Men." *Canadian Forum, 55*: 4-7.
McGregor, Douglas
　　1960. *The Human Side of Enterprise*. New York: McGraw-Hill.
McFarland, Joan
　　1979. "Women and Unions: Help or Hindrance?" *Atlantis, 4*:2.
McHale, John
　　1972. *World Facts and Trends*. New York: Collier Books, The Macmillan Co.
McKinney, John C. and Frank T. Vyver (eds.)
　　1966. *Aging and Social Policy*. New York: Appleton-Century-Crofts.
McMillan, Charles J., David J. Hickson, Christopher Hinnings, and Rodney E. Schneck
　　1973. "The Structure of Work Organizations Across Societies." *Academy of Management Journal, 16(December)*: 555-69.
McRoberts Hugh A. *et al.*
　　1976. "Francophone-Anglophone Differences in Mobility." *Sociologie et Societe, 8(2)*: 61-79.
Mechanic, David
　　1962. " Sources of Power of Lower Participants in Complex Organizations." *Administrative Science Quarterly, 7(December)*: 349-64.
Meissner, Martin
　　1969. *Technology and the Worker: Technical Demands and Social Processes in Industry*. San Francisco: Chandler Publishing Company.
Menzies, Heather
　　1981a. *Women and the Chip: Case Studies of the Effects of Informatics on Employment in Canada*. Montreal: The Institute for Research for Public Policy.
Menzies, Heather
　　1981b. *Informatics Case Studies (Supplementary Material to "Women and the Chip")*. Labour Market Development Task Force Technical Studies Series #23. Ottawa: Canada Employment and Immigration Commission.
Merton, Robert K.
　　1957. *Social Theory and Social Structure. Revised and Enlarged Edition*. New York: The Free Press.

Merton, Robert K., George G. Reader, and Patricia L. Kendall (eds.)
   1957. *The Student-Physician: Introductory Studies in the Sociology of Medical Education*. Cambridge, Mass.: Harvard University Press.
Merton, Robert K., Leonard Broom, and Leonard S. Cottrell, Jr. (eds.)
   1959. *Sociology Today: Problems and Prospects*. New York: Basic Books.
Mesthene, Emmanuel G., ed.
   1967. *Technology and Social Change*. New York: Bobbs-Merrill.
Mesthene, Emmanuel G.
   1970. *Technological Change: Its Impact on Man and Society*. Cambridge, Mass.: Harvard University Press.
Miles, Raymond E.
   1965. "Human Relations or Human Resources?" *Harvard Business Review, 43(July/August)*: 148-63.
Miller, Delbert C. and William H. Form
   1949. "Occupational Career Pattern as a Sociological Instrument." *American Journal of Sociology, 54(January)*: 317-29.
Miller, Delbert C. and William H. Form
   1964. *Industrial Sociology*. 2nd ed. New York: Harper and Row.
Miller, Delbert C. and William H. Form
   1980. *Industrial Sociology*. 3rd ed. New York: Harper and Row.
Miller, Gail
   1981. *It's a Living: Work in Modern Society*. New York: St. Martin's Press.
Miller, George A.
   1967. "Professionals in Bureaucracy: Alienation Among Industrial Scientists and Engineers." *American Sociological Review, 32(October)*: 755-68.
Miller, Richard M. and Fraser Isbester (eds.)
   1971. *Canadian Labour in Transition*. Scarborough, Ont.: Prentice-Hall.
Mills, C. Wright
   1940. "Situated Actions and the Vocabularies of Motive." *American Sociological Review, 5(December)*: 904-13.
Mills, C. Wright
   1951. *White Collar: The American Middle Classes*. New York: Oxford University Press.
Mills, C. Wright
   1959. *The Power Elite*. New York: Oxford University Press.
Mills, Donald L. and Donald E. Larson
   1981. "The Professionalization of Canadian Chiropractic," in David Coburn, Carl D'Arcy, Peter New, and George Torrance (eds.): *Health and Canadian Society: Sociological Perspectives*. Don Mills, Ont.: Fitzhenry and Whiteside.

Mitchell, Terence R. and Lee Roy Beach
1976. "A Review of Occupational Preference and Choice Research Using Expectancy Theory and Decision Theory." *Journal of Occupational Psychology, 49*: 231-48.

Mohr, Lawrence B.
1971. "Organizational Technology and Organizational Structure." *Administrative Science Quarterly, 16(December)*: 444-59.

Montagna, Paul D.
1977. *Occupations and Society*. New York: John Wiley and Sons, Inc.

Montgomery, Donald R.
1977. "The Canadian Labour Congress—Its Concerns and Goals," in Dodge, Ferrari and Jepson (eds.): *Industrial Relations in Canada: Towards a Better Understanding*. Ottawa: The Conference Board in Canada.

Moore, Wilbert E.
1960. "Notes for a General Theory of Labour Organizations." *Industrial and Labour Relations Review, 15*: 389-97.

Moore, Wilbert E.
1969. "Occupational Socialization." in David A. Goslin (ed.): *Handbook of Socialization Theory and Research*. Chicago: Rand McNally and Co.

More, Douglas M.
1962. "Demotion." *Social Problems, 9(Winter)*: 213-21.

Moy, J. and C. Sorrentino
1977. "An Analysis of Unemployment in Nine Industrial Countries." *Monthly Labour Review, 100(4)*: 12-24.

Mumford, Enid and Olive Banks
1967. *The Computer and the Clerk*. London: Routledge and Kegan Paul.

Neice, D., L. Snider, and E. Zureik (eds.)
1982. "Microelectronics—Information Technology and Canadian Society." Papers presented at a workshop at Queen's University, May 5-7, 1982.

Nichols, Theo, and Peter Armstrong
1976. *Workers Divided*. London: Fontana/Collins.

Nichols, Theo, and Huw Beynon
1977. *Living with Capitalism: Class Relations and the Modern Factory*. London: Routledge and Kegan Paul.

Norman, Colin
1981. "The New Industrial Revolution: How Microelectronics May Change the Workplace." *The Futurist, 15(1)*: 30-40.

Nosanchuk, Terrance A.
1972. "A Note on the Use of the Correlation Coefficient for Assessing

the Similarity of Occupational Rankings." *Canadian Review of Sociology and Anthropology, 9(4)*: 357-65.

Nosow, Sigmund and William Form (eds.)
1962. *Man, Work, and Society: A Reader in the Sociology of Occupations*. New York: Basic Books.

Olesen, Virginia L. and Elvi W. Whittaker
1968. *The Silent Dialogue: A Study in the Social Psychology of Professional Socialization*. San Francisco: Jossy-Bass.

OECD
1976. *Labour Force Statistics, 1961-74*. Paris: OECD.

O'Hara, Robert P.
1962. "Roots of Careers." *Elementary School Journal, 62(February)*: 277-80.

Oppenheimer, Martin
1975. "The Unionization of the Professional." *Social Policy 5(5)*: 34-40.

Ornstein, Michael D.
1981. "The Occupational Mobility of Men in Ontario." *Canadian Review of Sociology and Anthropology, 18 (May)*: 183-215.

Osipow, Samuel H.
1968. *Theories of Career Development*. New York: Appleton-Century-Crofts.

Osipow, Samuel H.
1973. *Theories of Career Development*. 2nd ed. Toronto: Prentice-Hall.

Osipow, Samuel H.
1979. *Theories of Career Development*. 3rd ed. Toronto: Prentice-Hall.

Ostry, Sylvia
1968. *"The Female Worker in Canada,"* Table 16. Ottawa: Queen's Printer.

Ostry, Sylvia
1971. "The Canadian Labour Market," in Richard U. Miller and Fraser Isbester (eds.): *Canadian Labour in Transition*. Scarborough, Ont.: Prentice-Hall.

Parai, Louis
1975. "Canada's Immigration Policy, 1962-74." *International Migration Review, 9(4)*: 449-78.

Parsons, Talcott
1960. Structure and Process in Modern Societies. Glencoe, Ill.: Free Press.

Parsons, Talcott
1968. "Professions," in Cavid L. Sills (ed.): *International Encyclopedia of Social Sciences, 12*: 536-47. New York: Macmillan.

Pavalko, Ronald M.
  1971. *Sociology of Occupations and Professions*. Itasca, Ill.: F.E. Peacock.
Peitchinis, Stephen G.
  1970. *Canadian Labour Economics: An Introductory Analysis*. Toronto: McGraw-Hill.
Peitchinis, Stephen G.
  1978. *The Effect of Technological Changes on Educational and Skill Requirements of Industry*. Department of Industry, Trade and Commerce, Ottawa.
Peitchinis, Stephen G.
  1979. "Some Evidence on the Effects of Technological Change on the Educational and Skill Requirements of Organizations." Discussion Papers Series, no. 48. Calgary: Department of Economics, University of Calgary.
Peitchinis, Stephen G.
  1980. *Technological changes and Employment*. Studies on Employment Effects of Technology. Calgary: University of Calgary, Alberta.
Peitchinis, Stephen G.
  1982. "Microelectronic Technology and Employment: Micro and Macro Effects," in David Neice, Laureen Snider, and Elia Zureik (eds.): *Workshop on Microelectronics—Information Technology and Canadian Society*. Kingston: Queen's University.
Perlman, Selig
  1949. *A Theory of the Labour Movement*. New York: Kelley.
Perrow, Charles
  1967. "A Framework for Comparative Analysis of Organizations." *American Sociological Review, 32(April)*: 194-208.
Perrow, Charles
  1970. *Organizational Analysis: A Sociological View*. Belmont, Cal.: Wadsworth.
Perrow, Charles
  1972. *Complex Organizations: A Critical Essay*. Glenview, Ill.: Scott, Foresman and Co.
Perry, Robert L.
  1971. *Galt, U.S.A.: The "American Presence" in a Canadian City*. Toronto: Maclean-Hunter.
Pike, Robert
  1970. *Who Doesn't Get to University—and Why: A Study of Accessibility to Higher Education in Canada*. Ottawa: Association of Universities and Colleges of Canada.
Pineo, Peter C. and John Porter
  1967. "Occupational Prestige in Canada." *The Canadian Review of Sociology and Anthropology, 4(1)*: 24-40.

Pineo, Peter C.
1976. "Social Mobility in Canada: The Current Picture." *Sociological Focus, 9(2)*: 109-23.

Pineo, Peter C., John Porter, and Hugh A. McRoberts
1977. "The 1971 Census and the Socioeconomic Classification of Occupations." *The Canadian Review of Sociology and Anthropology, 14(1)*: 91-102.

Pineo, P. and D. Looker
1983. "Class Conformity in the Canadian Setting." *The Canadian Journal of Sociology, 8(3)*: 293-317.

Popitz H., H.P. Bahrdt, E.A. Jures, and H. Kesting
1957. *Technik und Industriearbeit: Soziologische Untersuchungen in der Huttenindustrie*. Tubingen: Mohr.

Porter, John
1965. *The Vertical Mosaic: An Analysis of Social Class and Power in Canada*. Toronto: University of Toronto Press.

Porter, Marion R., John Porter and Bernard R. Blishen
1973. *Does Money Matter?: Prospects for Higher Education in Ontario*. Toronto: Macmillan.

Pugh, Derek S., David J. Hickson, Christopher R.J. Hinings, K.M. McDonald, C. Turner, and T. Lupton
1963. "A Conceptual Scheme for Organizational Analysis." *Administrative Science Quarterly, 8(December)*: 289-315.

Pugh, Derek S., David J. Hickson, Christopher R. Hinings, and C. Turner
1968. "Dimensions of Organization Structure." *Administrative Quarterly, 13(June)*: 65-105.

Pugh, Derek S., David J. Hickson, Christopher R. Hinings, and C. Turner
1969. "The Context of Organization Structures." *Administrative Science Quarterly, 14(March)*: 91-114.

Puxley, Evelyn
1971. *Poverty in Montreal*. Montreal: Dawson College Press.

Pyron, H. Charles and U. Vincent Manion
1973. "Preretirement Counseling," in John Cull and Richard Hardy (eds.): *The Neglected Older American*. Springfield, Ill.: Charles C. Thomas.

Rando, Jean
1972. "Toward an Organization of Working Women." *Women Unite*. Toronto: Canadian Women's Educational Press.

Regan, Thomas G.
1978. "Profiles of Physician Distribution in N.S." Unpublished paper.

Reiss, Albert J., Jr.
1961. *Occupations and Social Status*. New York: The Free Press.

Richardson, C. James
1977. *Contemporary Social Mobility*. London: Frances Printer Publishing.

Rico, Leonard
   1967. *The Advance Against Paperwork: Computers, Systems and Personnel*. Ann Arber, Mich.: Bureau of Industrial Relations, Graduate School of Business Administration. The University of Michigan.
Riley, Matilda White and Anne Foner
   1968. *Aging and Society*. Volume 1. New York: Russell Sage.
Riley, Matilda White, Anne Foner, Beth Hess, and Marcia L. Toby
   1969. "Socialization for the Middle and Later Years," in David A. Goslin (ed.): *Handbook of Socialization Theory and Research*. Chicago: Rand McNally.
Rinehart, James W.
   1975. *The Tyranny of Work*. Don Mills, Ont.: Longman Canada.
Ritzer, George
   1972. *Man and His Work: Conflict and Change*. New York: Appleton-Century-Crofts.
Ritzer, George
   1977. *Working: Conflict and Change*. Englewood Cliffs, N.J.: Prentice-Hall.
Roberts, Kenneth
   1968. "The Entry into Employment: An Approach Towards A General Theory." *Sociological Review, 16*: 165-84
Roberts, Kenneth
   1975. "The Developmental Theory of Occupational Choice: A Critique and An Alternative," in Geoff Esland, Graeme Salaman and Mary-Anne Speakmen (eds.): *People and Work*. London: The Open University Press.
Roberts, Kenneth
   1977. "The Social Conditions, Consequences, and Limitations of Careers Guidance." *British Journal of Guidance and Counseling, 5(January): 1-9*.
Robin, Jacqueline
   1981. *Quality of Working Life: Concepts and Programs for Change*. Ottawa: Labour Canada.
Robin, Martin
   1968. *Radical Politics and Canadian Labour, 1880-1930*. Kingston: Industrial Relations Centre, Queen's University.
Roethlisberger, Fritz
   1945. "The Foreman: Master and Victim of Double Talk." *Harvard Business Review, 23(Spring)*: 283-98.
Roethlisberger, Fritz and William J. Dickson
   1939. *Management and the Worker: An Account of a Research Program Conducted by the Western Electric Company, Hawthorne Works, Chicago*. Cambridge, Mass.: Harvard University Press.
Rogers, Theresa F. and Nathalie S. Freidman
   1980. *Printers Face Automation: The Impact of Technology on Work*

and Retirement among Skilled Craftsmen. Lexington, Mass.: Lexington Books (D.C. Heath).

Rosenberg, George
1970. *The Worker Grows Old*. San Fransisco: Jossey-Bass.

Ross, Aileen D.
1961. *Becoming a Nurse: Professional Nurses in Canadian Hospitals*. Toronto: Macmillan.

Ross, Aileen D.
1979. "Businesswomen and Business Cliques in Three Cities: Delhi, Sydney and Montreal." *Canadian Review of Sociology and Anthropology, 16(4)*: 425-35.

Roy, Donald
1952. "Quota Restriction and Goldbricking in a Machine Shop." *American Journal of Sociology, 57(March)*: 427-42.

Roy, Donald
1953. "Work Satisfaction and Social Reward in Quota Achievement: An Analysis of Piecework Incentive." *American Sociological Review, 18(October)*: 507-14.

Roy, Donald
1954. "Efficiency and 'the Fix': Informal Intergroup Relations in Piecework Machine Shop." *American Journal of Sociology, 60(November)*: 255-66.

Roy, Donald
1959. "Banana Time': Job Satisfaction and Informal Interactions." *Human Organization, 18*: 158-68.

Salamon, Graeme
1980. "The Sociology of Work: Some Themes and Issues," in Geoff Eslan and Graeme Salamon (eds.): *The Politics of Work and Occupations*. Toronto: University of Toronto Press.

Sales, Stephen M.
1969. "Organizational Role as a Factor in Coronary Disease." *Administrative Science Quarterly, 14(September)*: 325-37.

Sampson, William A. and Peter H. Rossi
1975. "Race and Family Social Standing." *American Sociological Review, 40*: 201-14.

Sayles, Leonard R.
1958. *Behavior of Industrial Work Groups*. New York: Wiley.

Sayles, Leonard R. and George Strauss
1966. *Human Behavior in Organizations*. Englewood Cliffs, N.J.: Prentice-Hall.

Schein, Edgar H.
1968. "Organizational Socialization and the Profession of Management." *Industrial Management Review, 9(2)*: 1-16.

Schein, Edgar H.
1970. *Organizational Psychology*. Englewood Cliffs, N.J.: Prentice-Hall.

Schein, Edgar H.
1974. "Careers Anchors and Career Paths: A Panel Study of Management School Graduate." MIT Working Paper 707-74. Cambridge: Massachusetts Institute of Technology.

Schermerhorn, R.A.
1970. *Comparative Ethnic Relations: A Framework for Theory and Research*. New York: Random House.

Schneider, Eugene V.
1969. *Industrial Sociology*. 2nd ed. New York: McGraw-Hill.

Science Council of Canada
1980. *The Impact of the Microelectronics Revolution on Work and Working*. Ottawa: Science Council of Canada, Committee on Computers and Communications.

Seashore, Stanley and David Bowers
1963. *Changing the Structure and Functioning of an Organization*. Ann Arbor, Mich.: University of Michigan Press.

Seidman, Joel, Jack London and Bernard Karsh
1951. "Why Workers Join Unions." *The Annals of the American Academy of Political and Social Sciences, 274*: 75-84.

Selznick, Philip
1966. *TVA and the Grass Roots: Study of Sociology of Formal Organization*. Berkeley: University of California Press.

Selznick, Philip
1969. *Law, Society and Individual Justice*. New York: Russell Sage.

Shapiro, Martin
1978. *Getting Doctored: Critical Reflections on Becoming a Physician*. Kitchener, Ont.: Between the Lines.

Shepard, Jon M.
1969. "Functional Specialization and Work Attitudes." *Industrial Relations, 8(2)*: 185-94.

Shepard, Jon M.
1971. *Automation and Alienation: A Study of Office and Factory Workers*. Cambridge, Mass.: MIT Press.

Shepard, Jon M.
1973. "Technology, Division of Labour, and Alienation." *Pacific Sociological Review, 13*: 161-73.

Shepard, Jon M.
1977. "Technology, Alienation, and Job Satisfaction," in Alex Inkeles (ed.): *Annual Review of Sociology, 3*: 1-21

Sheppard, H.L. and N.Q. Herrick
1972. *Where Have all the Robots Gone? Workers Dissatisfaction in the 70s*. New York: Free Press.

Sherlock, Basil and Alan Cohen.
1966. "The Strategy of Occupational Choice: Recruitment to Dentistry." *Social Forces, 44(3)*: 303-13.

Simon, Herbert A.
1947. *Administrative Behavior: A Study of Decision-making Processes in Administrative Organization*. New York: Macmillan.

Simon, Herbert A.
1957. *Administrative Behavior: A Study of Decision-making Processes in Administrative Organization*. 2nd ed. New York: Macmillan.

Simon, Herbert A.
1964. "On the Concept of Organizational Goal." *Administrative Science Quarterly, 9(June)*: 1-22.

Simon, Herbert A.
1977. "What Computers Mean for Man and Society." *Science, 195*: 1186-91.

Simpson, Ida Harper
1967. "Patterns of Socialization into Professions: The Case of Student Nurses." *Sociological Inquiry, 37*: 47-54.

Simpson, Ida Harper
1979. *From Student to Nurse: A Longitudinal Study of Socialization.* Cambridge: Cambridge University Press.

Simpson, Ida Harper and John C. McKinney (eds.)
1966. *Social Aspects of Aging*. Durham, N.C.: Duke University Press.

Simpson, Ida Harper, Jurt W. Back, and John C. McKinney
1966a. "Attributes of Work, Involvement in Society and Self-evaluation in Retirement," in Ida Harper Simpson and John C. McKinney (eds.): *Social Aspects of Aging*. Durham, N.C.: Duke University Press.

Simpson, Ida Harper, Jurt W. Back, and John C. McKinney
1966b. "Orientations Towards Work and Retirement and Self-evaluation in Retirement," in Ida Harper Simpson and John C. McKinney (eds.): *Social Aspects of Aging.* Durham, N.C.: Duke University Press.

Simpson, Ida Harper, Jurt W. Back and John C. McKinney
1966c. "Exposure to Information on, Preparation for Self-evaluation in Retirement," in Ida Harper Simpson and John C. McKinney (eds.): *Social Aspects of Aging*. Durham, N.C.: Duke University Press.

Simpson, Richard L. and Ida Harper Simpson
1959. "The Psychiatric Attendant: Development of an Occupational Self-image in a Low-status Occupation." *American Sociological Review, 24(June)*: 389-92.

Skinner, Denise A.
1980. "Dual-Career Family Stress and Coping: A Literature Review." *Family Relations, 29(4)*: 473-80.

Slocum, Walter L.
1974. *Occupational Careers*. 2nd ed. Hawthorne, N.Y.: Aldine.

Smelser, Neil (ed.)
    1965. *Readings on Economic Sociology*. Englewood Cliffs, N.J.: Prentice-Hall.
Smelser, N.J.
    1976. *The Sociology of Economic Life*. Englewood Cliffs, N.J.: Prentice-Hall.
Smith, Douglas A.
    1980. "Employment and Unemployment: The Impact of New Technology." *Canadian Business Management Developments, 1-16*: 165-71.
Smucker, J.
    1980. *Industrialization in Canada*. Scarborough, Ontario: Prentice-Hall.
Sofer, Cyril
    1974. "Introduction," in W.M. Williams (ed.): *Occupational Choice: A Selection of Papers from the "Sociological Review."* London: George Allen and Unwin Ltd.
Solomon, David N.
    1968. "Sociological Perspectives on Occupations," in Howard S. Becker, Blanche Geer, David Reisman, and Robert S. Weiss (eds.): *Institutions and the Person: Papers presented to Everett C. Hughes*. Chicago: Aldine.
Somers, Gerald, Arvid Anderson, Malcolm Denise, Leonard Sayles
    1975. *Collective Bargaining and Productivity*. Madison, Wis.: Industrial Relations Research Association.
Soothill, William E. (trans.)
    1968. *The Analects of Confucius*. 2nd ed. Book V, Section IX. New York: Paragon Book Reprint Corp. (Originally published by Shansi, 1910.)
Sorrentino, Constance
    1970. "Unemployment in the United States and Seven Countries." *Monthly Labour Review, 93(9)*: 12-23.
Spencer, Byron G. and Dennis C. Featherstone
    1970. *Married Female Labour Force Participation: A Micro Study*. Ottawa: D.B.S.
Spenner, Kenneth I.
    1983. "Deciphering Prometheus: Temporal Change in the Skill Level of Work." *American Sociological Review, 48*: 824-37.
Stebbins, Robert A.
    1970. "Career: The Subjective Approach." *Sociological Quarterly, 11(1)*: 32-49.
Stecklein, John E. and Ruth E. Eckert
    1958. *An Exploratory Study of Factors Influencing the Choice of College Teaching as a Career*. Washington, D.C.: Cooperative Research Pro Office of Education. Cited in Ronald M. Pavlako: 1971. *Sociology of Occupations and Professions*. Itasca, Ill.: F.E. Peacock.

Stelling, Joan and Rue Bucher
1972. "Autonomy and Monitoring on Hospital Wards." *Sociological Quarterly, 13(Fall)*: 431-46.

Stephenson, Marylee (ed.)
1973. *Women in Canada*. Toronto: New Press.

Stirling, Robert and Denise Kouri
1979. "Unemployment Indexes—The Canadian Context," in John Allan Fry (ed.): *Economy, Class and Social Realities: Issues in Contemporary Canadian Society*. Toronto: Butterworths.

Strauss, Anselm L.
1959. *Mirrors and Masks: The Search for Identity*. New York: Free Press.

Strauss, Anselm L.
1978. *Negotiations: Varieties, Contexts, Processes and Social Order*. San Fransisco: Jossey-Bass.

Strauss, Anselm L., Leonard Schatzman, Rue Bucher, Danuta Ehrlich and Melvin Sabshin
1963. "The Hospital and its Negotiated Order," in Elliott Freidson (ed.): *The Hospital in Modern Society*. New York: Free Press of Glencoe.

Strauss, Anselm L., Leonard Schatzman, Rue Bucher, Danuta Ehrlich and Melvin Sabshin
1964. *Psychiatric Ideologies and Institutions*. New York: Free Press.

Strauss, George
1963. "Notes on Power Equalization," in George Struther (ed.): *The Social Science of Organization*. Englewood Cliffs, N.J.: Prentice-Hall.

Strauss, George
1969. "Human Relations—1968 Style." *Industrial Relations 7(May)*:262-76.

Stromberg, Ann H. and Shirley Harkess (eds.)
1978. *Women Working: Theories and Facts in Perspective*. Palo Alto, Calif.: Mayfield Publishing.

Struther, George (ed.)
1963. *The Social Science of Organization*. Englewood Cliffs, N.J., Prentice-Hall.

Super, Donald E.
1953. "Theory of Vocational Development." *American Psychologist, 8*:185-90.

Super, Donald E.
1957. *The Psychology of Careers: An Introduction to Vocational Development*. New York: Harper and Row.

Super, Donald E.
1980. "A Life-Span, Life-Space Approach to Career Development," *Journal of Vocational Behaviour, 16(3)*:282-98.

Susman, Gerald I.
1972a. "Process Design, Automation, and Worker Alienation." *Industrial Relations*, *11*:34-45.
Susman, Gerald I.
1972b. "Automation, Alienation and Work Group Autonomy." *Human Relations*, *25(2)*:171-80.
Tannenbaum, Frank
1951. *A Philosophy of Labor*. New York: Alfred A.Knopf, Inc.
Taylor, Frederick W.
1911. *The Principles of Scientific Management*. New York: Norton and Company.
Taylor, Lee
1968. *Occupational Sociology*. New York: Oxford University Press.
Tenne, Ruth and Bilha Mannheim
1977. "The Effect of the Level of Production Technology on Workers' Orientations and Responses to the Work Situation," in Marie R. Haug and Jacques Dofney (eds.): *Work and Technology*. Beverly Hills: Sage.
Tepperman, Lorne
1975. *Social Mobility in Canada*. Toronto: McGraw-Hill Ryerson.
Tepperman, Lorne
1976. "A Simulation of the Social Mobility in Industrial Societies." *The Canadian Review of Sociology and Anthropology*, *13(1)*:26-42.
Terkal, Studs
1974. *Working: People Talk About What They Do All Day and How They Feel About What They Do*. New York: Pentheon Books.
Thompson, James D.
1967. *Organizations in Action: Social Science Bases of Administrative Theory*. New York: McGraw-Hill.
Thompson, Victor
1961. *Modern Organization*. New York: Knopf.
Thomson, Anthony
1984. "Nova Scotia Labour in the 1980s: Response to the Crisis." Paper presented at the 16th Annual Meetings of the Atlantic Association of Sociologists and Anthropologists. March 15-17, 1984, Fredericton, N.B.
Tilgher, A.
1958. *Homo Faber: Work Through the Ages* (Trans. by D.C.Fisher). Chicago: Henry Regnery.
Trist, Eric L.
1969. "On Socio-technical Change," in W.G.Bennis, K.D. Benne and R. Chin (eds.): *The Planning of Change*. New York: Holt, Rinehart, and Winston.
Trist, Eric L.
1981. "The Quality of Working Life and Organizational Improvement," in Raynold Dorion and Lucie Brunet (eds.): *Adapting to a*

Changing World: A Reader on the Quality of Working Life. Minister of Supply and Services Canada.

Trist, Eric L. and E.K. Bamforth
1951. "Some Social and Psychological Consequences of the Long-wall Method of Coal-mining." *Human Relations, 4(February)*:3-38.

Trist, Eric L., G.W.Higgin, H.Murray and A.B.Pollock
1963. *Organizational Choice: Capabilities of Groups at the Coal Fact Under Changing Technologies*. London: Tavistock Publications.

Tumin, Melvin M.
1953. "Some Principles of Stratification: A Critical Analysis." *The American Sociological Review, 18(August)*:387-93.

Turrittin, Anton H.
1974. "Social Mobility in Canada: a Comparison of Three Provincial Studies and Some Methodoligical Questions." *Canadian Review of Sociology and Anthropology, 11*:163-86.

Tyler, Leona
1951. "Relationship of Interests to Abilities and Reputation Among First Grade Children." *Educational and Psychological Measurement, 11*:255-64.

Tyler, Leona
1964. "The Antecedents of Two Varieties of Vocational Interests." *Genetic Psychology Monographs, 70*:177-277.

United States of America, Department of Labour
1965. *Dictionary of Occupational Titles*. 3rd ed.

United States of America, Department of Labour
1977. *Technology and Manpower in the Health Service Industry*, 1965-1975. Bulletin No.16.

United States of America
1964. *Manpower Report of the President*. U.S.Government Printing Office.

VanMaanen, John
1975. "Breaking in: Socialization to Work," in Robert Dubin (ed.): *Handbook of Work, Organization and Society*. Chicago: Rand McNally.

Vincent, Claude L.
1979. *Policeman*. Toronto: Gage.

Vollmer, Howard M. and Donald L.Mills (eds.)
1966. *Professionalization*. Englewood Cliffs, N.J.:Prentice-Hall.

Vroom, Victor H. (ed.)
1967. *Methods of Organizational Research*. Pittsburg: University of Pittsburg Press.

Wadel, Cato
1973. *Now Whose Fault Is That? The Struggle for Self-esteem in the Face of Chronic Unemployment*. St. John's: Memorial University of Newfoundland.

Walker, C.R.
1922. *Steel: The Diary of a Furnace Worker*. Boston: Atlantic Monthly Press.

Walker, C.R. and R.H.Guest
1952. *The Man on the Assembly Line*. Cambridge: Harvard University Press.

Walsh, Ruth M. and Stanley J. Birkin (eds.)
1979. *Job Satisfaction and Motivation: An Annotated Bibliography*. Westport, Conn.: Greenwood Press.

Warskett, George
1982. "The Revolution in Microelectronics: Prospect for Social Transformation," in D. Neice *et al.*: Papers presented at a workshop at Queen's University, May 5-7, 1982.

Warner, W. Lloyd and P.S. Lunt
1941. *The Social Life of a Modern Community*. New Haven: Yale University Press.

Warner, W. Lloyd and P.S. Lunt
1942. *The Status System of Modern Community*. New Haven: Yale University Press.

Warner, W.Lloyd and Anselm Strauss (eds.)
1959. Industrial Man. New York: Harper.

Warner, W.L., Robert J. Havighurst, Martin B. Loeb
1944. *Who Shall be Educated: The Challenge of Unequal Opportunities*. New York: Harper.

Warner, W. Lloyd, Marchia Meeker, and Kenneth Eells
1949. *Social Class in America*. Chicago: Social Science Research Associates.

Watson, Tony J.
1980. *Sociology, Work and Industry*. London: Routledge and Kegan Paul Ltd.

Webb, Sidney, and Beatrice Webb
1926. *Industrial Democracy*. London: Longmans, Green and Co.

Weber, Max
1930. *The Protestant Ethic and the Spirit of Capitalism*. London: Allen and Unwin.

Weber, Max
1946. "Politics as a Vocation," in H.H. Gerth and C.W. Mills, eds. and trans.: *From Max Weber: Essays in Sociology*. N.Y.: Oxford University Press.

Weber, Max
1947. *The Theory of Social and Economic Organizations*. Translated by A.M. *Henderson and Talcott Parsons*. New York: Free Press.

Weeks, David R.
1980. "Industrial Development and Occupational Structure," in Geoff

Esland and Graeme Salaman (eds.): *The Politics of Work and Occupations* (pp. 75-106). Toronto: University of Toronto Press.

Weiss, M.
1967. "Rebirth in the Airborne." *Transaction, 4(May)*: 23-26.

White, Julie
1980. *Women and the Unions*. Ottawa: The Canadian Advisory Council on the Status of Women.

White, Terrance
1980. "Formal Organizations," in Robert Hagedorn (ed.): *Sociology*. Toronto: Holt, Rinehart and Winston.

Whiteley, John M. and Arthur Resinkoff (eds.)
1972. *Perspectives on Vocational Development*. Washington: American Personnel and Guidance Association. 14(4): 3-12.

Whyte, William Foote (ed.)
1948. *Human Relations in the Restaurant Industry*. New York: McGraw-Hill.

Whyte, William Foote
1956. "Engineers and Workers." *Human Organization,*

Wilensky, Harold L.
1960. "Work, Careers and Social Integrations." *International Social Science Journal, 12*: 543-60.

Wilensky, Harold L.
1961. "Orderly Careers and Social Participation: the Impact of Work History on Social Integration in the Middle Mass." *American Sociological Review, 26(August)*: 521-39.

Williams, Jack
1975. *The Story of Unions in Canada*. Don Mills, Ont.: J.M. Dent and Sons (Canada) Ltd.

Williams, R. (ed.)
1973. *Tomorrow at Work*. London: British Broadcasting Corporation Publications.

Williams, W.M. (Ed.)
1974. *Occupational Choice: A Selection of Papers from the "Sociological Review."* London: George Allen and Unwin Ltd.

Wilson, S.J.
1982. *Women, the Family and the Economy*. Toronto: McGraw-Hill Ryerson Ltd.

Wirth, Louis
1945. "The Problem of Minority Groups," in R. Linton (ed.): *The Science of Man in the World Crisis*. New York: Columbia University Press: 347-72.

Woodward, Joan
1958. *Management and Technology*. London: Her Majesty's Stationery Office.

Woodward, Joan
1965. *Industrial Organisation: Theory and Practice*. London: Oxford University Press.

Woodward, Joan
1970. *Industrial Organization: Behaviour and Control*. London: Oxford University Press.

Work in America
1973. Report of a Special Task Force to the Secretary of Health, Education and Welfare. Cambridge, Mass.: MIT Press.

Wray, Donald
1949. "Marginal Men of Industry: the Foremen." *American Journal of Sociology, 54*: 298-301.

Wrong, Dennis H.
1964. "Social Inequality without Social Stratification." *Canadian Review of Sociology and Anthropology, 1(1)*: 5-16.

Zald, Mayer
1969. "The Power and Function of Boards of Directors: A Theoretical Synthesis." *American Journal of Sociology, 75(July)*: 97-111.

Zald, Mayer
1970. *Power and Organizations*. Nashville: Vanderbilt University Press.

Zaleznik, A.
1956. *Worker Satisfaction and Development: A Case Study of Work and Social Behavior in a Factory Group*. Boston: Division of Research, Graduate School of Business Administration, Harvard University.

Zelan, Joseph
1967. "Social Origins and the Recruitment of American Lawyers." *British Journal of Sociology, 18(March)*: 45-54.

Zeman, Zavis
1979. *The Impact of Computer/Communication on Employment in Canada: An Overview of Current OECD Debates*. Montreal: Institute for Research on Public Policy.

Zurcher, Louis A., Jr., David W. Sonenschein and Eric L. Metzner
1966. "The Hasher: A Study of Role Conflict." *Social Forces, 44 (June)*: 505-14.

Zwerman, William
1970. *New Perspectives on Organizational Theory: An Empirical Reconsideration of the Maryian and Classical Analyses*. Westport, Conn.: Greenwood.

Index